Postliberalization Indian Novels in English

Postliberalization Indian Novels in English

Politics of Global Reception and Awards

Edited by
Aysha Iqbal Viswamohan

ANTHEM PRESS
LONDON · NEW YORK · DELHI

Anthem Press
An imprint of Wimbledon Publishing Company
www.anthempress.com

This edition first published in UK and USA 2014
by ANTHEM PRESS
75–76 Blackfriars Road, London SE1 8HA, UK
or PO Box 9779, London SW19 7ZG, UK
and
244 Madison Ave. #116, New York, NY 10016, USA

First published in hardback by Anthem Press in 2013.

© 2014 Aysha Iqbal Viswamohan editorial matter and selection;
individual chapters © individual contributors

The moral right of the authors has been asserted.

All rights reserved. Without limiting the rights under copyright reserved above,
no part of this publication may be reproduced, stored or introduced into
a retrieval system, or transmitted, in any form or by any means
(electronic, mechanical, photocopying, recording or otherwise),
without the prior written permission of both the copyright
owner and the above publisher of this book.

British Library Cataloguing-in-Publication Data
A catalogue record for this book is available from the British Library.

Library of Congress Cataloging-in-Publication Data
The Library of Congress has catalogued the hardcover edition as follows:
Postliberalization Indian novels in English : politics of global reception and awards /
edited by Aysha Iqbal Viswamohan.
pages cm
Includes bibliographical references and index.
ISBN 978-0-85728-564-5 (hardcover : alk. paper)
1. Indic fiction (English)–History and criticism.
I. Viswamohan, Aysha Iqbal, editor of compilation.
PR9492.2.P67 2013
823.009'954–dc23
2013004506

ISBN-13: 978 1 78308 334 3 (Pbk)
ISBN-10: 1 78308 334 4 (Pbk)

This title is also available as an ebook.

In loving memory of my father, the late Dr Iqbal Ahmed

CONTENTS

Acknowledgements   ix

Foreword   xi
Tabish Khair

Introduction   xv

1. A Maverick Scholar: The Writings of Pankaj Mishra   1
   A. N. Dwivedi

2. Commodification of Post-Rushdie Indian Novels in English: Kunal Basu and the Politics of Decanonization   9
   Angshuman Kar

3. Marketing Lad Lit, Creating Bestsellers: The Importance of Being Chetan Bhagat   19
   Aysha Iqbal Viswamohan

4. Vikas Swarup: Writing India in Global Time   31
   Chinmoy Banerjee

5. *The God of Small Things*: Arundhati Roy's 'Made in India' Bookerboiler   41
   Chinnadevi Singadi

6. Aravind Adiga: The White Elephant? Postliberalization, the Politics of Reception and the Globalization of Literary Prizes   51
   John Masterson

7. 'The Multinational's Song': The Global Reception of M. G. Vassanji   67
   Laura Moss

8.	'Shreds of Indianness': Identity and Representation in Manju Kapur's *The Immigrant* *Letizia Alterno*	77
9.	Inside 'The Temple of Modern Desire': Recollecting and Relocating Bombay *Maria Ridda*	87
10.	Tabish Khair: Marketing Compulsions and Artistic Integrity *Om Prakash Dwivedi*	103
11.	Rohinton Mistry and the Canlit Imperative *Patricia Gruben*	113
12.	Amitav Ghosh: The Indian Architect of a Postnational Utopia *Sajalkumar Bhattacharya*	127
13.	Here, There and Everywhere: Vikram Seth's Multiple Literary Constituencies *Mala Pandurang*	141
14.	Whatever Happened to Kaavya Viswanathan? *Shaleena Koruth*	151
15.	Of Win and Loss: Kiran Desai's Global Storytelling *Sara-Duana Meyer*	167
16.	Immigrant Desires: Narratives of the Indian Diaspora by Chitra Banerjee Divakaruni *Tutun Mukherjee*	185

Glossary of Indian Words   195

List of Contributors   197

Bibliography   201

Index   215

ACKNOWLEDGEMENTS

To undertake articulation of any idea is a daunting task. It not only involves private discovery and reflection, but also collaboration and interaction with several like-minded people. It goes without saying that a writer, besides being always in need of concrete information and knowledge, also needs intellectual and emotional support from those whom s/he holds in high esteem.

I am, therefore, grateful to the following:

Prof. Bhaskar Ramamurthy (director, IITM); Prof. T. T. Narendran, Prof. Job Kurien (former deans, ICSR) and Prof. Krishnan Balasubramanian (dean, ICSR); and Prof. Ajit Kolar (chairman, Centre for Continuing Education, IITM) for providing facilities and infrastructure for this endeavour;

Tabish Khair for graciously writing the foreword, and all the other contributors who added value to this volume;

faculty and staff of the Department of Humanities and Social Sciences;

the library staff of IIT, Madras; Simon Fraser University, Vancouver; British Council Division, Chennai; English and Foreign Languages University, Hyderabad; and Shastri Indo-Canadian Institute, New Delhi;

the Anthem Press team: Janka Romero, for her suggestions at all stages of writing this book, Tej Sood, Partha Malik and the editorial staff;

the peers who added value to the manuscript via the review process;

my family: son Aneesh, husband Viswamohan, mother Dr (Mrs) M. Iqbal and father (late) Dr Iqbal Ahmed;

my dear research scholars, U. Gopika and Vimal Mohan John for their tremendous support during the various stages of this project.

Foreword

REDEFINING INDIAN WRITING IN ENGLISH

Tabish Khair

Language is not transparent. It conditions our understanding and narration of events. If this can be the case between dialects of the same 'language', imagine the extent of the challenge when one writes in a particular language about characters who do not – or who do not only – speak that language?

Unfortunately, to say this in the context of Indian writing in English is to show a red rag to two very different species of bull. The first, simpler, species is the language nationalist, who will usually conflate your discussion of the complexity of English (in India) with a dismissal of it. He – it is often a male – will claim that Indians 'should only write in Indian languages', glibly echoing a common colonialist rant despite the fact that English has been around in India for three centuries and is now an 'Indian language' – though it is a language that has a different relationship to many Indian realities and to other Indian languages than, say, Tamil, Hindi, Urdu or Bangla.

But to make this ancillary point, while recognizing the place of English in India, is to show a red rag to the other, subtler and more cosmopolitan, species of bull, who would then read it as a dismissal of Indian English writing or an attempt to question the 'authenticity' of Indian English. However, for Indian literature in English to be read on its own terms, both the particular problems and the particular possibilities of English as a language in India have to be addressed – these might or might not be the same in a diasporic or general 'postcolonialist' context. This leads us to another aspect of the problem of discussing Indian writing in English: postcolonialism.

It is impossible to read Indian literature in English without reference to postcolonial literature, and at the same time it is impossible to read it primarily with reference to postcolonial literature. In fact, one can argue that the tendency to read Indian literatures in English along postcolonial lines is often distortive: it slants the reading not only towards a particular selection of texts, but also towards a particular understanding of India and history. Hence, a literature written in a region with about four thousand years of extant literary texts is dated, effectively, about two hundred and fifty years back to the colonization of Bengal by the British East India Company. Sometimes, this tendency is resisted by incorporating a reference to 'classical' literature (though these are mostly Sanskrit texts retrieved by Orientalist scholarship), but even this leaves out about a millennia of thriving and cross-fertilizing literature in various languages, ranging from Sanskrit, Tamil and Farsi to more recent ones like Hindi and Urdu.

Again, even English in India exists in a situation that is very different from the one that obtains in such postcolonial states as Australia, New Zealand, Canada or Anglophone Caribbean. English is only one of many other spoken and written languages in India, all of which have thriving literatures. English is also a language that is not spoken uniformly across classes and lifestyles. It is hardly spoken by working-class Indians and in rural India, and it is mostly spoken with difficulty and reluctance in *taluk* (provincial) India. This observation, however, is difficult to make, as I have indicated above. It is mostly transformed into culturalist/nationalist reductionism – either celebrated or critiqued as a dismissal of the 'authenticity' of English writing in India, which it certainly is not.

The matter is not entirely different from the matter of postcolonialism. Indian English writing cannot be read without reference to the problems of English narration in an Indian context, but it should also not be read without reference to the possibilities. Similarly, while Indian fiction in English cannot be read as postcolonial fiction without doing violence to its complexities, it can also not be read entirely outside the discursive framework of postcolonialism.

Another area of mutual complexity – overlapping with what is usually practiced under the rubric of 'postcolonialism' in academia – is what has sometimes been called the Indian diaspora. It has come to represent the visible tip of the iceberg of Indian English writing in most critical accounts (let alone the media). However, any discussion of the literature of the Indian (or, more broadly, the South Asian) diaspora in the UK (and Europe) has to be carried out at various levels.

Any discussion of the South Asian (or Indian) diaspora also needs to address the massive movements of South Asian (and other Asian and African) peoples before European colonization. After all, the first recorded members of the South Asian diaspora to reach Europe in large numbers were probably the 'gypsies'. But, of course, 'gypsies' are not seen as belonging to the diaspora. In many ways, current discussion privileges the movements of certain kinds of people. First of all, it privileges the Eurocentric connection by implicitly repeating the colonialist myth of European colonization as the great connecting link. This is, as I have indicated in *Other Routes*, a false conception: Asians and Africans moved before European colonization as well as during and after it. Secondly, it privileges the movement of certain kinds of South Asians: usually anglophone South Asians like me who started moving out of South Asia in the 1940s and later; that is, in the postcolonial phase. Even here, there is a deep irony in the fact that Raja Rao, who wrote the excellent novel *Kanthapura* in 1938, is usually not read in diasporic terms. His novel is held up – correctly so – as one of the very few convincing Indian English texts about village life in India. There seems to be a gulf between him and visibly 'diasporic' South Asian writers like Salman Rushdie. But in actual fact, the very young Raja Rao is reputed to have written *Kanthapura* partly in a castle in France and continued to live in France and USA for the rest of his long life.

In fact, the South Asian diaspora goes back a long way even in the colonial and postcolonial context. There are sixteenth-century paintings and accounts of Indian servants in England. The number of Indian servants and lascars (mostly South Asian sailors) being taken to Britain increases in later centuries – and in many cases these servants and lascars seem to have been abandoned on the streets of Britain (and Europe) when their services were no longer needed.

From early on, a small number of Indian aristocrats and gentry also chose to go to Europe, either to travel (as Abu Taleb did in 1797) or to settle down (as Deen Mahomed did a generation before Abu Taleb). Incidentally, both Taleb and Mahomed wrote books about their travels: the former in Farsi (Persian) and the latter in English. Finally, in the early twentieth century, thousands of South Asian soldiers reached Europe to fight the two great tribal wars in Europe: World War I and World War II. During World War I, for instance, India contributed more soldiers to the British cause than all the other colonies (Australia, Canada, etc.) combined.

It is in this context that one has to situate the literature of the South Asian diaspora. True, Rushdie, Hanif Kureishi and co. might have made it particularly visible, but even before them there were writers like Attia Hosain (who stayed on in London in 1947 because she could not choose between Pakistan and India) and Raja Rao. And before Rao, Hosain and others, there were writers like Deen Mahomed and the thousands of invisible South Asians who moved to and across Europe: servants, nursemaids (*ayahs*), sailors, travellers, soldiers, traders, all the way back to probably the first 'gypsies'.

It is in the context of the above problems and possibilities, visibilities and invisibilities that this book seems to serve a crucial purpose. This is indicated by the fact that the papers in it cover not only writers of Indian origin who are visible in the West or in international postcolonialist contexts but also

Indian writers who have a greater significance in India than abroad. It is this intermixture of writers that requires attention today, in Indian English critical terms. Without it, Indian writing in English will inevitably continue to be largely defined elsewhere.

INTRODUCTION

From postcolonialism to the current times of globalization, India and her fiction in English have travelled a long journey. One of the crucial debates that have been at the centre of postliberalization literature is its reception, at home and abroad. As the title suggests, all essays in this volume focus on the reception of the seminal authors and their works of the postliberalization period. The watershed year for postliberalization was 1991, when economic reforms changed the urban Indian landscape. This was also the time when Indian writers of English caught the attention of the Western world like never before. My interest is particularly in such writers whose concerns are related to India in its immediacy and who came into literary prominence in postliberalized India. For this study, I attempt to analyse the perceptual shifts on the receivers (i.e. members of the English-speaking world) as a consequence of liberalization. This shift will be measured in terms of critical reception as well as reception at the university level in English-speaking countries.

Observers of Indian novels in English tell us that this is one of the best periods for the category of Indian writing in English, at least in terms of attention received. The number of successes speaks for itself: Salman Rushdie won the 'Booker of Bookers' (1993); Vikram Chandra won the Commonwealth Writer's Prize for *Red Earth and Pouring Rain* in the best first book category (1995); Arundhati Roy won the Man Booker for *The God of Small Things* and Amitav Ghosh won the Arthur C. Clarke Award for *The Calcutta Chromosome* (1997); Jhumpa Lahiri won the Pulitzer Prize for *Interpreter of Maladies* and V. S. Naipaul was awarded the Nobel in Literature (2000); Vikram Seth got a staggering sum of £1.3 million in advance for *Two Lives* (2003); Chetan Bhagat's *Five Point Someone* remained on the bestseller list for 70 weeks (2004); Kiran Desai won the Man Booker for *The Inheritance of Loss* (2006); Amitav Ghosh was shortlisted for *The Sea of Poppies* and Aravind Adiga won the Man Booker for *The White Tiger* (2008). While the accolades keep coming, criticisms toward the celebrity status of Indian writing cannot be ignored, and this anthology attempts to map the voices of scepticism as well. It is therefore no accident that many of the essays are concerned with the nature of book trades, distribution, marketing and circulation, along with award politics, and how these elements have a formative effect on reception of books. Excessive market play and the position of English as a global language inform the trends in reception of contemporary novels in English from India. Academics blame the publishing industry for various gimmicks and ploys to ensure sales. In this context Pankaj Mishra says, 'We don't have a critical culture in English […] we rely on celebrity endorsements to assess a piece of writing.'[1] However, the brighter side is that today all kinds of genres are explored and experimented with, including historical, thrillers, chick/lad lit, campus fiction and children's fiction.

Despite their unprecedented success, Indian novelists in English are constantly at the receiving end of salvos. Jerry Pinto summarizes the usual complaints against these authors who, according to the critics:

1. don't understand India,
2. live abroad and don't get India right,
3. get paid obscene quantities of money,
4. get all the attention in the media,
5. never translate them (critics perhaps mean that these global writers never translate Indian literature in other languages).[2]

Pinto of course debunks several myths of the above misconceptions, as does Shashi Deshpande elsewhere while debating the politics of awards and reception of certain acclaimed novels.[3] Further, if hype and star status of an author could sell a book, then Adiga's *Between the Assassinations* (2008) and Rushdie's *The Enchantress of Florence* in the same year would have been the bestsellers. However, the fact is both these novels vanished without a trace.

While discussing the pool of talent in Indian novels in English, Khushwant Singh makes a list of writers who he regards as 'significant' and rates as 'the best in the last 60 years'.[4] The aim of the present volume is to document those Indian novelists from postliberalized India who have received acclaim at critical and university levels; for example, they receive positive reviews in eminent newspapers and magazines, are interviewed by high-profile talk-show hosts on television; their works are adapted for films and prescribed in university syllabuses; and they are invited as professors/writers-in-residence and are on distinguished committees, including the literary prize-giving ones.

The essays in this volume posit:

1. What are those cultural and critical frameworks that define literary reception?
2. Has there been a marked shift in the reception of Indian novelists in English postliberalization as compared to earlier novelists?

3. What about the attitude of the award-giving bodies? Does a freer economy c/overtly determine these awards?
4. Do marketing strategies by the big publishing companies play a significant role in making the works of some authors more visible (e.g. bidding wars between publishers, much-publicized advances/royalties, etc.)?
5. To what extent are the works of these writers driven by the dictates of the market?
6. Do our commercially/economically driven media influence critical/commercial perceptions?
7. Are there certain thematic concerns and representations that are deemed 'prize and attention worthy' and do these factors influence the critical/commercial reception of the novels?

A brief overview of the anthology is presented thus:

A. N. Dwivedi's essay on Pankaj Mishra focuses on Mishra's role as a chronicler of our times. Dwivedi notes that Mishra's rise coincides with the phenomenon of postliberalization. While Mishra's inspirations are the European masters, his sensibilities are essentially Indian and are reflected in his travelogues and nonfiction writings. Mishra is credited with bringing the small town back into literary writing, and is one writer who cannot be accused of writing books to suit Western tastes. Dwivedi argues that Mishra's steadfast refusal to play the media game could be one of the reasons for the lack of attention bestowed upon him.

Since his literary debut, Salman Rushdie has been recognized as one of the most powerful figures of postcolonial fiction. Angshuman Kar addresses the construct of decanonization pertaining to the writers of the post-Rushdie generation in 'Commodification of Post-Rushdie Indian Novels in English: Kunal Basu and the Politics of Decanonization'. Kar argues that against the forces of marketing and canonizing, a writer like Kunal Basu must bide his time before receiving his rightful attention.

One of the biggest success stories of contemporary India is Chetan Bhagat, who with five bestselling novels to his credit is decidedly a literary superstar. A self-proclaimed 'Karan Johar/Salman Khan' of literature, Bhagat positively revels in his mass appeal. Although constantly shunned by the upmarket literary critics, Bhagat's is a voice that needs more attention. My paper, 'Marketing Lad Lit, Creating Bestsellers: The Importance of Being Chetan Bhagat', attempts to address this gap, and analyses the writer's place and his voice in postliberalized India.

Chinmoy Banerjee analyses Vikas Swarup's extraordinary success in 'Vikas Swarup: Writing India in Global Times', as a consequence of synthesizing globalization and marketing forces. Swarup, through mastering certain codes and tropes, has positioned himself as a writer of our times through *Q & A* (2005) and *Six Suspects* (2008). Banerjee traces the trajectory of Indian novels in English from Raja Rao to Amit Chaudhuri, writers who have struggled to cope with notions of authenticity and language, and situates Swarup as someone who seems indifferent to these serious literary concerns.

The God of Small Things evokes strong reactions among readers across the globe, its author's perhaps the strongest. Chinnadevi Singadi tackles the 'whys' and 'buts' of the politics of reception for the writer–activist. Singadi interrogates the West's preoccupation with India's filth, caste and superstitions, and how prestigious award bodies respond to the 'ugly' representation of the Third World.

One of the most controversial books of our times, as far as awards go, is Aravind Adiga's *The White Tiger*. John Masterson, in 'Aravind Adiga: The White Elephant? Postliberalization, the Politics of Reception and the Globalization of Literary Prizes', explores the combined phenomenon of globalization, postcoloniality and subalterity implicit in Adiga's novel. Masterson feels that a divisive work like this indicates the effectiveness with which it opposes the erasing of difference necessary for globalization.

Laura Moss looks at Vassanji's multinational identity in 'The Multinational's Song: The Global Reception of M. G. Vassanji'. Vassanji's refusal to be pigeonholed by the expectations of nationality or genre echoes the increasing desire of global subjects to think about the constructs of identity and place. It is not surprising, therefore, that Vassanji can be marketed as an African, South Asian, Canadian writer. This perhaps, for Moss, accounts for Vassanji's global reception.

Letizia Alterno's 'Shreds of Indianness: Identity and Representation in Manju Kapur's *The Immigrant*' focuses on the immigration experience and forced categorization. At the core of Kapur's works are the themes of migration, cultural transition, adaptation and identity and gender across national contexts, and Alterno invites us to read how significant these issues are in the context of the postliberalization Indian scenario.

Maria Ridda, in her 'Inside 'The Temple of Modern Desire': Re-collecting and Re-locating Bombay', explores the impact of globalization and the plethora of possibilities it has launched on the urban spaces of India's largest and fastest growing city, Mumbai. Essentially a study of Suketu Mehta's *Maximum City* (2004) and Vikram Chandra's *Sacred Games* (2006), the article investigates how the books themselves introspect the cosmopolitan character of urban Mumbai through an intertextual study of Bollywood cinema, which envisages the core of Indian sentiments, visualizing the dreams and desires of a heterogeneous multitude in a quasi-real manner that compliments the city's translucent nature.

Om Prakash Dwivedi assesses the impact of globalization on Tabish Khair and wonders why a major talent like his is not receiving the attention it deserves. Dwivedi admires Khair's felicity for sketching life and characters from rural India and underprivileged backgrounds, an atypical trait in any contemporary writer. Khair's ability to infuse fiction with history and his Rushdie-like ability to introduce magical realism into his writings is also explored in 'Tabish Khair: Marketing Compulsions and Artistic Integrity'.

Patricia Gruben discusses issues of critical reception for Rohinton Mistry and considers how his 'Parsiness' forges a unique identity for him in Canada. The writer also reflects on the perception of Mistry's work as a realist in 'Rohinton Mistry and the Can-Lit Imperative'. Mistry's humanistic impulses and depiction of family values are also discussed as contributing factors toward his popularity.

Sajal Bhattacharya considers Amitav Ghosh as 'The Indian Architect of a Postnational Utopia' and details Ghosh's preoccupation with borders and nationalities, and with institutionalized sufferings. It is seen that Ghosh's role as an anthropologist shapes his role as a fiction writer. Bhattacharya maintains that while Ghosh enjoys worldwide popularity, he retains his essential Indian flavour, which underscores his positive reception at global level.

Vikram Seth's uniqueness among contemporary Indian writers and his refusal to be bracketed within categories of nationalistic diaspora forms the central thrust of this paper. Mala Pandurang's 'Here, There and Everywhere: Vikram Seth's Literary Constituencies' discusses his literature and biography, correlating his identity as a global migrant and his diverse creative output. Seth's unique migratory subjectivity is also examined in the light of his many geo-cultural locations and his ability to be 'at home' everywhere. Locating his last two (distinctively international) works within the period of India's economic liberalization, Seth's attempts to escape the restrictive boundaries of nationalism is also examined.

Dramatic reversal of fortunes defined Kaavya Viswanathan's career, and Shaleena Koruth's provocative 'Whatever Happened to Kaavya Viswanathan?' traces the decline and fall of the young writer. Koruth unfolds the sordid saga of strategizing and plagiarizing that underpinned the *Opal Mehta* (2006) controversy. Wheeling-dealing, marketing and packaging all form an integral part of the modern publishing set-up. For Koruth, the blame lies as much as with the publicity machinery and the big publishing houses as with Viswanathan herself.

Sara-Duana Meyer, in 'Of Win and Loss: Kiran Desai's Global Storytelling', examines Kiran Desai as the celebrity novelist and Indo-American author of 'the erstwhile league of diaspora literature'. The chapter follows the major themes in her work, studying her as a storyteller oscillating between the global and the local. The paper also proposes an analysis of the distinct cultural markers in her novels, amid accusations of her exoticization of the Indian experience. A study of her views on hybridization, globalization and migration is also attempted. The reality of a global commodification of cultural differences is seen in the light of Desai's visibility, marketability and prominence. The paper finally attempts to decode her strategy of retrieving and representing her 'Indianness'.

'Immigrant Desires: Narratives of the Indian Diaspora by Chitra Banerjee Divakaruni' by Tutun Mukherjee reads Banerjee's novels as a testament to the pains and pleasures of the diaspora. Prof. Mukherjee understands the implicit contradictions in the lives of the immigrants and realizes that this category of writing cannot be completely free of romanticization of India. Her essay asks if 'being visible and reader-friendly minimizes the need for this body of literature to address economic and sociopolitical issues that immigrants face in their new environments'.

I am aware that the novelists missing in the present anthology are many and significant. Some notable absentees are: Amit Chaudhuri, Anurag Mathur, Anita Nair, Jhumpa Lahiri, I. Allan Sealy, Kiran Nagarkar, Manil Suri, Mukul Kesavan, Manjula Padmanabhan, Namita Gokhale, Shashi Deshpande, Upamanyu Chatterjee, Hari Kunzru, Anita Rau Badami, David Davidar, Anuja Chauhan, Tarun Tejpal, Abha Dawesar, Jaishree Misra, Neel Mukherjee, Rukun Advani, Shobha Narayan, Shobha De, Karan Bajaj, Ashok Mathur, Amitava Kumar … the list goes on. But perhaps there will be another book, another day.

Notes and References

1 Sheela Reddy, 'The Blurb Bubble', *Outlook*, 4 December 2006. Online: http://outlookindia.com/fullprint.asp?choice=1&fodname=20061204&fname=AWriters+(F)&sid=1 (accessed 24 July 2011).

   In the same article it is further mentioned, 'Sometimes it's not just readers who get taken in; even publishers/distributors get swayed by blurbs, as debut writer Edward Luce discovered recently. Luce says he didn't realise how crucial blurbs were for sales here until his own book was launched. When his distributors in India, Penguin, discovered that the jacket of *In Spite of the Gods* carried blurbs by two heavyweights, Dalrymple and Amartya Sen, they doubled the order from 5,000 copies to 10,000, Luce Claims.'

2 Jerry Pinto, 'The Write Moment', *Outlook*, 31 December 2006, 163.

3 While discussing celebrity writers – Arundhati Roy, Kiran Desai and Aravind Adiga in particular – Shashi Deshpande remarks: 'There were many who admired Roy's book […]. The response to Desai's book, good or bad, was muted. Adiga's book has had a lot of adverse reactions […]. The writer's only job is not to present realities. And what the reader expects, however dark the book, is some redeeming quality.' (Shashi Deshpande, 'Debating Spaces', *Hindu*, Literary Review, 1 February 2009, 1.)

4 Khushwant Singh, 'Queen's Ransom', *Outlook*, 20 August 2007, 118. Singh lists, among others, Vikram Seth's *A Suitable Boy*, Amitav Ghosh's *Shadow Lines*, Kiran Nagarkar's *Cuckold*, Arundhati Roy's *The God of Small Things*, Jhumpa Lahiri's *Interpreter of Maladies*, Jaysinh Birjepatil's *Chinnery's Hotel*, Anita Rau Badami's *The Hero's Walk*, Tabish Khair's *Filming: A Love Story* and M. G. Vassanji's *The Assassin's Song*. He adds, 'Though more than half of them are now foreign nationals, their themes are Indian and the applause they get abroad resonates in India. They return to India periodically to be garlanded and to get fresh material, and now also earn handsome royalties in rupees.'

Chapter One

A MAVERICK SCHOLAR: THE WRITINGS OF PANKAJ MISHRA

A. N. Dwivedi

One of the relatively recent signatures in contemporary Indian English writing, Pankaj Mishra, shot into the limelight with his work in fiction and nonfiction. Not much attention has been paid to him in the academic world for very long; in this paper my attempt has been to address this gap. But for a few reviews appearing in newspapers and literary journals (as the endnotes reflect), and the critical articles of Rahul Gairola (2003), Padmaja Challakere (2004), Jill Didur (2009) and Dwivedi (2009), no sustained efforts in the form of a book have been made to throw light on Mishra's works and achievements. These reviews and articles evoke a mixed response to his writings. More critical attention is called for because Mishra happens to be an author of the postliberalization period. But for his *Butter Chicken in Ludhiana: Travels in Small Town India* (1985), all his works appeared after 1991 – once the process of liberalization and globalization in India had begun, the resonance of which was particularly felt in metropolitan cities.

Pankaj Mishra was born in the small town of Kannauj, Uttar Pradesh, in 1969. He did his undergraduate course at the University of Allahabad, which had been a centre of attraction for his maternal family: 'Three generations of my mother's family had gone to the University in Allahabad.'[1] Having spent three years at Allahabad (1985–88), Mishra proceeded to Benares in the winter of 1988 for an intensive self-guided reading. He describes Benares as 'the holiest city of the Hindus, where people come either ritually to dissolve their accumulated "sins" in the Ganges, or simply die and achieve liberation from the cycle of rebirths'.[2] He started attending the library of the Benares Hindu University where he discovered Edmund Wilson and his books, many of them being 'collections of reviews of books'.[3] He avidly read them along with several thought-provoking works by other authors, like Schopenhauer, Turgenev and Flaubert.

Mishra then shifted to Delhi to pursue his graduate studies at the School of Languages, Jawaharlal Nehru University. In the meantime, he began publishing insightful reviews of Indian fiction in English and Western fiction on India in *The Pioneer*, a daily from Delhi. Mishra completed his MPhil and then took up a travel writing project, which resulted in *Butter Chicken*, a travel book, mapping his journey across several North Indian small towns. Rahul Gairola posits that *Butter Chicken* is Pankaj Mishra's first novel, but the brief biography of Mishra published in *The Romantics* (1999) mentions this as his debut novel.[4] *The Romantics* is a predominantly autobiographical work and the protagonist Samar represents the author to an extent. Mishra was offered $450,000 as an advance from Random House for the novel – the second largest 'monetary nod' for an Indian writer in English, according to Robert Marquand in the *Christian Science Monitor*.[5]

Two books by Mishra came out in quick succession: first, *An End to Suffering: The Buddha in the World* (2004) – a memoir about his experience researching the life of Gautama Buddha, the Enlightened One – and second, *Temptations of the West: How to Be Modern in India, Pakistan and Beyond* (2006) – a travelogue taking him to some historically and politically significant cities in India, and later through Kashmir, to Pakistan and Afghanistan, culminating in a visit to Nepal and Tibet. Mishra's essays and reviews have been appearing at regular intervals in national and international journals as well as periodicals of repute, including the *New York Review of Books*, the *New Statesman*, *Granta*, the *Times Literary Supplement*, the *Guardian* and *Outlook*.

The Romantics, written over a period of about nine weeks, is the only fictional work that Mishra has produced to date.[6] It narrates the story of a 20-year-old university student called Samar, who studies at the University of Allahabad and later shifts to Benares to pursue the works of Edmund Wilson and other Western philosophers. He regards Wilson as his 'own Guru, long dead but [...] more real than anyone I actually knew during that winter'.[7] To him, Wilson's was 'an extraordinarily cohesive sensibility'.[8] Another great influence upon Samar is that of Gustav Flaubert and his *A Sentimental Education* (1869). According to Jill Didur, Flaubert's disaffected protagonist, Frederic Moreau, serves as 'a partial model for Mishra's narrator, Samar'.[9]

At the Benares Hindu University, Samar meets Rajesh, a politically active Brahmin student leader recommended by another student leader named Vijay of Allahabad. Samar is drawn to Rajesh because both of them are keenly interested in Wilson. The theme of the East–West encounter comes out vividly in *The Romantics*. While the ancient city of Benares struggles to cope with the modern India, Samar comes into contact with a number of people, both Indians and non-Indians: the old Panditji and his beleaguered wife living in separate rooms for the past 15 years, their son Arjun and his wife

Sitadevi, their servant Shyam, Miss West, Mark, Debbie, Sarah, Catherine and her exploitative Indian boyfriend Anand. Of these, Samar draws closer to Miss West and Catherine, especially to the latter. Whereas his relationship with Miss West is one of friendliness, his relationship with Catherine is one of infatuation. Commenting on the ending of the novel, Jill Didur observes, 'Mishra's novel concludes with Samar in a secular, exilic mode, eschewing belonging and ready to begin a contrapuntal accounting of the past and his place in the nation.'[10]

Butter Chicken focuses on small towns (not in the popular tourist destinations) like Murshidabad, Muzaffarnagar and Kottayam. In undertaking his travels, Mishra has no real itinerary or planned route. He is not so much interested in sights as in observing the transformation of Indian society under the myriad new influences affecting the country. There is much in this book about the effect of television, fast-food restaurants, rapidly expanding multistorey hotels and newer means of transportation. Though he may not be as sharp in wit as Paul Theroux or as ponderous as V. S. Naipaul in his observations, Mishra connects with the locals and he is funny and thoughtful with an ironic style.

In his itinerary, Mishra comes to Kottayam and meets, among others, Mary Roy, principal of the Corpus Christi School. He carries an introduction from a casual acquaintance, Arundhati Roy, who is Mrs Roy's daughter now living in Delhi in an illicit relationship with a Hindu man. Here it may be noted that Mishra's acquaintance with Arundhati Roy might have been 'casual' in 1985, but later it grew deep and he did his best to promote her novel, *The God of Small Things* (1997), which eventually earned for her the Booker Prize in 1997. In the acknowledgement section of *The God of Small Things*, Arundhati Roy has expressed her indebtedness to Mishra for 'flagging it off on its journey into the world.'[11] However, the unusual interest shown by him in the international promotion of the novel cost him dearly – he was fired from his position at HarperCollins in India.

Butter Chicken evoked a mixed response from readers and reviewers. Some of them consider it as a work of 'sharp insight'[12] that endeavours to discover 'the huge and diverse land that is India', but the same review also criticizes it as 'somewhat lacking in focus and direction'.[13] Mishra, too, remains queasy about his work: 'It is a fake book, a dishonest book by a dishonest writer. I completely suppressed some part of myself, the part that belongs to small town India in order to mock at it. I borrowed a voice, and maintained a constant distance between myself and the experience.'[14]

In *An End to Suffering*, Mishra agonizes over the rise of religious extremism and its offshoot, majoritarianism. He thinks that the disappointment of the postcolonial Indians is due to 'the uneven distribution of modernity's promises.'[15] To illustrate this, Mishra narrates the story of his visit to his college friend

Vinod's family home in rural North India in the late 1980s. He meets Vinod there and then recounts the young man's feeling of bitterness over his failure to shine in the colonial education system, which would have enabled him to get out of his family's feudal, Brahminical way of life. Vinod exclaims with sorrow, 'I went with such high expectations', but he finds utter chaos and confusion on the campus. He is appalled to discover a miserable situation there: 'Teachers not showing up for classes, the exams being delayed for months, sometimes years. Criminals roamed the campus with guns and homemade bombs.' Disappointed, Vinod becomes one of 'the Hindu nationalists who were then rising to power on a wave of anti-Muslim violence across North India'.[16] *An End to Suffering* makes, in a way, an ironic interpretation of caste-based politics and modernity that 'provides young men like Vinod, self-identified with Hindu majoritarian culture, extra leverage in the increasingly global capitalist environment fostered by economic liberalization in India during the early nineties'.[17] Though Mishra seems to be identifying himself with Vinod and his situation, he maintains a distance from the Hindu majoritarian thinking because this kind of thinking only accentuates the suffering of those who live on the margins of modernity. Mishra tries to explore, through this memoir of sorts, the source of his own sense of 'futility and doom', of fear and disenchantment in the postcolonial Indian society, suggesting thereby the truth that the 'end to suffering' will come when the benefits of modernity are equally distributed across the social spectrum.[18]

Temptations, unlike *Butter Chicken*, is notable for its range and scope. It focuses not only on some cities of India but also on Kashmir, Pakistan, Afghanistan, Nepal and Tibet. In his foreword, the author emphatically declares, 'Western ideologies, whether of colonialism, or of communism and globalization, have confronted the countries I visited – India, Pakistan, Afghanistan, Nepal and Tibet – with the same challenge: modernize or perish.'[19] And Benares bears 'the most garish symbols of the entrepreneurial energies unleashed by the liberalization of the Indian economy, which would transform Benares in the way they had already transformed other sleepy small towns across India'.[20] As a travelogue, *Temptations* presents a first-hand account of various places, persons and events within and beyond India. Mishra's previous attempts at travelogue writing have obviously made him more focused and mature. As a result, *Temptations* is anything but 'a fake book'.

Apart from being a distinguished novelist and travel writer, Mishra is also a prolific writer of insightful essays, such as 'Edmund Wilson in Benares', 'A New, Nuclear India', 'Death in Kashmir', 'Behold the Good European' and 'A Sepulchral Chill in the Soul'. Of these essays, the first three appeared in the *New York Review of Books* and the last two in the *New Statesman*.[21] 'Edmund Wilson in Benares' shows Mishra's attraction towards Wilson while living in Benares and his intensive reading of his books. 'A New, Nuclear India' critiques India's (then) recently acquired nuclear capabilities and its possible ramifications, while 'Death in Kashmir' charts out the breathtaking landscape of Kashmir, later besmeared with religious fanaticism and bloodshed. 'Behold the Good European' is a reflection on the manners, behaviour and culture of a good European, whereas 'A Sepulchral Education in the Soul' brings out the coldness of Flaubert's Frederic Moreau. Reviewing a revised edition of this work, Mishra comments on Moreau: '[He] dreams a great deal but nothing comes of his grand plans for success in art, business, journalism and politics. His shallow love affairs peter out.'[22]

The resonance of the open door policy and the economic liberalization of India in the early 1990s is repeatedly felt in Mishra's works. In this context, *The Romantics* and *Temptations* come immediately to one's mind. In *The Romantics*, Samar finds the city of Benares old and dusty in the initial stage, but he notices a gradual transformation. Modern concrete and glass hotels are seen in the new parts of it, and the 'new middle-class prosperity has at last come to Benares'.[23] Under the impact of liberalization, some palpable changes have taken place. Mishra hits the mark as he details the discontents of globalization: 'those ghostly fast-food places and beauty parlours and so-called Italian restaurants and the hotels with discotheques'.[24] In *Temptations*, an identical description of the city of Benares is found: 'a rash of fast-food outlets, video-game parlors, and boutiques, the most garish symbols of the entrepreneurial energies unleashed by the liberalization of the Indian economy'.[25] Speaking of Ayodhya, Mishra suggests that this city, after the demolition of the Babri Masjid by the Hindu *karsevaks* (zealots) in December 1992, is now ready for 'new lucrative connections to the global economy', and is an exemplar of 'the profound modernity of religious nationalism'.[26] The incident of demolition coincided with the upsurge of nationalistic sentiments and economic liberalization in India, instilling a ray of hope in Mishra for the future prosperity of the city of Ayodhya.

We live in times when critical reception of any work of art is determined by publishers and an army of media strategists. Book writing is more of a media event than a literary one, and in some instances we even witness Bollywood personalities launching books of new, and sometimes well-known, writers. Mishra, however, largely remains untouched by such publicity shenanigans. Perhaps due to this conscious avoidance of hype, the reception to his works has often been a mixed one. A case in point is the reception of *Butter Chicken*. *The Romantics* was more fortunate. Reviewing it for The *New York Times Book Review*, Akash Kapur remarks, 'For all the poignancy of the moment, there is something labored about Mishra's language, its explicitness suggesting a first-time author too insecure to let the story speak for itself. This is a recurring problem in *The Romantics*. Although Mishra has a wonderful capacity for detail and psychological portraiture, his narrative is cluttered with thematic elucidation and explanations, many of them as dry as that "emanation [...] from unknown ancient times."'[27]

Kapur's review of the novel praises Mishra's 'wonderful capacity for detail and psychological portraiture' but calls in question his laboured language and cluttered narrative. Commenting on *The Romantics*, which went on to win the *LA Times* Art Seidenbaum Award for First Fiction, Margery Sabin remarks, 'He shares the revulsion of many radical intellectuals for the greed and callousness of the new global consumer economy that has left the vast majority of the subcontinent's population in the same impoverished misery as before.'[28]

Sabin's review evidently appreciates Mishra's concerns for 'the vast majority of the subcontinent's population' (i.e. poor Hindus). The opinion of Shirley Chew about the novel is also worth quoting here: 'Mishra's writing has a lovely potency [...]. [A] subtly layered and compelling first novel.'[29] Likewise, *Temptations* was favourably received by many. The reviewer of the *Observer* found it, 'Thoughtful, intelligent and rigorous [...] a deep, insightful study of the very notion of modernity.'[30]

Irrespective of the hype, Mishra has remained steadfast in his output. Like Tabish Khair, here is a writer who is persistent in his depiction of the 'real' India, with all her warts and blemishes, along with her inherent sheen. Innately low-key and publicity shy, Mishra has emerged as one of the most remarkable Indian writers of our fast-changing times. He voices the concerns felt by most educated middle-class people of India, while offering a nonpopulist critique of our sociopolitical and cultural ethos. And therefore, I believe, this is a voice that is worthy of more critical attention.[31]

Notes and References

1 Pankaj Mishra, *The Romantics* (London: Picador, 1999), 8.
2 Mishra, *Temptations of the West: How to Be Modern in India, Pakistan and Beyond* (London: Picador, 2006), 3.
3 Ibid., 6.
4 Rahul Gairola, 'Pankaj Mishra (1969–)', in *South Asian Novelists in English: An A-to-Z Guide*, ed. Jaina C. Sanga (Westport, CT and London: Greenwood Press, 2003), 158–60.
5 Robert Marquand, 'Not New Export: Prose Passages from India', *Christian Science Monitor*, 1 February 2000. Online: http://www.csmonitor.com/2000/0201/p1s4.html (accessed 17 January 2013).
6 *The Romantics* captured my attention because he is a fellow alumnus of the University of Allahabad. See: A. N. Dwivedi, 'Allahabad in Pankaj Mishra's *The Romantics*: A Partly Corrective View', *Parnassus* 1 (2009): 7–12.
7 Mishra, *Temptations of the West*, 5.
8 Ibid., 7.
9 Jill Didur, '"An Unremembered Time": Secular Criticism in Pankaj Mishra's *The Romantics*', *Journal of Commonwealth Literature* 44, no. 2 (2009): 67.
10 Ibid., 82.

11 Arundhati Roy, acknowledgements to *The God of Small Things* (New Delhi: IndiaInk, 1997).
12 Customer review by 'vvp', Amazon.com. Online: http://www.amazon.com/Butter-Chicken-Ludhiana-Travels-Small/dp/0330444123/ref=sr_1_1?ie=UTF8&qid=1358432551&sr=8-1&keywords=Butter+Chicken+in+Ludhiana (accessed 17 January 2013).
13 Review of *Butter Chicken*, Complete Review. Online: http://www.complete-review.com/reviews/mishrap/bcinludh.htm#basic (accessed 17 January 2013).
14 See Mishra's interview with Jerry Pinto: '*Butter Chicken in Ludhiana* Was a Dishonest Work by a Dishonest Writer', *Times of India*, 16 January 2000, 16.
   Editor's note: Amitava Kumar recalls the impact of *Butter Chicken*: 'That book was a sardonic look at the attitudes that went with what Mishra called India's "shabby borrowed modernity". *Butter Chicken* signalled a growing interest among writers and readers in understanding the ways in which a new economy was beginning to find root in the whole of India.' (Amitava Kumar, *Bombay-London-New York: A Literary Journal* (New Delhi: Penguin, 2002), 41.)
15 Didur, 'An Unremembered Time', 66.
16 Mishra, quoted in *South Asian Novelists in English: An A-To-Z Guide*, ed. Jaina C. Sanga (Westport, CT: Greenwood Press, 2003), 161.
17 Didur, 'An Unremembered Time', 66.
18 Mishra, *An End to Suffering*, 133–4.
19 Mishra, foreword to *Temptations of the West*, n.p.
20 Mishra, *Temptations of the West*, 4.
21 **Editor's note:** The fact that Mishra is directly influenced by the American writer and literary critic Edmund Wilson is pointed out by Challakere: 'The popularity of *Romantics*, indicated by the number of favorable reviews it has received, makes us wonder to what degree Mishra's admiration of Edmund Wilson points to Mishra's own ambitions.' Padmaja Challakere, 'Pankaj Mishra', *South Asian Literature in English: An Encyclopedia*, ed. Jaina C. Sanga (Westport, CT: Greenwood Press, 2004), 263.
22 Mishra, 'A Sepulchral Chill in the Soul', *New Statesman*, 16 February 2004. Online: http://www.newstatesman.com/node/147304 (accessed 24 March 2011).
23 Mishra, *The Romantics*, 3.
24 Ibid., 266–7.
25 Mishra, *Temptations of the West*, 4.
26 Ibid., 151.
27 Akash Kapur, 'Sentimental Education', *New York Times*, 27 February 2000. Online: http://www.nytimes.com/books/00/02/27/reviews/000227.27kapurt.html (accessed 17 January 2013).
28 Margery Sabin, 'Pankaj Mishra and Postcolonial Cosmopolitanism', *Raritan* 21, no. 4 (2002): 200; cited from Jill Didur, *Journal of Commonwealth Literature* 44 (2009): 76.
29 Shirley Chew, cover blurb of Pankaj Mishra, *The Romantics*.
30 *Observer*, cover blurb of Pankaj Mishra, *Temptations of the West*.
31 **Editor's note:** For more details on Mishra's sociopolitical concerns, see his interview with Sarah Fay, 'Pankaj Mishra', *Believer*, March 2007. Online: http://www.believermag.com/issues/200703/?read=interview_mishra (accessed 12 May 2010).

Chapter Two

COMMODIFICATION OF POST-RUSHDIE INDIAN NOVELS IN ENGLISH: KUNAL BASU AND THE POLITICS OF DECANONIZATION

Angshuman Kar

In the last PhD entrance test conducted by our department, almost ninety per cent of the 55 students who appeared before the Research Advisory Committee (the board in our university that conducts the test) to defend their proposals expressed their willingness to do the research on writers other than British. Eighty per cent of this ninety per cent, surprisingly, wanted to work on writers of Indian origin. Seventy percent of this eighty per cent chose fiction writers. Availability of research materials and the number of the PhDs done on these writers – which is still no match to the works done on canonical British writers and which, in a way, lessens the burden of the researcher in terms of the review of the existing research works on the writer of his/her choice – may have determined the choice of these candidates who would work in a rural university of a developing country like ours. But their choice of Indian writers writing fiction in English clearly shows how popular these writers have become in Indian academia. Indian English writers started getting global attention when decanonization, both as a theoretical paradigm and as a literary practice, began to shape the production of literary texts across the world.[1] But at the end of the first decade of the twenty first century, one has to admit, decanonization itself has almost taken the shape of a reverse canonization that invariably involves the politics of exclusion/inclusion. The halo seems to hang over a select few fortunate writers, whereas others, if not in darkness, are at least shadowed by the luminaries. This essay, by focusing on the fiction of Kunal Basu, would like to examine the issues that are mediating the production and consumption of post-Rushdie Indian novels in English, and in so doing it would also try to show

how these issues are inseparable from the politics of decanonization. In this context, it has also to be mentioned that though Rushdie came to fame in the early 1980s, the 'Rushdie phenomenon' did not impact on Indian English novels until the early 1990s, a time when India gradually started entering into the postliberalization phase of its economy. An examination of the production and consumption mechanics of post-Rushdie Indian English novels, therefore, in a way, becomes an examination of the factors that contribute to the production and consumption of postliberalization Indian English novels as well.

To a 'postcolonial' academic or writer writing in English, decanonization is often synonymous with an attempt to reread/rewrite texts produced by white, colonial British writers; s/he usually ignores the politics of class and gender that went into the making of the British canon.[2] Such a trend of equating decanonization with decolonization perhaps began with Rushdie's famous essay 'The Empire Writes Back with a Vengeance' (1982), where he shows how the writers of the erstwhile colonies have started subverting the essentially colonial constructs and stereotypes of European literatures.[3] This trend gained momentum when Rushdie's phrase was appropriated by Bill Ashcroft et al. in their worldwide famous book, *The Empire Writes Back: Theory and Practice in Postcolonial Literatures* (1989). In the Indian context, these attempts at writing back – which have not only stuck to rereading/rewriting texts produced by the colonizers but has also included attempts at celebrating the native past – have unquestionably produced some of the great masters of Indian English fiction. However, if we look back at the path that Indian English fiction has already trodden, it would be wrong to say that the processes of decanonization have always had an anticolonial overtone. Texts that celebrate Indian national culture, examine the processes of nation building and their impact on the Indian populace after independence, foreground the problems of the Indian migrants in different multicultural countries of the world and map the trajectory of a transnational future, have earned not only worldwide fame for some of the Indian English writers but also places of honour in English literature syllabuses in universities across the globe. In the last 30 years, almost all of the prestigious prizes of the world have been given to various English writers of Indian origin. Apart from Rushdie (whose *Midnight's Children* (1981) has won the Booker Prize, the Booker of Bookers and also the Best of the Booker), many other writers have also won distinguished prizes. Arundhati Roy has won the Booker Prize for her *God of Small Things* (1997), the Commonwealth Writers' Prize has been received by Rohinton Mistry for *Such a Long Journey* (1991) and Vikram Seth for *A Suitable Boy* (1993), Jhumpa Lahiri became the first Indian to win the Pulitzer Prize for her *Interpreter of Maladies* (1999) and Kiran Desai became the youngest woman to win the Man Booker Prize for *The Inheritance of Loss* (2006). Amitav Ghosh, apart from many other awards, has recently won the controversial Dan David

Prize, the monetary worth of which is $1 million. Prizes, indeed, have brought both fame and money. M. K. Naik and Shyamala A. Narayan have informed us that Vikram Seth's *A Suitable Boy* 'was sold to Faber and Faber for a sum of one million pounds, for the UK rights alone'.[4] In this context, it is particularly interesting that Kiran Desai's *The Inheritance of Loss* has sold 190,000 copies in India alone.[5] Because Indian English fiction is selling in the market, for a young debutant of Indian English fiction, finding a publisher is perhaps no more a big problem if s/he has either a foreign education or a foreign job, or at least a place for staying abroad. Thus, whereas Anand's *Untouchable* was rejected by 19 British publishers in 1935, Amit Chaudhuri's first novel, *A Strange and Sublime Address* was published by Heinemann in 1991.[6] There is little doubt that the success of Rushdie and his followers in the Western market – particularly the success of the Indian diaspora writers, most of whom either write about India or about problems of acculturation in their host land – is the cause of this change in the attitude of foreign publishing houses to Indian writers. The increase in the number of the English-educated, middle-class Indians and the huge market that they offer have also attracted foreign publishing houses either to open branches in India or to bring out Indian/South Asian versions of a book in an affordable price that suits the consumer of a Third World/developing country. The viability of the market for Indian English fiction is also behind the emergence of some *deshi* publishing houses, like Rupa paperbacks, who are not only publishing new works but also inexpensive editions of the old British classics. The next section of the essay will address how marketing and the factors that determine the character and movements of a literary market are heavily mediating the production and consumption of postliberalization and post-Rushdie Indian English fiction.

Though the great trio of Indian English fiction (Anand, Rao and Narayan) could have very successfully created a market for themselves, the present boom of Indian English fiction owes largely to the success of Rushdie. The impact of Rushdie's success on his successors is clearly marked by two books published recently on the history of Indian English literature. If the chapter on contemporary Indian English novelists in M. K. Naik and Shyamala A. Narayan's *Indian English Literature 1980–2000: A Critical Survey* (2001) is titled '*Midnight's Children*'s Children: The Novel II', the title of such a chapter (by John Mee) in Arvind Krishna Mehrotra's *An Illustrated History of Indian Literature in English* (2003) is 'After Midnight: The Novel in the 1980s and 1990s'. Both the titles clearly indicate how the Rushdie phenomenon shaped the face of contemporary Indian English fiction. Mee posits, 'The 1980s witnessed a second coming for the Indian novel in English. Its messiah seems to have been Salman Rushdie. The appearance of *Midnight's Children* in 1981 brought about a renaissance in Indian writing in English which has outdone that of the 1930s.'[7]

Mee, in fact, has pointed out a few features of *Midnight's Children* that have become the features of most of the major Indian English novels of the time: 'a certain postmodern playfulness, the turn to history, a new exuberance of language, the reinvention of allegory, the sexual frankness, even the prominent references to Bollywood'.[8] In fact, a close examination of some of the works of the contemporary big names of Indian English fiction shows that Rushdie's turn to history (the history of the subcontinent in particular) has, in the hands of the contemporary writers, become an engagement with the idea of India the nation-state and the trope of Indianness. Most of the novels of Amitav Ghosh, for instance, examine the positionality of India on a global sociopolitical scale sometimes by going back to the past and exploiting colonialism as a setting and sometimes drawing on the cultural specificities of some particular regions of India. Cultural specificities of a particular region of India have also been exploited by Arundhati Roy to tell a universal tale that questions the larger issue of nation through a personal romance. In fact, the interface of the narrative of the individual and that of the nation seems to be the most important lens through which the history of Partition is seen in *The Shadow Lines* (1988), an inevitable choice of the syllabus designers of Indian English literature at almost every university in the world that offers a course on Indian English, South Asian English and/or postcolonial writers. Vikram Seth's *A Suitable Boy*, through a story of matchmaking, actually narrates the sociopolitical changes taking place in India after independence. Tharoor's *The Great Indian Novel* (1989), similarly, for examining the present-day Indian reality uses the story of *Mahabharata*. The so-called 'diaspora' writers of Indian English literature like Jhumpa Lahiri and Kiran Desai are also negotiating with 'India' and 'Indianness' either by presenting Indian exotica under veil or by making the most of the problems of acculturation that Indian migrants experience in their host countries or by making the Indian reality subject to a foreign gaze. An overview of the post-Rushdie and postliberalization Indian English novels, therefore, shows manifold negotiations of the novelists with 'India' and 'Indianness'. Mee explains the scene thus:

> Many of the novelists seem to regard India's wealth of literary and mythical tradition as freely available to rewrite in the present. A different perspective might construe this trend as the self-serving attempt by section of the elite to represent their own modernity in terms of continuity with India's past, papering over the cracks in the national imaginary, as it were, to affirm their own authenticity. Similarly the celebration of plurality and openness could be understood as doing the ideological work of economic liberalization, presenting Indian identity in terms of the shifting surfaces of late capitalism, privileging mobility and cosmopolitanism over local

cultures and communities [...]. It is also true that marketers of the Indian novel in English have also shown great canniness. There has developed, over the past few years, a sense that India sells abroad.⁹

Mee's observations, apart from questioning the motives of the contemporary Indian English writers (most of whom have come with an elite background), have laid bare one truth: the commodification of 'India' in contemporary Indian English fiction. Because the correspondences between a writer and his/her agent/publisher take place in the 'private' domain and a select innocent few of them are made public during a writer's lifetime, and because a writer while talking about the forces of motivation that worked behind the production of a text almost always remains silent about the forces of market, it is impossible for us to know whether a writer writing in English is now asked by the agent or the publisher to put 'India' into his/her writing.¹⁰ In this context, one idea can be deduced: an Indian English writer writing on India need not encounter the unsolicited advice of the editor that Raja Rao had to face at the time of the publication of *Kanthapura* in 1938.¹¹ Still, Mee's contention that 'India sells abroad' necessitates at least two observations. First, India not only sells abroad, India sells within India as well. The sale of *The Inheritance of Loss* in India could alone be a testimony to this claim. There is little doubt that postliberalization Indian English novels have become novels of the higher middle class, by the higher middle class, for the higher middle class. This category wants to know about India, desires to demarcate its role in nation building and aims to foresee their problems of acculturation in the host land, in case they migrate. This brings us to the second observation on Mee's thesis: only India of a particular kind sells in the literary market. A purely historical novel about India's past, even if it exploits Indian exotica to the extreme, does not seem to have good prospects. Recent past of India sells; remote past sells too, if used to make sense of the present. The fact that the success of *The Shadow Lines* is relatively greater than that of any one of the other novels by Ghosh not only attests to this fact but also shows that even the non-Indian readers of Indian English fiction love to see India represented in specific ways.¹²

In the context of the above discussion, it is really interesting to take up the fiction of Kunal Basu, a management teacher at Oxford University by profession. To date, Kunal Basu has written four novels – *The Opium Clerk* (2001), *The Miniaturist* (2003), *Racists* (2006), *The Yellow Emperor's Cure* (2011) – and a collection of short stories, *The Japanese Wife* (2008). Though Basu seems to be a writer of great merit and promise, it seems that he has not yet achieved the kind of attention – both public and critical – that he deserves. True, the title story of *The Japanese Wife* has been filmed by Aparna Sen and his novels have received enthusiastic reviews in important magazines and journals such as the *Times Literary Supplement*, the *Guardian*, *Sydney Morning Herald*, *Kirkus Review* and the like, but reception of Basu seems to fall short of the expected standard.[13] He has not yet grabbed any literary awards, neither has he been able to make a significant entry into the university syllabuses. Each of his books – as he himself has mentioned in an email conversation with this writer – has sold about 20,000 copies. *The Japanese Wife*, perhaps because of the film, has sold around 50,000 copies, no match to the sales of Kiran Desai's *Inheritance of Loss*. It could be argued that when academics write fiction, often the elitist style of writing acts as a barrier to their success in the market. Though Basu is an Oxford academic, this charge does not stand against him, as he writes in an English that is elegant but not inaccessible to the average reader. It could also be said that often a writer is not that well received in the market because s/he is published by small publishing houses that lack in their promotional strategies. This cannot be said about Kunal Basu. Most of his books have been published by reputed publishing houses like Penguin and HarperCollins and in the email conversation mentioned above Basu himself has acknowledged his indebtedness to his publishers, as they regularly send out prepublication review copies to newspapers, magazines, TV and radio channels, schedule interviews with the press, coordinate his appearances at literary festivals, arrange book tours and in India even give press advertising and point-of-sale support in bookshops. In fact, one of the reasons behind the relatively low reception of Basu could be his decision to not tell the stories of the NRI (nonresident Indian) life, stories that have – as we have argued already – a ready market. Writers of the Indian diaspora, who unquestionably contributed significantly to the creation of a steady market for Indian English fiction, mostly write stories on relatively easier and palatable problems of the NRI life without serious examination of the interactions among different diaspora communities or of the impact of the changes in the nature of capital, transnational trade, globalization and in the immigration policies of host countries in the face of terrorist threats. Such 'safely' written diaspora stories have got such a market that sometimes it seems that even a very short stay in any of the developed countries entitles an Indian writer to write about 'simplistic' diaspora experiences and makes him/her more privileged than those Indian English novelists who have never been abroad. Basu, however, is least interested in telling such NRI stories. In an interview with this author, published in the first issue of the Bengali version of *India Today* in 2006, Basu clearly said, 'I get bored telling known stories of the known world. For example, the lives of NRIs never attract me. I think that the life of an NRI is extremely boring, and there's no story in a boring life.'[14]

Writers of the Indian diaspora do write about India too, and in representing India they hardly come out of the trajectory designed by Rushdie. India, in fact, is present in Kunal Basu's work, but this India is not the kind of India that sells in the market. It would be unwise to think that Basu in his fiction is incapable of using an India that sells in the market. Born nine years after Indian independence, Basu spent his youth in Kolkata, which was stormed by the Naxalite politics in the late 1960s and the early 1970s. During his student years in Jadavpur University, he became actively involved in politics. He recalls, 'The Emergency in 1975 took me into the "underground". These were dangerous but heady days. There was the thrill of the moment, unlike the routine of daily bickering we know as politics. There were grand illusions, a glimpse of utopia [...] Campus life meant carousing with forbidden books, weapons [...] whispering secrets in the ears of comrades. There were trips to the margins, taking us far beyond our comfort zones.'[15]

This uncovering of Basu's past by the writer himself indicates that he is well aware of experiences about the recent past of India that can have a very good prospect in the market. But Basu, to his credit, has not marketed these experiences to gain recognition (or monetary benefit). *The Opium Clerk*, for instance, explores the dynamics of the nineteenth-century opium trade and the India that we see in the novel is the India of a remote past seen through Hiran, the protagonist of the tale. Basu's second novel, *The Miniaturist*, narrates the story of a miniaturist, Bihjad, the son of the chief artist of Akbar. Set in sixteenth-century India, the story documents, on the one hand, the great Mughal culture and art and, on the other, records the crisis of an artist confronting a bitter reality. Basu's third novel, *Racists*, in no way is related to India. This is, perhaps, the first Victorian novel written by a contemporary Indian English writer that addresses the great nineteenth-century debate on race. In this context, it is interesting to point out that the India of recent times (though not exactly the one that sells in the market) does figure in the title story of *The Japanese Wife*, and this story has also been picked up by a renowned Indian filmmaker.

At this juncture, one needs to ask the old question again: who determines what sells in the literary market? Is it the writer, who once sure of the market value of a particular brand of writing goes on repeating him/herself? Is it the publisher who, with his/her innovative 'promo' techniques, can create a demand in the market even for a mediocre work or, relying on the feedback of the market taken by highly professional market surveyors, accepts only those manuscripts that have a product value, whatever their literary merits are? Are all these issues related to larger issues of globalization and liberalization and of the role of capitalism and its nexus with print and audio-visual media? Or is it the academic who, for professional reasons, writes papers and publishes books on these authors and even instructs a budding researcher to choose any one of these 'talked about' writers for his/her dissertation. I am, in context of this essay, particularly interested in exploring the last of the four questions asked above.

The list of the papers presented in any seminar or conference on Indian English literature (or postcolonial literature in general) often reflects how some contemporary, big, award-winning names overshadow both the names of the past masters and those of the less-known but promising writers of the present. The titles that these presenters choose for their papers clearly show a preference for issues related to India studies. India, Indianness, pan-Indian identity, preindependence, postindependence, nation, nationality, nation-state, transnationalism, postnationalism – these are some of the terms that regularly feature in the titles of the papers presented in these conferences. Sometimes some of these terms figure in the titles of the seminars as well. What is true for a seminar/conference is also true for a critical book. Edited volumes on the representation of the issues mentioned above in Indian English fiction are produced in abundance. Commercial viability of critical books on Indian literature is determined by whether academics and researchers consume the materials available in these books in order to reproduce more material along similar lines. So, writers work on certain issues, academics work on them further and these works are then published and consumed by other academics who then again work on these same issues. Consequently, a limited number of issues and a handful of names continue to dictate the market and the academia. This has been the scenario for at least the last two decades in India and an exit from this vicious circle, right now, seems almost impossible. What has worsened the situation is the fact that in most cases academics also act as reviewers, appointed by magazine or newspaper literary editors. The study of James Curran, in this context, offers interesting insights. In his study of the 'frameworks of the cultural values and social networks that bind together magazine and newspaper literary editors, publishers and novelists', Curran shows 'how a relatively small literary network shapes the acquisition, hierarchical promotion and critical judgements made about books and authors'.[16] His social networks seem to exclude academics, but if we look at the Indian situation, this can hardly be done. Academics very often run independent magazines and journals in India. Many a time, these publications do not even require a sponsor because they are run by the financial support of the contributors. There is little doubt that these journals and magazines, where one can buy a publication, are further aggravating the situation. One last thing before I conclude: in the name of worshipping the poststructural/postmodern philosophy of uncertainty/indeterminacy, present-day academics, unlike old stalwarts like Prof. Iyengar or Prof. Naik, seldom measure the merit of a literary work and take it as a suitable site for applying the latest culture theories. This is significantly contributing to the perpetuation of the vicious circle mentioned above. Had these academics been a little bit more judgemental, things could have been different.

So, Indian English writing that emerged as a part of the processes of decanonization during the colonial period in India seems to have converted itself into a process of reverse canon formation. Inclusion in this canon is not always being done on the basis of the literary merit of the work included; exclusions, similarly, are being monitored by extraliterary concerns that mediate the production and consumption of these works. This, however, does not mean that all the writers included in the canon do not deserve a place there. The point is: some of them could be and should be replaced by some others who are excluded. Time, of course, is the greatest adjudicator in this respect. In the final analysis, issues that mediate the production and consumption of texts and control the politics of inclusion/exclusion in the canon cannot compete with the unbiased, indifferent tick of the clock. A canon, therefore, is created, destroyed and re-created: once in the canon does not necessarily mean always in the canon. A writer like Basu, therefore, should wait for his turn.

Notes and References

1. In this context, one has to remember the work by critics like K. R. Srinivasa Iyengar, M. K. Naik and C. D. Narasimhaiah; these critics not only made the Western academia familiar with the first masters of Indian English writers but also proved the merit of their works by unhesitatingly giving their judgment on the value of the works of these writers.
2. In his *Postcolonial Literature: An Introduction*, Promod Nayar writes, 'Decanonization is a two-step process: (i) the process of re-reading this literature for its colonial/imperial themes (ii) re-writing the texts from an anti-colonial (even native) point of view.' See Pramod K. Nayar, *Postcolonial Literature: An Introduction* (Delhi: Pearson Longman, 2008), 239.
3. Salman Rushdie, 'The Empire Writes Back with a Vengeance', *Times*, 3 July 1982, 8.
4. M. K. Naik and Shyamala A. Narayan, *Indian English Literature 1980–2000: A Critical Survey* (Delhi: Pencraft, 2001), 35.
5. See 'Penguin India Bags Rights for Kiran Desai's New Novel, *Pamuk*', *Hindu*, 6 October 2010. Online: http://www.thehindu.com/arts/books/article816256.ece (accessed 2 November 2010).
6. Naik and Narayan, *Indian English Literature*, 35.
7. John Mee, 'After Midnight: The Novel in 1980s and 1990s', in *An Illustrated History of Indian Literature in English*, ed. Arvind Krishna Mehrotra (Delhi: Permanent Black, 2003), 318.
8. Ibid.
9. Ibid.
10. We can know these inside details only when all the correspondences between a writer and his/her agent/publisher are made public, once the copyright period is over.
11. Malcolm Barnes, Rao's editor for Allen and Unwin, objected to Rao's colloquial English and even advised him to go for a more anglicized title for the book in place of the Indianized *Kanthapura*. For a detailed treatment of the issue, see Ruvani Ranasinha,

South Asian Writers in Twentieth-Century Britain: Culture in Transition (Oxford: Clarendon Press, 2007).

12 Even a cursory look at the syllabuses of Indian English literature of different universities in India and abroad illustrates the sweeping victory of *The Shadow Lines* over other works of Ghosh in terms of the number of entries. To date, *The Shadow Lines* has also been the only one of his novels on which independent critical anthologies have been published.

13 Navtej Sarna, who reviewed *The Opium Clerk* in the *Times Literary Supplement*, hailed the novel as 'a first novel of rare assurance, imaginatively set and richly textured with tales that spin away into elliptical orbits'. (Navtej Sarna, 'God's Own Medicine'. Online: http://navtejsarna.com/br_opium.htm (accessed 2 November 2010).)

14 Kunal Basu, 'Sahitya Amar Kaache Kalpnaar Uraan', interview with Angshuman Kar in *India Today*, 4 September 2006, 98–9 [translation mine].

15 Kunal Basu, 'Kunal Basu Unrehearsed: A Conversation with Amitava Roy', interview with Amitava Roy in *Romancing the Strange: The Fiction of Kunal Basu*, ed. Subir Dhar et al. (Kolkata: Avantgarde Press, 2004), 7.

16 Keith Negus, 'The Work of Cultural Intermediaries and the Enduring Distance Between Production and Consumption', *Cultural Studies* 16, no. 4 (2002): 513. Also see James Curran, 'Literary Editors, Social Networks and Cultural Tradition', in *Media Organisation in Society*, ed. James Curran (London: Arnold, 2000), 215–39.

Chapter Three

MARKETING LAD LIT, CREATING BESTSELLERS: THE IMPORTANCE OF BEING CHETAN BHAGAT

Aysha Iqbal Viswamohan

If chick lit is popular fiction by, for and about young women (or 'tweens'), then lad lit can be explained as a fictional genre with books written by men and focusing on twentysomething male characters, particularly about those who are self-absorbed, nonconformist and afraid of commitment.[1] While some critics may object to the general candy floss nature of the genre, what remains unchallenged is its enormous popularity among target readers, occasionally resulting in successful films. Notable examples include *Bridget Jones's Diary* (1996), *Sex and the City* (1997), *The Devil Wears Prada* (2003) and, to an extent, *He's Just Not That Into You* (2004) – all produced by big Hollywood studios, featuring major box office stars. Quite similar in tone are the 'guy's books': Nick Hornby being the accepted big daddy of the genre, along with Matt Dunn, Michael Weinreb, Michael Chabon and Eric Jerome Dickey (and to some degree Toby Young and Aaron Karo's selected works).[2] Some common themes that readers of this category are familiar with include masculine insecurities, competition at college or the work place, sexual fantasies, drug addiction, relationships, heartbreaks, family issues and obsession with sports. Like chick lit, lad lit too has a cult following, and some of the notable screen adaptations are *High Fidelity* (2000), *How to Lose Friends and Alienate People* (2008), *About a Boy* (2002) and *Wonder Boys* (2000), featuring A-list names such as Michael Douglas, Toby Maguire, Hugh Grant and John Cusack, in roles reinforcing the belief that 'boys will be boys'.

Tween lit, of both the chick and lad variety, is a relatively recent phenomenon in India. Anurag Mathur's *The Inscrutable Americans* (1991) can be termed, however loosely, as an exemplar of lad lit. The symptoms are present full-on: self-discovery, travel, *Bildungsroman*, coming of age, liberal use of Hinglish and an obsession with losing virginity. The novel traces the life of Gopal, a twenty-year-old who travels to America and goes through a series of comical situations because of cultural differences. Published by Rupa, *The Inscrutable Americans* created a record in Indian publishing history for not only being the most-sold Indian book but also for being the only book to feature on the bestseller list for eleven years.

That was during the early 1990s, when the names that mattered in the Indian novels in English marquee were confined to Salman Rushdie, Anita Desai, R. K. Narayan, Nayantara Sehgal and Khushwant Singh. With the gradual passage of time and a sudden shift in the economic landscape, observers of Indian writing in English noticed a dramatic change in the literary scene. An unprecedented exposure and accessibility to global publications (including books, lifestyle and fashion magazines), along with international films and television programs, paved the way for a new kind of fiction portraying the lives of (mostly urban) protagonists who were ambitious, chic and brand conscious, were the products of elite institutes and were unafraid to question the 'sacred cows'.

While Swati Kaushal's *Piece of Cake* (2005), Rupa Gulab's *Girl Alone* (2007) and Advaita Kala's *Almost Single* (2010) are a few popular chick lit novels set in India, the grandmaster of lad lit is undoubtedly Chetan Bhagat. Bhagat graduated from the Indian Institute of Technology (IIT) in Delhi in 1995 and then did his MBA from the Indian Institute of Management (IIM) at Ahmedabad in 1997. While working in an investment bank in Hong Kong, he hit upon the idea to write a novel on his days and experiences at the IIT Delhi.

True to the lad lit genre, Bhagat's debut novel *Five Point Someone: What Not to Do at IIT* (2004) maps the lives of three students at IIT Delhi who are unable to cope with the system. Their poor grades brand them as underperformers in IIT society and test everything else they hold important – friendship, love, ambition and responsibilities. Like most works of this genre, *FPS* explores the question of success and its importance in other aspects of life. Chetan peppered the story with all the right ingredients make it market friendly (though the manuscript was rejected twelve times): parental pressure, familial obligations, gender roles, dating, sex, drugs, suicide, geeky students, nerdy professors – just about every teen issue is addressed. Vaguely philosophical, with a funny take on campus life in one of the country's most prestigious institutes, *FPS* was an instant chartbuster and retained its number one position on most of the 'Top Ten Reads' lists for several years.

For some, Bhagat pulled it off because 'he was the first – there was novelty. More of the same starts tasting like a samosa made from yesterday's bhaji, fried in *utra hua tel*.'[3] Further, Bhagat must have anticipated a substantial readership for the book because it breaks many myths about an institute of formidable repute. The price factor, too, played a role. Bhagat ensured that the work was priced under Rs 100 to make it accessible to target readers, while most works by the 'elite' writers come in around Rs 500. A writer without a hyphenated existence, Bhagat was the mastermind of a website promoting the book, offering a monthly contest and his own email address for fan letters, feedback, etc. This market savvy paid off as sales topped fifteen thousand in just the first six weeks (making the book a bestseller in India's English-language fiction market).

In an article in the *New York Times*, Barbara Crossette observed, 'Writing in English, these authors [Indian writers in English] are able to present their disarmingly intimate and often unconventional images of India to readers beyond their nation's borders.'[4] This observation, made way back in 1990, still holds true today. Indeed, emboldened by critical and commercial success, Indian writers in English are pulling out all the stops in their work. Prof. Tapan Basu has further elaborated, 'Market has developed indeed in India for Indian writing in English on a dimension and proportion in which such a market never existed in our country prior to the mid-1980s.'[5] Truly, Indian writing in English is witnessing an era of endless opportunities, both in terms of experimentation with the novelty of themes and style as well as in its commercial viability.

It is in this connection that Kushal Gulab explores yet another phenomenon: publishers seeking potential writers. Gulab elaborates:

> Over the last year or so, V. Karthika, editor in chief at HarperCollins India, has actively sought writers to write the kind of books that Indian writers haven't written in English so far or at least not in volumes. She's looked for writers who'll do chick lit, who'll do thrillers, who'll do contemporary urban stories, who'll write for young adults. In short, writers who write the kind of books that the majority of us like to read. Books that are not highbrow, that tell a good story without necessarily probing the murky depths of human experience, that entertain and are simply a damn good read.[6]

Clearly, writers from India had never had it this good. Taking a cue from the trend, Chetan Bhagat, a student of business and marketing, packed his debut novel (and subsequent works) with appropriate doses of commercial ingredients, the right amount of humour and the essential 'all's well' feeling of a lad lit. He sensed that the Indian middle class 'has an appetite for literary entertainment that falls between the elite idiom of the cultivated literati, who might be familiar with the novels of Amitav Ghosh or Salman Rushdie, and the Indian English of the street and the supermarket. Theirs is the Indian English of the outsourcing generation. For these people, there is only one author: Chetan Bhagat.'[7]

With *FPS*, apart from marketing a very lucrative genre, Rupa also worked at building up the debuting writer's reputation. The company launched a full-throttled media blitzkrieg about Bhagat's impressive credentials, including graduation from IIT Delhi, his stint at IIM Ahmedabad and his successful banking career in Hong Kong. The book was reviewed by leading dailies and magazines, and the publishers capitalized on the reviews by highlighting adjectives such as 'fun-filled', 'breezy' and 'racy and raunchy' for the publicity material. To strengthen the viability of *FPS*, an effective marketing strategy was employed by the publishers through their brochures. Trying to make sense of the remarkable success of *FPS*, a scholar posits, 'While readership profiles are not available, I would argue that Rupa's market lies as much in what are called the B centres as in the bigger cities of India. This audience, belonging largely to the middle and lower sections of the middle class, is exposed to metropolitan sensibilities through the media and has an aspirational attitude towards them – the same audience, in fact, which is also making Rupa's *Five Point Someone: What Not to Do at IIT* a national bestseller.'[8]

Set in the early 1990s, *FPS* details the lives of three 'IIT-ians' – Hari, Ryan and Alok. Although the three have been school toppers, their lives and grades at IIT are in a mess. The writer establishes his intentions at the outset: 'This is not a book to teach you how to get into IIT or even survive it' (1). Evidently, the idea that underpins the book is spelt out loud and clear: have nonstop fun without wrecking your brains by searching for something deeper. Needless to say, although the backdrop of *FPS* is elitist, its appeal is universal. Any urban college student would identify with Pink Floyd, grass and vodka; action films and scooter rides to plush markets 'to check out girls' (36); fretting over grades and insipid food in mess; hatching a plot to steal question papers from the office of the head of the department; and having an affair with the director's daughter – the novel caters to practically every adolescent fantasy.

To make his work accessible to its target readers, Bhagat uses an abundance of digestible humour: Alok's family is described as poor, but 'not World Bank ads type starving poor' (33); 'calling an IIT-ian a commerce student was one of the worst insults, like a prostitute calling her client a eunuch' (56); 'tearing his rotis like a famished Unicef kid' (37); [describing a typical Hindi film heroine] 'she bathed in the rain, played tennis in mini-skirts and wore sequined negligees to discos. Since all her hobbies involved wearing less or transparent clothing, the audience loved her' (37); [on a topper] 'he had put enough oil in his hair to cook an entire Kumaon dinner' (93); and there are his tongue-in-cheek references to family planning documentaries (87).

The IIT-ians are known for their distinct 'campus language' and Bhagat makes liberal use of terms like 'insti', 'arbit', 'prof', 'muggu' and 'fundoo'. At the same time, the author makes sufficient use of the linguistic variety of

Indian English too: 'Like samosas-chutney, idli-sambhar or rajma-chawal, Floyd and vodka are in a combo-class of their own' (81); 'drop-shrop it' (65); 'paranthas' (35), etc. Thus, Bhagat combines the Indian part of his language and its own argot with slang from abroad, making the language extremely palatable and reader-friendly. This 'abrogation of standard English is the sign of a certain cultural weightlessness'[9] and one of the many reasons of Bhagat's appeal.[10]

Bhagat's influences are obvious. The angst-ridden teen voice echoes *Catcher in the Rye* (1951) and the drug-filled 'insti' roof scenes recall the raves of Pakistani writer Mohsin Hamid's *Moth Smoke* (2000). The elitist youngsters retaining their Indianness is a nod at Agastya Sen from Upmanyu Chatterjee's *English August* (1988). A heady mix of high and low brow, with liberal doses of pop culture and home-grown common sense, Bhagat serves us a world that is thrilling and racy, with occasional dark tones, yet always instantly recognizable.

Buddy literature goes hand-in-hand with lad lit and Bhagat overdoses on the tropes. The cover of *FPS* is strewn with definitions, axioms and popular proverbs on and about friendship. It is interesting to observe how thematically close the book is to the cult buddy film *Dil Chahta Hai* (2001). The film, directed by Farhan Akhtar, depicts typical Generation X young urban men, their lives, loves and aspirations. As the film caught the imagination of the urban, upper middle–class youth, it was evident that forces of globalization and economic liberalization would henceforth influence popular art and literature from India (Bhagat yet again pays homage to the music of *Dil Chahta Hai* in the Bed Lounge and Bar scene of *One Night @ the Call Center*).

Bhagat's success can also be attributed to his willingness to reach out to his audience. The market-savvy writer has an attractive and interactive website, where he provides information about his novels, his art, answers questions, encourages visitors to email him and claims to look forward to their feedback.[11] Taking on the mantle of a modern day spiritual guide, Bhagat asserts in the *Hindu*, 'One day a boy wrote to me that he wanted to commit suicide after failing to make it to IIT but when he read *Five Point Someone* he came out of the negative thought. To me this is the success of literature.'[12] Needless to say, such effective measures go a long way in forging a bond with readers and, dare I add, leading to better sales. The book's affordability (Rs 95, 'for an international-quality paperback version, a never-before in Indian publishing – only to make this book accessible to all' says the author's website, rather helpfully) played no minor role in making it a runaway success.

There is no denying the impact *FPS* had on the average reading public and on the young college-going population, and Bhagat's follow-up *One Night @ the Call Center* (2005) was yet another attempt to appeal to his captivated audience. In simplistic terms, its themes are universal, namely: ex-girlfriend, bad boss and God, and that is half the marketing battle won. The narrative mirrors the alienation and angst of the call centre, a current metro phenomenon, a symbol of India's rapidly globalizing economy. While regular Indians sleep, a sizeable population of young, skilled and upwardly mobile professionals works through the night, functioning on US time under made-up American names. They enjoy a lifestyle that is a cocktail of premature affluence and conspicuous consumption. It is a subculture that merits closer examination and Bhagat milks it for all its worth.

Bhagat's second outing, too, follows his well-trodden path of exploiting contemporary market forces to the hilt. The novel explores a topical theme; that is, the lifestyle and attitudes of those working in call centres. The author cleverly reinforces every possible stereotype about this industry and lends a touch of controversy through his anti-American discourse, while providing a dose of palatable pop spirituality. In keeping with their 'Indian' image, Rupa cashed in on the spiritual angle of the novel with the publicity material loudly proclaiming, 'It was the night they got a phone call. That phone call was from God.'

ON@TCC begins in a typical self-help guide style by asking the readers to write something that they fear, get angry about and don't like about themselves. From the outset, it is established that the novel is targeted at the yuppie reader raised on a composite culture of Cosmo-Vogue 'how to...' reading. Told through the eyes of the protagonist Shyam, it tells the story of globalized environment, thwarted ambitions, sexual repression, the generation gap, pop psychology, unrequited love, cultural conflict, mounting pressures of patriarchal set-ups and so on. To allow his readers to locate the characters, Bhagat introduces every stereotype: Shyam, the 'loser' hero on the verge of losing his job as well as the woman he loves (echoes of Mohsin Hamid's Dara from *Moth Smoke*); Priyanka, the self-righteous and upright girl; Esha, the aspiring model; Radhika, the sari-clad housewife who knits during office hours while her sales manager husband cheats on her; Vroom, the 'misfit' who loves living on the edge (shades of Ryan from *FPS*); Military Uncle, a retired army man, abandoned by his son and daughter-in-law; Bakshi, the unscrupulous and lecherous boss; Priyanka's mother, a hysterical gold digger, desperate to hook up her daughter with an NRI; and Ganesh, a Lexus-driving Microsoft professional, who fails to win over Priyanka's heart (and hand).

Besides these characters, Bhagat characteristically fills the story with identifiable locations, spaces and language. In an interview, the writer explains his language preference: 'It is easy to impress someone by using multi-syllable words. It is much more difficult to write simply. Just because you don't need a dictionary to understand my book, it does not mean it cannot have emotions. Flowery language kills humour. Anyway, it is not my cup of tea.'[13]

Sample these: 'He is MSGroom 1.1 – deluxe edition' (70); 'A door bitch is the hostess who stands outside the disco. And if your waist is more than twenty-four inches, or if you were not wearing something right out of an item number, the door-bitch will raise an eyebrow at you like you are a fifty-year-old aunty' (99); 'The other girls were just for fun. They are channel surfing' (133); 'So what serious channel am I? The BBC?' (133); 'Only women think there is a reason to thank people if they listen to them' (158); 'Vroom said in an insanely cheerful, radio jockey voice' (161); 'You've cluttered my life enough, now stop cluttering my mailbox' (165); 'Your humor has a tumor' (175); and much more.

Although *ON@TCC* offers more space to women characters than *FPS*, Bhagat retains the lad lit flavour, with sufficient male bonding, guy talk and some adrenalin-rushing action. But what makes it a controversial work is the underlying theme of anti-Americanism. Making Vroom his mouthpiece, Bhagat is aggressive in his attacks on American politics, culture and lifestyle and he got it right this time too, bagging yet another chartbuster. The reviewers were not as kind, however: 'Silly books with silly ideas are common enough, but this is among the more outrageous ones we've seen in a while. But what is truly troubling is that it was a success in India, that there were readers who apparently bought into this and who approve of what happens.'[14] The book faced more flak and one reviewer says, 'The story has an interesting premise, but it's one of the worst-written books I've ever read, falling somewhere between bad high school love poem and sixth-grade book report. You'll laugh out loud. The hilarity will be entirely unintentional.'[15]

The criticism, however, did not deter the book-buying public. As in his earlier attempt, author-signed copies of *ON@TCC* could be bought directly from Bhagat's website for international delivery, with the promise of personalized copies for the buyer. In the first month after its release, the book sold more than 100,000 copies: 'The sales have been stunning. I do not know of any other book which has sold so many copies in such a short time in India', says publisher Kapish Mehra of Rupa.[16] Bhagat takes the criticisms in his stride, making no bones about his lack of 'elitist' literary ambitions: 'I have not written it for the cocktail circuit. It is unfair to compare Bart Simpson with Shakespeare, though both are brilliant in their own ways. My books touch the Indian middle class, where I also come from. I understand their problems and can make them entertaining.'[17]

Bhagat is apparently easy to translate onto film and Bollywood came calling for Bhagat's second bestseller. The film, titled *Hello* (2008), features Salman Khan playing a man the storyteller meets on a train. Those who have read the novel will know that this is quite a bit of casting. The 'man on the train' is none other than Bhagat himself, discussing his past and future writings, thus giving *One Night* a touch of metafictional narrative. Continuing his track record of hawking his wares to perfection, Bhagat's website gives us a link which leads to a captivating publicity still of the film, featuring a host of popular actors.

A media favourite (not to mention wonderfully media savvy), Bhagat was elated when producer-director Vidhu Vinod Chopra adapted *FPS* as *3 Idiots* (2010). However, once the film was released, the author felt scorned that he was merely 'acknowledged' at the end of the credit rolls, and was not given the credit, he felt, he justly deserved. A battle of words ensued, where the firebrand producer and the film's leading man Aamir Khan accused Bhagat of resorting to cheap publicity gimmicks. Bhagat immediately recanted and apologized to all concerned: 'I love Aamir Khan', he declared. 'I also apologise to all his fans.'[18] The film, which went on to become one of the highest all-time grossing, draws on Bhagat's knack of storytelling and penchant for blending humour with sentiment. Fans of *FPS* were quick to note the similarities: the hostel ragging, romancing the irascible director's daughter, drinking vodka on the 'insti' roof, a sly mugger called Venkat and a suicide attempt – it is all there, with slight variations.

Following the unsavoury incident triggered by *3 Idiots*, Bhagat was compelled to lie low for a while, but not for long. His *2 States* (2009) hit the market and was catapulted to the status of a bestseller. A tale of interstate marriage between a Punjabi boy and a Tamil Brahmin girl, the writer's diehard fans are treated to the trademark Bhagatisms: 'Another South Indian had conquered the world of academics' (ix); 'Girls like Ananya become instant pin-ups in our testosterone-charged, estrogen-starved campus' (3); 'uncle looked up and down at me as if I had questioned him about his secret personal fantasies' (47); [on arriving in Chennai] 'Almost ninety percent of the people were dark complexioned. Of these ninety percent, eighty percent had dabbed talcum that gave them a grey skin tone. I understood why Fair and Lovely was invented' (76); [On Tamil actors] 'The heroes' pictures make you feel even your uncles can be movie stars' (77). Bhagat's eager followers lap up such one-liners and instances of earthy humour. He certainly gives the audience what it wants.

On December 24, 2009, during one of his several promotional tours for *2 States*, in Chennai, Bhagat's penchant for reinforcing stereotypes was on full display as he launched into a detailed analysis for the 'big' question: 'Why do Punjabi women prefer Tamil women?' He typically brought the house down as he did a power point presentation of his findings. Capitalizing on his ability to connect with the audience, largely comprising those under 25, Bhagat demonstrated yet again that his popularity with masses remains uncontested.[19] The writer, whose first novel won him the Society Young Achievers' Award in literature, has been vilified by critics and run down by the intelligentsia. Still, he has a phoenix-like ability to rise from the ashes, and reportedly his take on the sensitive issue of the Gujarat riots of 2002, *The 3 Mistakes of My Life* (2008), is adapted for a Hindi film, *Kai Po Che* (2013), produced by UTV Spotboy. This time, we are informed, Bhagat will be coscripting it.

That Bhagat's success story spawned off a spate of fiction set in elite educational institutes of India therefore does not come as a surprise.[20] A divisive writer – few writers divide readers the way Bhagat does – it is fashionable to 'hate' him. Notwithstanding the opinion of the cognoscenti, this self-professed 'Salman Khan among writers' continues his phenomenal success story by keeping the audience sufficiently entertained. After all, who needs snobbish critics and upmarket publishers when you have a cult following?[21]

Scholars feel that in contemporary times 'we do not have a space for the irresponsible misfit, which means we do not have a space which is at an angle to power. In India, everybody is some way in some kind of nexus of power. We need to regain that space for the irresponsible.'[22] Let me stretch this statement a little and consider how Bhagat's oeuvre fits Chaudhuri's observation. It is evident that on the surface Bhagat's characters are global aspirants; but at the core they are plagued with the regular insecurities of an average misfit. Bhagat positively revels in being the champion of the underdog. Hari of *FPS*, Shyam Mehra (or Sam Macy) of *ON@TCC*, Krish of *2 States* and Gopal of *Revolution 2020: Love, Corruption, Ambition* (2011) are ordinary young men, who have to rough it out at improving their chances in a lopsided society. Bhagat's heroes inevitably invite their readers to identify with the underdog where, at the end, the loser takes it all. Therefore, we cheer when Hari in *FPS* tames Prof. Cherian; rejoice when, in true Hindi film fashion, Bakshi, the Hitlerian boss, gets his comeuppance in *ON@TCC*; feel elated when the 'boys next door' Govind and Krish beat the odds in *3 Mistakes* and *2 States*; and we positively partake in his redemption when Gopal, the loser-turned-corrupt hero from *Revolution 2020* is endorsed by the writer with, 'You are a good person' (296). It is this emotional connect, this relatedness and ability to motivate an average middle-class youth to aspire and attain the elusive Indian Dream, that gives the writer his immense mass appeal.

I maintain that attitudes towards marketing and marketability of Indian writing in English vary across the writing field. The discerning ones who expect the angst of a Holden Caulfield (*Catcher in the Rye*) or the pseudo intellectual ramblings of a Howard Kirk (*The History Man*, 1975) in popular literature will end up in disappointment, since for the majority of readers it is the upbeat quality and the entertainment quotient of the writing that matters. Bhagat's fiction and related commercial values are, therefore, symptomatic of the general moral and intellectual climate of our times.

Notes and References

1. See Shaleena Koruth's 'Whatever Happened to Kaavya Viswanathan?' elsewhere in this volume.
2. See, for instance, how an average passage in Hornby reads:
   'How about we stay in tomorrow night? Watch a DVD?' she said.
   I didn't say anything.
   'Or we can go out, if you want. I'll take you to Pizza Express.'
   I still didn't say anything.
   'Pizza Express and the cinema. How about that?'
   'No, you're all right', I said, as if she was being nice to me and offering me something. I mean, she was, in a way. She was offering me a pizza and a film. But in another way, she was just trying to stop me doing what I wanted to do, and she knew it, and I knew it. (Nick Hornby, *Slam* (London: Penguin, 2007), 47)
3. Rashmi Bansal, '"Anything for You, Ma'am?" No Thanks!', *Youth Curry* (blog), 22 June 2006. Online: http://youthcurry.blogspot.com/2006/06/anything-for-you-maam-no-thanks.html (accessed 17 April 2010).
4. Barbara Crossette, 'A Generation Writing in English is Broadening the Fiction of English', *New York Times*, 13 February 1990. Online: http://www.nytimes.com/1990/02/13/books/a-generation-writing-in-english-is-broadening-the-fiction-of-india.html?pagewanted=2&src=pm (accessed 12 April 2010).
5. Tapan Basu, 'Contemporary Indian Writing in English: Is There a Market in India for This Text?', 2007. Online: http://www.open.ac.uk/Arts/ferguson-centre/indian-lit/workshops/london-workshop2007-tapan-basu.htm (accessed 9 July 2009).
6. Kushal Gulab, 'Desperately Seeking Writers', *Hindustan Times*, 23 September 2007. Online: http://www.open.ac.uk/Arts/ferguson-centre/indian-lit/documents/pub-doc-kushal-gulab-sept07.htm (accessed 11 September 2009).
7. Robert McCrum, 'Chetan Bhagat: The Paperback King of India', *Guardian*, 24 January 2010. Online: http://www.guardian.co.uk/books/2010/jan/24/chetan-bhagat-robert-mccrum (accessed 12 January 2010).
8. Shvetal Vyas, 'Marketing and promotion of Indian Writing in English', 2007. Online: http://www.open.ac.uk/Arts/ferguson-centre/indian-lit/workshops/london-workshop2007-tapan-basu.htm (accessed 9 July 2009).
9. John Mee, 'After Midnight', in *An Illustrated History of Indian Literature in English*, ed. Arvind Krishna Malhotra (New Delhi: Permanent Black), 321.
10. *FPS* continued its phenomenal success story as the Madras Players staged an adaptation of the play in Jan, scripted and directed by Nikhila Kesavan. An excellent device to appeal to the college-going spectators was to rope in actual IIT students to play the main leads, and following the play's success many critics credited Bhagat with promoting the cause of theatre among Generation X.
11. Chetan Bhagat, 'Welcome to Fan Café'. Online: http://www.chetanbhagat.com/fancafe/ (accessed 5 January 2013).
12. See 'The Inside Story', *Hindu*, 31 May 2007. Online:http://www.hindu.com/mp/2007/05/31/stories/2007053150870100.htm (accessed 8 March 2010).
13. Chetan Bhagat, 'One Night @ the Call Centre', interview by Raju Lalwani, 28 October 2005. Online: http://in.rediff.com/getahead/2005/oct/28night.html (accessed 19 April 2009).

14 See review of *One Night @ the Call Centre*, the Complete Review. Online: http://www.complete-review.com/reviews/india/bhagatc.htm (accessed 9 May 2010).
15 Fofatlal, 'One Night @ Bad Fiction Hell', *Sepia Munity* (blog), 1 May 2006. Online: http://www.sepiamutiny.com/sepia/archives/003318.html (accessed 8 December 2010). Also see the review by Mark Baumer, 'One Night @ the Call Center', 2005. Online: http://everydayyeah.com/content/one-night-call-center-chetan-bhagat (accessed 8 August 2010).
16 TiVo Community Forum, 'Bestselling Indian Author Paints Grim View of Outsourcing Jobs', 30 December 2005. Online: http://archive2.tivocommunity.com/tivo-vb/showthread.php?t=279178 (accessed 23 December 2013).
17 Ibid.
18 Chetan Bhagat, 'I Love Aamir Khan', *Hindu*, 5 January 2010. Online:http://beta.thehindu.com/arts/article75901.ece (accessed 8 April 2010).
19 A. R. Rahman, noted music director from India, says, 'I've seen the effect Chetan has on his readers. He often writes about following your dreams and not bowing to others' expectations. That isn't easy in India, where family opinion matters and some professions are regarded as more serious than others. [...] It's great to see brave young people giving their dreams a chance. Chetan's writing inspires that kind of bravery.' (A. R. Rahman, 'The 2010 Time 100', *Time*, 29 April 2010. Online: http://www.time.com/time/specials/packages/article/0,28804,1984685_1984940_1985518,00.html (accessed 12 May 2011).)
20 'When his book inexplicably climbed up the bestseller list, the very publishers who'd looked down their noses at him, went chasing after his clones. They signed on any IIT or IIM graduate who thought he had a book in him.' ('The Lo-Cal Literati', *Outlook*, 18 July 2011, 32–3.)
21 'Most publishers are very fake. The only writers they admire are those who are popular in the UK. [...] Books that work in UK are tailor-made for them, not for us.' (Chetan Bhagat, *Outlook*, 18 July 2011, 36.)
22 Amit Chaudhuri, 'I Wish Indian Writing in English Were Less Triumphant', Deutsche Welle, 3 October 2006. Online: http://www.dw.de/i-wish-indian-writing-in-english-were-less-triumphant/a-2186200 (accessed 21 September 2010).

Chapter Four

VIKAS SWARUP: WRITING INDIA IN GLOBAL TIME

Chinmoy Banerjee

Vikas Swarup[1] is an extraordinarily successful writer. His first book, *Q & A* (2005), received a number of awards, including the Boeke Prize in South Africa (2006) and the Prix Grand Public at the Paris Book Fair (2007), sold well in the popular market across the world and has so far been translated into 34 languages (though it has sold translation rights in 42 languages). It was distinguished by being nominated for 'Most Influential Book of the Year' in 2008 by Kingstone Bookstore, the biggest chain in Taiwan. Its success skyrocketed when it was made into a British film by Danny Boyle with the title *Slumdog Millionaire* (2008), which was widely acclaimed by critics, received eight Oscars in the US, was hugely successful across the globe (except in India, until the Oscars) and assured Swarup's marketability. Following the triumph of the film, *Q & A* was reissued as *Slumdog Millionaire*, though the title – created by Simon Beaufoy for his award-winning screenplay – was much reviled in India and is significantly different from the book. Under this title, the book won the Heathrow Travel Product Award in 2009. Swarup's second book, *Six Suspects* (2008) was immediately picked up for film rights and is being produced by Paul Raphael's Starfield Productions under BBC Films and being scripted by John Hodge, who wrote the screenplay for Danny Boyle's *Shallow Grave* (1994) and *Trainspotting* (1996). The book has already sold translation rights in 24 languages and is being produced as a radio play by Radio 4 in Britain. Swarup was also honoured at the Synergies Summit in Washington, DC in 2009 with Anil Ambani and Azim Premji, two giants of India's globalized economy. Swarup is now a marketing phenomenon and an international celebrity.

Though several Indian writers in English, particularly Salman Rushdie, Vikram Seth and Arundhati Roy, have achieved publishing success and celebrity status since the 1980s, Vikas Swarup's success is distinctively a product of the intersection of the Indian economy in its globalized phase and the history of English writing in India. Rushdie, Seth and Roy, as well as Amit Chaudhuri, Amitav Ghosh, Pankaj Mishra and Vikram Chandra, have in their various ways made the question of whether India could be written in the colonial master's language obsolete and irrelevant. This was a question that necessarily faced earlier generations of writers in English who had to struggle against the authority and wealth of vernacular literatures in India and the colonial status of English writing in India in the English-speaking world. How an indigenous subject could be written about in the master's language was a problem that vexed all colonized people, and was reflected on and resolved to varying degrees in Africa and the Caribbean as well as India. Raja Rao's experiment with language in *Kanthapura* was a bold attempt to bend English to the texture of Indian life, as Chinua Achebe would do in Nigeria. The spectacular success that Indian writers in English have achieved since the 1980s is primarily a result of the indigenization of the language in India and the decline of metropolitan authority. Salman Rushdie and Amit Chaudhuri could be seen as two poles of this resolution: Rushdie creating a flamboyant language affirming an Indian difference within English and Chaudhuri using the language without any bending to produce what might be called a Bengali novel in English. However, coming in the wake of these writers who opened a space for Indian writing in the international market and particularly in academic courses on world literature, Vikas Swarup has achieved his spectacular success with utter indifference to the problem that his predecessors had struggled to resolve. Swarup's oblivion to the question of language and authenticity, the problem of finding a language adequate to the specificity of experience, marks his work as a product for the globalized market. The quest for an authentic Indian voice in English is not relevant to him because English as the language of the global market is a deterritorialized vehicle for the communication of information, not an inflected medium for embodying a socioculturally located subject.

Swarup's success makes his work a valuable site for investigating the 'genius' that holds the key to the cash register in the globalized market and coming to know the reader/consumer at the other end of the transaction. Swarup has noted that the basis of his success is ease of communication. As he says in an interview published with the 2008 edition of *Slumdog Millionaire*: 'What a writer writes must, in the final analysis, be accessible to the reader. If the writer cracks a joke the reader doesn't get, then what's the point?' (10).

Swarup's language, from whatever narrative position it is uttered, is the language of the urban Indian elite generously sprinkled with cliché. His attempts at mimicry succeed only in the rendering of journalistic jeremiad in *Six Suspects* but fail dismally in all other cases, producing the tedious caricature of American 'white trash' when it is consistent. Everywhere else the language is authorial. It is a naive mixture of registers that range from purple prose to colloquialism and slang, jargon, sociological journalese and operatic rhetoric. The barely literate Ram Mohammad Thomas (RMT) sets the tone for everything to follow at the opening of *Slumdog Millionaire*: 'They came for me late last night, when even the stray dogs had gone off to sleep. […] There was no hue and cry. […] Only the old owl on the tamarind tree hooted at my arrest. […] I should have kicked and screamed. Protested my innocence, raised a stink, galvanized the neighbours' (9). It is tempting to read this combination of 'hue and cry', 'raised a stink' and 'galvanized' as a parody of Indian English but it is difficult to fathom the purpose of such parody.

He speaks of 'Asia's biggest slum' and explains, 'when you live on the brink of penury in an urban wasteland where you jostle for every inch of space […] you are conditioned to believe that one day there will be a warrant with your name on it. […] The brain is an organ we are not authorized to use' (10). It is not likely that someone in RMT's situation would have access to the levels of language and information that he displays but this potpourri would not be unfamiliar to the middle-class reader in India or make any demand on people looking for an easy read anywhere. Cliché has currency everywhere.

Sometimes there is an address to a particular community with information unavailable to others. Readers familiar with the Indian print media would recognize the woman who rescues RMT from torture as being built from matrimonial columns: of 'average height and slim build', she has 'nice teeth and lovely arched eyebrows' and 'a certain presence' (21). The recognition probably functions as an in-joke for the Indian reader (an image of the ideal bride), though what such a stylistic joke is doing in this specific context is an awkward question. Similarly, RMT's adoptive father, Dominic Thomas, was last seen 'buying a train ticket to Bhopal with a shotgun in his hand' (43). While all readers would possibly enjoy the cliché, Indian readers would know that someone of Dominic's status could not acquire a shotgun in India or board a train with it, adding a layer of absurdity to the comedy. The language in such use shows a self-consciousness that passes through the lowly narrator to connect author and reader in a bond of class privilege as possessors of the language.

Self-consciousness in Swarup's writing seems to function solely as a cement of social status since the writing is otherwise conspicuously unaware of its cliché-ridden stylistic incongruity: RMT's scream 'is a piercing cry that shatters the stillness of the morning like a bullet' (55). Swarup even likes the expression enough to repeat it a few pages later. With no claim to education, RMT speaks of 'middle-class soaps on Doordarshan' (78); he advises Salim regarding a fortune teller: 'These chaps are con men' (82); and he soars operatic in his denunciation of Bombay: 'There are a million people like me, packed in a two-hundred-hectare triangle of swampy urban wasteland where we live like animals and die like insects. [...] Dharavi residents come from the dusty backwaters. [...] They come to Mumbai, the city of gold, of dreams in their hearts of striking it rich and living upper-middle-class lives. But the gold turned to lead a long time ago, leaving behind rusted hearts and gangrenous minds' (132). In *Six Suspects*, Shabnam Saxena shows the same taste for rhetorical flourish, prophesying the fate of the many women who write to her: 'Their brittle dreams of stardom would crumble against the nightmarish reality of sexual slavery' (34). In another section of the same book, the words 'emanated' and 'funeral dirge' rub against 'chicken shit' in the description of Little Andaman (39).

Within the general blindness to language, however, there is occasional self-consciousness in the form of jokes, as we have noted. 'Munna Mobile', the petty thief in *Six Suspects*, indulges in wordplay: 'Ramesh is a serial adulterer. [...] Suresh is a serial adulterator' (52). He is 'bonking' the wife of one of his employers, of whom he says condescendingly, 'I could have tolerated their boorishness' (53). Since the thief has no claim to this language of status, the language functions here as a social bond between author and reader. Similarly, in the account of Onge culture, a number of words such as 'torale', 'ingetayi' and 'ongkobowkwe' are used as exotic objects and left to be understood by the context. Yet one word is presented with a double translation: '"Kujeli" exclaimed Pemba, which was the Onge equivalent of "Oh shit!" though its literal meaning was "The pig has pissed!"' (49). The translation is both conspicuous and redundant, with the redundancy functioning only to extract humour from the social and cultural distance between the author-reader and their object.

But both blindness and self-consciousness perform a bonding of status between author and reader that makes the consumption of exoticism comfortable. RMT finds Mustafa and Punnoose, two thugs working for Babu Pillai (who would likely speak Bombay Hindi), committing malapropism in English when they attempt 'to prevent us from mixing too much with those they mispronounce as "handiclapped" kids' (93). The manager of a *chawl*, presumably speaking in Marathi, says, 'We Indians have this sublime ability to see the pain and misery around us, and yet remain unaffected by it' (71). Swarup sees no need to render the difference between languages of his representation because everything is contained in the language of his class.

Undoubtedly the most important key to Swarup's success is his use of enigma as the dominant code of his narratives. Both his novels foreground this code: *Q & A* is constructed around the enigma of RMT's ability to answer the questions at the quiz show and *Six Suspects* around the question of which out of the six suspects killed Vicky Rai. The frames of both are familiar, being located respectively in the global circulation of television quiz shows and the board game *Clue*, which gives the enigmas set within them an immediate popular appeal. By overdeveloping this code, Swarup frees himself of the need to develop character and setting beyond mere functionality. Emotional engagement is created by constructing the characters on the binary of oppressor/oppressed and curiosity is generated by placing them in a variety of exotic settings. Being binary functions, the characters have only as much cultural specificity as is needed to make them vehicles of the globally popular dream of reversal, that the low shall be high and the oppressor receive his just rewards, so that, paradoxically, it is their very 'thinness' that gives them their marketplace 'universality'.

The enigmas are created with considerable cleverness and resolved with surprising twists. This is so extreme that, although Swarup's novels are related to 'whodunits', they differ in not allowing the reader any engagement in the deciphering of the mystery. Authorial cleverness positions the reader as a purely passive consumer of the solutions produced. The novels are based entirely on chance, such as the chance that RMT would be asked the very questions for which he would have the answers, and chance is the means by which the author resolves all difficulties while holding a surprise trick up his sleeve for the end: the motive for RMT's presence at the quiz show, it will turn out, was not the money but retribution, and the real killer of Vicky Rai is none of the suspects whose stories have been told but a previously unknown avenger. The novels are 'page turners' because the passive reader is assured of a happy solution to the unpleasant but titillating problems of torture, rape, incest, violent abuse, corruption and murder that provide the lure for the story.

Swarup establishes this contract with the reader early by the use of the first-person, present-tense narrative: *Q & A* opens with a scene of torture being narrated in the present by the protagonist: 'I have been arrested. For winning a quiz show' (9); 'I shall be dead in approximately six minutes' says 'The Thief' at the beginning of his tale in *Six Suspects* (51). Samuel Richardson introduced this mode of narration in the eighteenth-century epistolary novel as a means of registering the urgency of situations on a socioeconomically constructed interiority, occasionally producing the kind of absurdity that Henry Fielding gloriously ridiculed in *Shamela* (1741). But while Richardson's technique contributed historically to the production of the bourgeois subject in and through the novel, Swarup purchases curiosity at the cost of absurdity because his addressee is the global consumer in search of an entertaining product.

Coherence of point of view is obviously of little importance for this product. In the process of being tortured, RMT sees himself as a starving

African child – Swarup's reader apparently needing the reference to visualize a similarly malnourished child in India. As we have noticed, neither RMT's language nor his critical views and access to information in general have any credible location in his point of view, and the same can be said of the first person narration of 'Munna Mobile' in *Six Suspects* and the 'journal' of Shabnam Saxena. Swarup always speaks through his puppets and uses the first person primarily for the construction of the enigma that its limited vision enables. Neither the stylistic nor the technical crudeness of the work offers any barrier to popular consumption; rather, it defines Swarup's market. One could also add to the definition of this market the juvenile genres of cloak-and-dagger adventure, such as the tales of the Australian diplomat spook, the quest of the Little Andaman tribal for the stolen sacred stone or the slapstick adventures of the trailer park American, Larry Page, among the 'terrorists' in Kashmir. These adventures are situated within the anthropological exoticism of Onge tribal magic and the custom of communal prostitution in the Bedia tribe, the orientalism of the fort of Jaisalmer with its fiery Rajput woman, the colonial exotic of the voodoo priestess and the Dickensian exotic of the beggar business in Mumbai.

Swarup blends this exoticism with an apparently critical element to engage sympathy for the suffering underdog and indignation at the callousness of an unjust society. The India of his books is the land of orphanages where boys are routinely sodomized, of slums that would become tourist destinations, operations for the production of crippled beggars, *chawls*, *dabbawalas*, feudal 'Rani Sahebas', gangsters and gangster politicians, rich people who get away with murder, police torture, dying tribes, arrogant and oppressive bureaucrats, Maoists and Kashmiri terrorists. These things are not unfamiliar to Indians who witness, read about and see them on television and films. Yet an India constructed from these elements, through Swarup's use of open-ended forms, is no different from the India of snake charmers and *fakirs*. Writing for the global market has required updating of the colonial image, creating an India out of the circulation of images in print, television, film and the Internet. The product is a combination of familiarity and strangeness that sells.

Swarup's picture is not untrue. Indian society is brutally unjust. Poor orphan children are left entirely at the mercy of those who have power over them to be raped or sold into sex slavery or crippled beggary. The poor live in abysmal conditions amidst enormous wealth. The police are brutal and corrupt, torturing and murdering with impunity. Politicians are corrupt and linked to crime and business interests. The rich live in arrogant disregard of the laws of the land. In a supposedly secular country, minority Muslims are burnt alive by Hindu mobs. The modernizing state destroys the way of life and livelihood of tribal people, over whom it operates as a colonizer. The state has not brought justice for the victims in Bhopal of the worst industrial disaster in the world. Swarup confronts the horrors of an India seeking status as a global economic power with indignation or comic satire. This is not new, since this aspect of India is subjected to constant critique within India, though such criticism is often met by chauvinistic protest. However, Swarup uses this material for sensationalism, sentimentality, melodrama and comedy, though he presents it as criticism. The hero of his product of entertainment is ineffectual middle-class outrage, satisfied with expressing itself through the theatrical voice of RMT or Arun Advani, the investigative journalist in *Six Suspects*.

Impotence and hopelessness are the hidden underside of Swarup's stories of the underdog striking it rich and the oppressor coming to a bad end. These dreams not only offer compensation for powerlessness but also absolution from responsibility, since in the absence of any hope and agency they find wish fulfilment through luck and the avenger figure. RMT's narrative is a series of lucky coincidences that make possible what agency he has for survival and vengeance: a weak railing enables him to push the drunken Shantaram to death for raping his daughter, a gun turns up in his hand to shoot a bandit for molesting a girl travelling on a train and another gun comes to his hand through a voodoo victim so that he can attempt to avenge Neelima Kumari and Nita, though it actually enables him to hit the jackpot of revenge, winning a billion Rupees and buying the woman he loves. In *Six Suspects*, it turns out happily that the killer of Vicky Rai is none of the suspects in custody (some of whom had personal motives for the murder) but an unknown avenger performing an act of social retribution on behalf of the outraged middle class. The novels offer vigilantism as the only recourse in the face of social injustice. As in all popular art, this is the fantasy solution to the problem of injustice, through which people's dissatisfaction is transmuted into a consumable product. Clint Eastwood in Hollywood and Amitabh Bachchan in Bombay have achieved iconic stature in this process.

But a more serious service to the dominant ideology than the containment of social criticism through the merchandising of fantasy is rendered by Swarup's trivialization of actual challenges to the most severe oppressions by the Indian state: the onslaught of modernization in collaboration with national and multinational corporations against the aboriginal people (*adivasis*), and the enormously oppressive military occupation of Kashmir and the denial of democracy to its people, leading to a prolonged and bloody uprising. These are areas of profound conflict in which the oppressed have taken up arms against the state. They deserve a risk-taking criticism in which many Indian intellectuals are engaged. Swarup, however, chooses to conform to the official and popular views by ridiculing the resistance. He uses the loss of tribal identity to generate sympathy for the exoticized Onge as the victims of bureaucratic exploitation but ignores the struggle for forestland and livelihood that defines the *adivasis* of Jharkhand, Chhattisgarh, Lalgarh and contiguous areas on the Indian mainland.

That Swarup's success as a writer should be involved with his works being made into British films is a phenomenon of considerable significance since the books are intimately related to Bombay cinema. Swarup thematizes Bombay cinema through a representation of its stars, producers, directors, fans and magazines. He also reflects on its formulas, stereotypes, fantasies and mixture of genres. RMT offers the following paradigm of 'Hindi' cinema: 'Armaan plays a gangster […] with a heart. He loots the rich and distributes money to the poor. In between he falls in love with the heroine […] and fulfils his mother's wish by taking her on a pilgrimage […] that's the story till the interval' (29). The other half of the film completes the paradigm: 'Armaan and Priya will now sing a song in Switzerland, before Priya is murdered by a rival gang. Then Armaan will kill hundreds of bad guys in revenge, expose corrupt politicians and police officers, and finally die a hero's death' (32). Within the frame of this self-consciousness, Swarup constructs narratives in the mode of the popular cinema he parodies. The name Ram Mohammed Thomas is clearly based on the title of the popular 1977 film *Amar Akbar Anthony* (a formulaic 'lost and found' film where the three protagonists represent three different communities in India, namely, Hinduism, Islam and Christianity) and embodies the same secular nationhood that Bombay cinema as a whole promotes. Swarup's 'criticism' of Indian society is the theme of innumerable other films from the Bombay industry, and the vigilantism and rule of luck that dominate his books are common features of Bombay cinema. The mixture of comedy, violence, melodrama, pathos, criticism and preaching in the books makes them mirrors of Indian popular cinema. At the closest point of the relationship, Swarup's writing becomes the script for the film:

> Then, all of a sudden I pick up Shankar in my arms and proceed toward the lighted palace. […] I climb on the table and place Shankar's body gently in the middle, in between a creamy vanilla cake and a bowl of rasgullas. The waiters stand as still as statues. […] I look directly at her with as much contempt as I muster and speak. Mrs. Swapna Devi, if this is your palace, and you are its queen, then acknowledge the prince. I have come to deliver the dead body of your son Kunwar Shankar Singh. (273)

Salman Rushdie has also used Bombay cinema as a theme and as a mode of narration, particularly in *Midnight's Children* (1981), *The Satanic Verses* (1988) and *The Moor's Last Sigh* (1995). But while Rushdie's use of cinema affirms it as a dynamic medium for narrating India, offering an indigenous equivalent of magical realism, Swarup's use is both positioned in superiority and as mimetic at the same time. Rushdie found semantic density in Indian popular cinema that he could weave into his writing; Swarup has mimicked a semantically denuded version of the cinema to find success in the market. Indian popular cinema, which has historically been unable to break into the mainstream global market, finds carriage to this market in Swarup's fiction. With Danny Boyle's film, Bombay cinema arrives into the Western mainstream. While Swarup is superior and reductive in his self-consciousness, Boyle thematizes, mimics, alludes to and is affirmatively self-conscious in relation to Bombay films.

This throws a paradoxical light on the histories of film and English writing in India in their relation to the global market. It is well known that although Indian popular cinema has a large market across the world, it has not been able to break into the mainstream market in the West. Its conventions are too distinct for transportation into a market dominated by its own conventions. However, the internal dynamics of Indian cinema, the wider circulation of Indian films through the new Indian diaspora and the exchanges between India and the diaspora have led to the production of a large number of films of technical excellence and considerable semiotic density within the conventions of popular cinema. Ketan Mehta's *Mangal Pandey: The Uprising* (2005), Amol Palekar's *Paheli* (2005), Mani Ratnam's *Guru* (2007), Vidhu Vinod Chopra's *Eklavya* (2007) and Rituparna Ghose's *Chokher Bali* (2003) are only a few examples of the excellence of Indian popular cinema since the 1990s. Even with this excellence, Indian cinema has not made it into mainstream distribution in the West – except in the works of Gurinder Chadha, Mira Nair, Shekhar Kapur and Deepa Mehta – but it has brought into the Indian popular market an artistic quality that had previously been the province of 'art' films. The dichotomy of art cinema and popular cinema has disappeared in the new Indian cinema. But with the work of Swarup, a new divide between literature and popular writing has opened up in the domain of Indian writing in English in the world.

Note

1 Vikas Swarup was born in Allahabad in a family of lawyers. After education in Allahabad University he joined the Indian Foreign Service in 1986. He has served in Turkey, UK, South Africa and Japan.

Chapter Five

THE GOD OF SMALL THINGS: ARUNDHATI ROY'S 'MADE IN INDIA' BOOKERBOILER

Chinnadevi Singadi

Arundhati Roy's *The God of Small Things* (1997) was the first ever Indian novel in English to win the Booker Prize. In this paper I attempt to highlight the problematic position that the novel occupies in relation to the writer's self-acknowledged activism, which is in part rooted in her personal experiences, and the role of the market in shaping India's literary production.

Suzanna Arundhati Roy (1961–) was born in the state of Assam. Roy's mother, the social activist Mary Roy, is a Syrian Christian from the state of Kerala. Her father was a Bengali who managed a tea plantation in Assam. Roy and her brother were still very young when her parents divorced. Mary Roy returned to her parents who lived in Aymanam, a small conservative rural town in Kerala. Mary Roy's unsuccessful marriage, divorce and supposedly 'shameful' return gendered obdurate hostility towards herself and her children. Under these circumstances, Roy and her brother were deprived of formal education, leading Mary Roy towards starting an informal school of her own. Perhaps the seeds of rebellion with a cause were sown in young Arundhati at precisely that point.

The God started off as stray thoughts keyed into her first computer. It took Roy four and a half years to bring her book to the finish line. In a now well-known story, she gave a copy of the manuscript to Pankaj Mishra, the editor at the HarperCollins India division, who in turn passed it on to British literary agent David Godwin, who arrived at Roy's door with a fat check within three days of receiving the book. The book topped the *Sunday Times* bestsellers list in London and was the first Indian author after Rushdie to make it to the top seventeen on the *New York Times* bestsellers list. In India it sold more copies than did any other novel in the English language. Filmmakers from many parts of the world, including Hollywood, approached Roy for rights to film the book, all of which she plainly declined.

Now, Roy spends most of her time virtually hitch-hiking across the globe, talking and writing, to give the world what she thinks is the insider's view of every possible *andolan* (protest) and human rights violation. Roy's activism is futuristic and well-meaning but her hysterics and the sense of doom she pegs to all that she says and does are a bit on the offensive side.

'Pity the nation that has to silence its writers!'[1] Arundhati fumes. And quite characteristically, the first of her scorching political essays was 'The End of Imagination', a tirade against the Vajpayee-led BJP government after the 'successful' detonation of nuclear devices in Pokhran, Gujarat in May 1998. Equally charged and equally defiantly, she takes up the cause of the Narmada valley in her next essay 'The Greater Common Good' (she donated her Booker prize money to the cause). In this well-researched, statistically corroborated report on dam projects in Gujarat, she cries foul at the politics of dam making.

In 2001, Roy staged a *dharna* outside the Indian Supreme Court along with other members of the *Narmada Bachao Andolan* (Save the Narmada movement), including Medha Patkar, protesting against the court's decision to vacate the stay on further construction of the Sardar Sarovar dam in the Narmada valley. This concern for the people and the world around her is at the heart of her novel.

The God is set in Kerala, in the remote village of Ayemenem (as it is spelled in the book), where Roy actually spent her childhood. Roy's rendition of Ayemenem is clearly in line with the expectations of readers in the West, who are curious to know more about this tropical paradise they have heard and read about: 'May in Ayemenem is a hot, brooding month. The days are long and humid. The river shrinks and black crows gorge on bright mangoes in still, dustgreen trees. Red bananas ripen. Jackfruits burst. Dissolute bluebottles hum vacuously in the fruity air. Then they stun themselves against clear windowpanes and die, fatly baffled in the sun' (1).

The God is as much about Ayemenem as it is about Estha and Rahel, the boy-and-girl twin protagonists of the novel, the youngest in the Ipe family, and their divorced thirty-one-year-old mother Ammu. The ebb and flow of the Meenachil River that runs through Ayemenem seems to have impinged on the members of the Ipe family, a respectable Brahmin Syrian Christian family, who keep returning and re-returning, in turn lending the narrative its rhythmic flashbacks and flashforwards.

The plot begins in the 1990s and returns and re-returns to the 1960s. The major world events of the '60s – the moon landing, the farmer revolt in West Bengal that spiralled into the Naxalite movement, the E. M. S. Namboodiripad (first Communist chief minister of Kerala) factor in Kerala politics, the Vietnam

War, Ramu Kariat's film adaptation of T. S. Pillai's *Chemmeen* (The prawn) and Robert Wise's 1965 release, *The Sound of Music* – are all meticulously woven (some overtly, some disguised) into the narrative web, lending the book the deceptive aura of a national allegory. The History House (converted later into a hotel) is the most concrete avatar of history in the book. But the truth is there is no history per se in the book (Roy herself makes this very clear in one of her interviews), only the 'remnants' of history. The remnants serve as the postcolonial backdrop against which Roy's postmodern performance is 'staged' (or rather 'constructed' in the architectural sense of the term). Roy is aware of the formula for success, that which worked for Rushdie, and does not shy from duplicating his strategies: the autobiography, the bits of history, the play with words – even the pickle factory (over which Roy claims more rights, saying her uncle actually owns one).

The narrative begins with the return of Rahel from America to Ayemenem. Having come to know that her brother Estha, older by eighteen minutes, had been re-returned by their father, Rahel returns to Ayemenem to reclaim what little she can of the past that they shared. In Kerala, and in India in general, it is unacceptable for a married woman to leave her husband and return home to her parents: 'In Kerala everyone has what is called a *tharavaad*, your ancestral home. If you don't have a father, you don't have a *tharavaad*. You're a person without an address. "No address", that's what they call you.'[2] No wonder Michiko Kakutani, in his review of *The God* in the *New York Times*, says that Roy's novel is 'Faulknerian in its ambitious tackling of family and race and class, Dickensian in its sharp-eyed observation of society and character' and is infused with an 'inexorable momentum of tragedy'.[3]

With *Midnight's Children* (1981), Rushdie regenerated the tradition of Indian literature in English; with *The God*, Roy regenerated the English language itself. She bequeaths the language with a lyrical, amorphous, malleable, feminine quality never before associated with the English language. Roy's metaphors and similes are the most spectacular segments of her prose, minus of course the overdone scaffolding. The capitalizations are arbitrary, the breakup/bridging of words architecturally meaningful and the typographical arrangement of words on the page momentarily lends it a canvas feel. Her images walk briskly into each other, bringing myriad visuals into single frames: '[Father Mulligan] had young Baby Kochamma's aching heart on a leash, bumping behind him, lurching over leaves and small stones. Bruised and almost broken' (24). Page after page, the novel is a visual treat; Kerala, and by extension India, becomes a photo album. Roy's use of English introduces the readers to a whole new range of linguistic aerobics. The Booker jury was expectedly enamoured.

Merritt Moseley observes, 'The literary prize-giving season in Britain, like the soccer season, lasts almost all year round.'[4] Moseley also points out that the prizing schedule is steered by the publishing cycle.⁵ Very few new books are published in November or December, the dead of winter. Sales of books peak during the Christmas season. This places the Booker at the peak of the prizing season and lends it an importance that establishes Booker as 'the gold standard' (1998) in prizing.⁶

The Man Booker Prize is sponsored by Britain's Man Group PLC, a major alternative investment management company that manages investments of around $60 billion.⁷ Originally a British sugar company founded some two hundred-odd years ago in colonial Demerara (now Guyana), with the independence of the colony the company relocated to London in the 1960s and made its foray into book publishing. Towards the end of the decade, the company instituted the Booker Prize for literature in English. Today the prize has grown to be one of Britain's most prestigious cultural institutions. 'We had the cash; we came home; what were we to do?' wallows Sir Michael Caine, former chairman of Booker PLC.⁸ This brief history makes it plain that the Booker means business and indeed makes no claims otherwise. Consider the following we-can-make-you-rich campaign screaming into your face from the Man Booker Prize official website: 'Every year the Man Booker Prize winner is guaranteed a huge increase in sales, firstly in hardback and then in paperback. There is spin-off too in global sales of books, in future publishing contracts and in film and TV rights. Besides the fortune, the winner of the Man Booker Prize can also be sure of fame. The announcement of the winner is covered by television, radio and press worldwide.'⁹ Under 'About the prize' it reads, 'The prize […] has the power to transform the fortunes of authors and even publishers.'¹⁰

Thanks to the Booker, Britain continues to *rediscover* its erstwhile *colonies*, through the written word. There is a huge prizing industry out there in the West, growing at an unprecedented pace and is indulging in strategic prizing for private commercial gain. The role of the 'tour guide' being played out by the Booker is, today, at its industrious best and makes for the single central 'plot' of the 'success stories' of Salman Rushdie, and postliberalization Indian novelists Arundhati Roy, Kiran Desai and Aravind Adiga.

Graham Huggan in *The Postcolonial Exotic: Marketing the Margins* calls attention to a link 'between postcoloniality as a regime of value and a cosmopolitan alterity industry.'¹¹ The alterity industry best illustrates a gigantic parasite feeding off cultural difference or, more precisely, the exotic. Huggan's 'exotic' is not an 'inherent *quality* to be found 'in' certain people, distinctive objects, or specific places' but a certain way of perceiving things that 'effectively manufactures otherness'.¹² He concurs with Aijaz Ahmad's compelling view that Third World literature in English is a product of the imaginings of the West and asserts that the Third World has indeed been successfully fashioned into a '*global* merchandising tool'.[13] And '"Indianness"', he goes on to say, 'is conceived of largely [...] an infinitely rechargeable, universally applicable market tool'.[14] Knowing this, Indian writers writing in English successfully indulge in 'strategic exoticism'.[15] The bottom line is: selling the exotic is the *mantra*.

Victor Segalen, in his *Essay on Exoticism*, attempts to explain how the colonial 'comes into being with the desire for native trade relations of the most commercial kind. For the colonial, Diversity exists only in so far as it provides him with the means of duping others'.[16] He goes on to define the 'Diverse' as everything and anything that is 'foreign, strange, unexpected, surprising, mysterious, amorous, superhuman, heroic, and even divine, everything that is *Other*'.[17] It is this diversity that forms the core of most of the winning stories recounted earlier in this essay.

Geographical diversity as manifested in climates, fauna and flora is the simplest form of diversity. To Segalen it is a 'vulgarized Diversity'. Such diversity, he believes, gives birth to 'false values'. The treatment of 'colonial' and 'exotic' as equivalents is the outcome of such false values. Among the several kinds of exoticisms he discusses, he calls the 'Exoticism in latitude' the 'first born', which he says is 'responsible for the camel, the Negro, the Palm trees'[18] and, in this case, God's Own Country, Kerala. Roy's 'God's Own Country' is both diverse and vulgar, with lurid descriptions of dead bodies and faeces.

How could this India, in its fiftieth year of Independence, have failed to capture the imagination of the Booker jury? *The God* was awarded the Booker Prize in October 1997 and Roy became a literary celebrity overnight. The work has been translated into forty languages and has sold more than six million copies across the globe. India's 50 years of freedom had been reduced to some three hundred and fifty pages of filth and froth. With five generations of sad, selfish, spurious men and women erratically appearing and disappearing amidst deaths, drownings, accidents, funerals, coffins, obituaries, squashed frogs, squashed dogs and squashed Veluthas, the narrative makes sure you never have a chance to breathe. In her review of *The God*, Ritu Menon calls it a 'chronicle of deaths foretold'.[19]

Merritt Moseley attributes Roy's 1997 win to 'an Indian momentum' inside the Booker camp, committed to make up for its misses – Rohinton Mistry's *A Fine Balance* the previous year and Rushdie's *The Moor's Last Sigh* the year before.[20] He sounds apparently miffed by the 'irritating quantity of typographical archness' in Roy's book and tags it a 'Rushdie rough draft'.[21]

The manner in which the (now legendary) dramatic 'discovery' of Roy's book unfolded in the media lent fairy tale appeal to the author, making her a Cinderella of sorts. Imagine this: having completed *The God* around May 1996, Roy handed a copy of the manuscript to writer and literary agent

Pankaj Mishra, then editor at HarperCollins in India. He immediately dashed off copies of the manuscript to Transworld, Jonathan Cape and British literary agent David Godwin. Godwin auctioned the British rights for previously unheard-of amounts. HarperCollins bought the British rights and Roy chose to give the American rights to Random House. The mammoth advances of more than a million dollars she received were virtually unprecedented for a book by an unknown author. Permission to translate the book into 18 languages earned Roy another half a million pounds in advance. Roy's publishers embarked on a promotional tour across the world and advertised the book and its young, slim, beautiful, 'authentically' Indian author through every medium possible, even as she faced obscenity charges back home for the erotic intercaste lovemaking episode that unfolds in the last three pages of the book. Sabu Thomas and G. M. Idikkula, small-time lawyers from Pathanamthitta in Kerala, had filed the case accusing her of 'violat[ing] all decency with her description of oral sex. That's an unnatural phenomenon and unheard of in Kerala. It pollutes the minds of the people.'[22] Elisabeth Bummiler in the *New York Times* observes, 'Mr Thomas's summons is not tragic news for Ms. Roy's American publisher, Random House, whose representatives are happy to talk about an obscenity complaint that can help sales in the United States.'[23] Much bigger factors converged in favour of Roy. Thanks to the publication of *The God* coinciding with India's Golden Jubilee celebrations, like Rushdie's midnight's child Saleem Sinai, Roy had her 'destinies indissolubly chained to those of [her] country'.[24]

In his introduction to *The Vintage Book of Indian Writing, 1947–1997*, Rushdie writes, 'The prose writing – both fiction and non-fiction – created in this period by Indian writers *working in English* is proving to be a stronger and more important body of work than most of what has been produced in the 16 "official languages" of India.'[25] He celebrates Roy's sensational debut in no mean way: 'The Keralan writer Arundhati Roy has arrived to the accompaniment of a loud fanfare. Her novel, *The God of Small Things*, is full of ambition and sparkle, and written in a highly wrought and utterly personal style.'[26] Not everyone was so gung-ho though. Lakshmi Gopalkrishnan, for instance, accuses Roy of cleverly 'incubating' the book for four and a half years to deliberately time it when she did.[27] Padmini Mongia, one of the first critics to highlight the role of marketing in the success story of *The God*, in her article 'The Making and Marketing of Arundhati Roy', engages in understanding the emergence of what she calls a 'Roy phenomenon' following the publication of the book. Roy's 'home grown' and 'authentically' Indian image was forcibly blended with her audacious cosmopolitanism to escalate the exotic value of her book in order to boost sales.

Mongia renders, quite painstakingly, a detailed description of the book's cover (referring to the Random hardback edition), which according to her 'is stereotypically evocative of the tropical: lushness, overgrowth, moisture and colour. Hardly different visually from a tourist brochure or travel guide, Roy's novel holds out the same sensual promise as those publications would.'[28] On the inside jacket, an equally alluring 'winsome author photo greets the reader', where Roy 'is luminous',[29] much like the flowers on the cover. Somini Sengupta makes a similar observation in the *New York Times*: 'Roy is gazing dreamily, beckoning the reader to open her debut novel.'[30] Huggan describes her as 'incorrigibly photogenic'[31] and Reena Jana seems totally floored by Roy's 'literary lioness persona', 'remarkably tiny' frame, 'curly black hair' and 'childlike, saucer eyes and cheekbones that erupt the moment she talks or smiles'.[32] Elsewhere there has been talk about her diamond nose ring, her sharply visible collarbones, her blue jeans, white shirt, her platform shoes and what not. With so much talk about her charm doing the rounds it is not surprising that *People Magazine* included Roy in their list of '50 Most Beautiful People in the World' in 1998. Roy's hairdo seems to attract attention too: '[Roy] cut off her unruly mane last year because she did not want to be known "as some pretty woman who wrote a book,"' writes Celia Dugger in the *New York Times* in November 2001.[33]

Ritu Menon, in her review, writes, '*The God of Small Things* is a seduction from start to finish.'[34] Talking about 'physical crafting', Roy herself revealed on several occasions that she did have control over the design details of the book. The commodification of postcolonial fiction begins right from the cover. More important, however, is the language. Evidently, 'the lushly romantic images' and the use of 'Conradian primitive myths' are evidences of the fact that Roy is aware of the 'profitable *Heart of Darkness* industry', and skilfully rolls out the carpet of 'imperial imaginary' as a '*strategic* exoticism, designed to trap the unwary reader into complicity with the Orientalisms of which the novel so hauntingly relates'.[35] *The God* is custom made in this sense. It is architectured 'to stand in metonymically for India itself as an object of conspicuous consumption'.[36]

Marta Dvorak's reading of *The God* takes off on a similar course. According to her, Roy's book exposes what she calls the 'neocolonial commodification' of India and Indian by putting on display those very codes of belief that its writer otherwise condemns. She goes on to say that 'with its domesticated mythological sensibility, its topographical details, its interpolation of Malayalam words, and descriptions of every sphere of social life […] the novel also satisfies the western reader's taste for the exotic'.[37]

Readers of *The God* would perhaps agree that, for most part, Roy serves her readers with the authentic sights, sounds, smells, colours and tastes of Ayemenem. She walks Estha all over Ayemenem, enabling in effect a guided tour of the village: the 'river that smelled of shit, and pesticide', fish that 'suffered from fin-rot and had broken out in boils', 'Gulf-money houses', 'cheap soft-porn magazines' with 'ripe, naked women' on the covers hanging from the ceilings in 'ration shops that sold rice, sugar and bananas' (13). Through the Plymouth window on the way to Cochin and back, the twins show us 'squashed frogs', 'frog-shaped stains on the road', 'squashed crows', 'squashed dogs', 'feathers', 'mangoes', 'spit', 'vomit streaks on buses' and a dead temple elephant among other things (61–82). While the car is at the level crossing, we get to see beggars with bandages, men with trays selling *vadas* on banana leaves, lepers with soiled bandages begging at car windows and a naked, armless lunatic, perched on a milestone with his genitals dangling. At the Abhilash Talkies, Roy takes her readers straight into the toilets where we see Ammu tell Rahel to 'balance in the air to piss. She said that Public Pots were Dirty. Like Money was. You never knew who'd touched it. Lepers. Butchers. Car mechanics. (Puss. Blood. Grease.)' (94). Roy walks her readers through *only* the dark, ugly, smelly, wretching, carcassed parts of Kerala to effectively 'stage' a sick and ailing India. Sadly, in moments like these, Roy's novel tends to read like an epitaph to her home, to God's Own Country, Kerala.

The God is over a decade and a half old, yet the furore over it continues. Universities in the West embraced the book soon after its successful run for the Booker and canonized Roy. However, in India, the book was considered taboo and many universities across India remained reluctant to include it in their literature programmes. Things have changed since and it is now common to see the book on the reading lists of college students and the book itself has reached the humblest of book displays on the roadside. Love her or hate her, as the cliché goes, we cannot ignore Roy. But the latest from Mumbai is that Rohinton Mistry's *Such a Long Journey* (1991) has been forcibly thrown out of the Mumbai University syllabus by the RSS organization and its cousins for its alleged anti-Marathi content.

There are a few good single-author studies available on *The God*. Julie Mullaney's *Arundhati Roy's The God of Small Things: A Reader's Guide* is an easily accessible, slim, pocketsize guide published in 2002 as part of the Continuum Contemporaries series. The guide introduces the thematic concerns that are central to *The God*, followed by a section on the novel's reception and a brief mapping of its commercial success. A more recent book-length study is Alex Tickell's *Arundhati Roy's The God of Small Things*, published in 2007 as part of Routledge Guides to Literature. 'Language, Hybridity and Dialogism in *The God of Small Things*' was specially commissioned for the guide. On the whole, Tickell's guide is the most extensively researched study guide on *The God* to date and the good news is that it is easily accessible. The book now remains one of the most read, discussed and analysed novels of postliberalization writing.

Notes and References

1. Arundhati Roy, 'The End of Imagination', in *The Algebra of Infinite Justice* (New Delhi: Penguin, 2002), 5–6. The dedication to the essay reads, 'For marmots and voles and everything else on earth that is threatened and terrorized by the human race.' The essay is available online: http://www.flonnet.com/fl1516/15160040.htm.
2. Arundhati Roy, *The Shape of the Beast* (New Delhi: Penguin, 2009), 33.
3. Michiko Kakutani, 'Melodrama as Structure for Subtlety', *New York Times*, 3 June 1997. Online: http://www.nytimes.com/1997/06/03/books/melodrama-as-structure-for-subtlety.html (accessed 16 August 2012).
4. Merritt Moseley, 'The Booker Prize for 2000', *Sewanee Review* 109, no. 3 (Summer 2001): 438. Online: http://www.jstor.org/stable/27549063 (accessed 14 December 2011).
5. Ibid.
6. Merritt Moseley, 'Recent British Novels', *Sewanee Review* 106, no. 4 (Fall 1998): 676. Online: http://www.jstor.org/stable/27548605 (accessed 14 December 2011).
7. The Man Group, 'About Us'. Online: https://www.man.com/GB/about-us (accessed 31 December 2012).
8. Quoted in Graham Huggan, *The Postcolonial Exotic: Marketing the Margins* (London: Routledge, 2001), 105.
9. Man Booker Prize, 'FAQs'. Online: http://www.themanbookerprize.com/prize/about/faqs (accessed 19 September 2010).
10. Ibid.
11. Huggan, *The Postcolonial Exotic*, 12.
12. Ibid., 14.
13. Ibid., 65. Also see Aijaz Ahmad, *In Theory: Classes, Nations, Literatures* (London: Verso, 1992), Chapter 7.
14. Ibid., 66.
15. Ibid., 81.
16. Victor Segalen, *Essay on Exoticism: An Aesthetics of Diversity*, trans. and ed. Yael Rachel Schlick (Durham, NC: Duke University Press, 2002), 35.
17. Ibid., 67.
18. Ibid.
19. Ritu Menon, 'The Age of Innocence', *Women's Review of Books* 14, no. 12 (September 1997): 3. Online: http://www.jstor.org/stable/4022771 (accessed 30 September 2010).
20. Merritt Moseley, 'Recent British Novels', 678.
21. Ibid.
22. Chindu Sreedharan, 'Booker or Not, Arundhati's Still in the Dock', *Rediff On The NeT* 15 October 1997. Online: http://www.rediff.com/news/oct/15case.htm (accessed 19 September. 2010).
23. Elizabeth Bummiler, 'A Novelist Beginning with a Bang', *New York Times*, 29 July 1997. Online: http://nytimes.com/1997/07/29/books/a-novelist-beginning-with-a-bang.html (accessed 18 October 2010).
24. Salman Rushdie, *Midnight's Children* (New York: Alfred A Knopf, 1981), 11.
25. Salman Rushdie and Elizabeth West, eds, *The Vintage Book of Indian Writing, 1947–1997* (New York: Vintage, 1997), viii.
26. Ibid., xix.
27. Lakshmi Gopalkrishnan, 'Booker Snooker', *Slate*, 26 October 1997. Online: http://www.slate.com/id/1837 (accessed 10 November 2010).

28 Padmini Mongia, 'The Making and Marketing of Arundhati Roy', in *Arundhati Roy's The God of Small Things*, ed. Alex Tickell (New York: Routledge, 2007), 105.
29 Ibid.
30 Ibid. For more on 'Indo Chic' see Saadia Toor, 'Indo-Chic: The Cultural Politics of Consumption in Post-Liberalisation India', *SOAS Literary Review* 2 (2000). Online: http://www.soas.ac.uk/soaslit/2000_index.htm
31 Huggan, *The Postcolonial Exotic*, 77.
32 Reena Jana, interview with Arundhati Roy, 'The Salon Interview: Arundhati Roy', *Salon*, 30 September 1997. Online: http://www.salon.com/1997/09/30/00roy/ (accessed 10 October 2010).
33 Celia Dugger, 'An Indian Novelist Turns Her Wrath on the US', *New York Times*, 3 November 2001. Online: http://law.gsu.edu/ccunningham/fall03/India-RoyContempt Case.htm (accessed 24 December 2012).
34 Ritu Menon, 'The Age of Innocence', 1–4.
35 Huggan, *The Postcolonial Exotic*, 77.
36 Ibid., 81.
37 Quoted in Alex Tickell, ed., *Arundhati Roy's The God of Small Things*, 77.

Chapter Six

ARAVIND ADIGA: THE WHITE ELEPHANT? POSTLIBERALIZATION, THE POLITICS OF RECEPTION AND THE GLOBALIZATION OF LITERARY PRIZES

John Masterson

[Prizes] like the Booker [might] be seen to operate to some extent at least as what Frederic Jameson calls 'strategies of containment' […] for the redirecting of oppositional energies into the mainstream of Western metropolitan cultural thought.

(Graham Huggan, *The Postcolonial Exotic*)[1]

Instead of confirming the victory of reform, the awarding of the Nobel Prize in literature to authors from Columbia, Egypt, South Africa, Nigeria, Mexico, Saint Lucia, and Afro-America in an almost unbroken succession in the 1980s and early 1990s gave ongoing lessons in the varieties of containment, and it is here that sublimation and cosmopolitanism have been largely identical.

(Timothy Brennan, *At Home in the World*)[2]

Standing around books, even books in a foreign language, you feel a kind of electricity buzzing up towards you […]. It just happens, the way you get erect around girls wearing tight jeans. Except here what happens is that your *brain* starts to hum.

(Aravind Adiga, *The White Tiger*)[3]

Set against a backdrop of celebrity authors and big budget book clubs, the global literary prize safari has arguably never been as high profile. With the international credit crisis still crunching, many multinational corporations continue to promote their more 'people-friendly' sides by investing in artistic awards. If the benefits of such associations are hard to quantify, they are multifarious. Yet, as Huggan and Brennan point out above, certain socioeconomic – and arguably political – imperatives bubble beneath the surface of such cultural largesse.[4] The resonant qualifying term linking both epigraphs is 'containment'. From their historico-materialist standpoints, the value of the exposure given to texts and authors shortlisted for, let alone winning, such awards is inherently ambiguous. If bringing benefits, they oftentimes incur exacting costs. Writers and texts associated with the Indian subcontinent have dominated what we could term the 'Bookerscape'.[5] This is reflected in the incredulity expressed by various commentators following the absence of any South Asian authors on the 2009 Booker longlist.[6] It was even starker following Aravind Adiga's controversial 2008 win for *The White Tiger* (2008).

This analysis explores that novel alongside *Between the Assassinations* (2008), considering how both explore the poetics and politics, promises, potentialities and pitfalls of globalization, probing how this in turn corresponds with the business of and discourses surrounding literary prizes. It can therefore be seen in relation to what Sarah Brouillette identifies as greater 'attention [to] the question of the intersections between literature and globalization'.[7] 'Intersections', 'interconnections' and 'disconnections' are all keywords throughout what follows. As Brouillette argues, '[I]f all signs indicate that the discussion of the literary will remain a key interest for those working at the intersections between contemporary politics and culture, attention to the global workings of the publishing industry can lead to precisely the sort of materially-oriented scholarship critics have long deemed necessary.'[8]

While Brennan's and Huggan's 'materially oriented scholarship' continues to inspire, Brouillette's intervention enables a revision of some of their underlying assumptions. Much ink has been spilled about the quality of Adiga's work and whether his Booker triumph signals a devaluing of the prize's benchmark status. In the following, I reassess the bases upon which these value judgements are founded, considering how far the works themselves, while circulating within the networks of transnational capitalism, heighten the reader's awareness of certain 'strategies of containment', be they economic or cultural. As my third epigraph suggests, there are moments where *The White Tiger* self-reflexively invites its reader to think about 'the global workings of the publishing industry' (and, arguably, the literary prize circuit itself) in a more nuanced manner.[9] If 'postcolonial' texts are commodity fetishes, setting publishers' pulses racing in anticipation of projected profit margins, they might still get their readers' brains humming with counterhegemonic urgency.

At their strongest, they can challenge overly prescriptive models of passive literary consumers and complicit producers.

Adiga's Booker triumph must be viewed in relation to those of other winners over the last forty years. V. S. Naipaul (Trinidad), Nadine Gordimer (South Africa) and Ruth Prawer Jhabvala (Anglo-India) all received the prize in the 70s. Yet it was Salman Rushdie's success with *Midnight's Children* in 1981, which would go on to receive the Booker of Bookers in 1993 before the Best of the Booker title in 2008, that is still regarded as a pivotal point in the prize's dense history.[10] The familiar names of Amis and Golding gradually ceded to those of Coetzee, Ondaatje, Hulme, Okri, Ishiguro and Roy. When you include Margaret Atwood (Canada), Peter Carey (Australia), Roddy Doyle, John Banville and Anne Enright (all Irish) and the Glaswegian *enfant terrible* James Kelman, the winners' roll call has assumed a distinctly un-English hue over the past few decades.[11] With awards in 2006 and 2008 respectively, Kiran Desai and Aravind Adiga complete the line-up for my 'postcolonial' purposes. Yet, rewinding to the eighties context with which their work is so intimately preoccupied, its significance cannot be divorced from broader socioeconomic, political and intellectual factors.

Both *The Inheritance of Loss* (2006) and *Between the Assassinations* display an awareness, however pained, of postcolonial theory, most notably that associated with Gayatri Spivak.[12] This reflects Desai's and Adiga's academic training, as well as their commitment to reappropriating those terms most readily used and abused by an invariably Western academe. For an India attempting to situate itself within the whirlwind of socioeconomic 'liberalization', debates surrounding 'subalternity' have a material rather than metaphoric resonance. It was in the embryonic stages of the postliberalization period that Spivak posed the original, seemingly irresolvable question, 'Can the Subaltern Speak?'[13] When considering Adiga's work, her revised conclusion in *A Critique of Postcolonial Reason* remains particularly enlightening.[14]

At the close of her 'History' chapter, Spivak traces disconcerting lineages between the suicide of 17-year-old Bhubaneswari Bhaduri in 1926 and the position of her 'elder sister's eldest daughter's eldest daughter [who] is a new U.S. immigrant and was recently promoted to an executive position in a U.S.-based transnational'. While Bhaduri's death was initially a mystery, Spivak addresses certain historiographic aporias, recording how 'she was a member of one of the many groups involved in the armed struggle for Indian independence. She had been entrusted with a political assassination. Unable to confront the task and yet aware of the practical need for trust, she killed herself'. In the final paragraphs, we fast-forward to her distant relative. Having quoted Lenin's identification of the shift from an old capitalism to new imperialism during 'the crisis of 1900–1903', Spivak pens an endnote to the globalized century par excellence while offering speculations on the one to come: 'Today's program of global financialization carries on that relay. Bhubaneswari had fought for national liberation. Her great-grandniece works for the New Empire. This too is a historical silencing of the subaltern.'[15] Besides specific references to assassinations, renewed wrestling with questions of subalternity, representation and resistance, alongside attention to the economic base, provides a provocative springboard into Adiga's work.

At the close of *Between the Assassinations*, Adiga includes a chronology of events affecting the town of Kittur. In a suitably Orwellian move, given Adiga's preoccupation with the levelling of difference, even dissent, intrinsic to globalizing processes, he begins in 1984. As its title suggests, the book is framed around the assassinations of Indira Gandhi and her son Rajiv. While providing the transnational reader who might be unaware of India's turbulent politics during this period with a useful sense of context, it is arguably the manner in which these events are presented that is most revealing. Both opening and closing entries focus on how the Gandhi assassinations (on 31 October 1984 and 21 May 1991 respectively) were relayed to news consumers. The BBC is responsible for transmitting events in the former case, while in the latter it is CNN. Metonymically, this shift from one global media provider to another represents a changing of the guard.[16] As much of the collection demonstrates, real money and power, ranging from property developers to media tycoons, now lies in the hands of predominantly North American companies. Adiga's turn to the '80s is thus a strategic attempt to trace the complex lineages of that globalized web within which India remains thoroughly entangled. As P. A. O'Hara maintains, 'Since the 1970s, globalization has especially taken a decidedly neo-liberal turn [...] accelerating production rather than protecting the environment; advancing the interests of the US and its allies rather than the Middle East, Africa and Latin America [...] the way in which globalization has been undertaken is not neutral [it is] imbued with internal contradictions that variously promote *and* inhibit socio-economic and politico-cultural progress.'[17]

While India is conspicuously absent, as in Brennan's epigraph, this should be supplemented by Rajan Harshe's assertion that 'India is reflecting some of the most significant trends that have been unleashed under globalization.'[18] Both *The White Tiger* and *Between the Assassinations* unleash suitably provocative reflections on postliberalization India.

Adiga's terse chronology enables him to gesture towards this wider cultural and economic context. The detail that the live broadcast of Indira Gandhi's cremation proved 'a major boost to the number of TVs sold in Kittur' (352) has a satirical edge that concentrates rather than dilutes the power of his critique.[19] Indeed, the true scale of globalization's reach can be measured by the extent to which the Gandhi assassinations morph into mass media events vying for spectatorial attention with the 1987 Cricket World Cup held in India and Pakistan. Yet, it is perhaps the reference to the erroneously titled 'First Gulf War' that most clearly shows why Adiga has turned to events twenty years earlier in a bid to reflect on their lineages in the 'historical present'. Rather than providing figures of the dead or dying, Adiga defamiliarizes the conflict. Framing it from a local perspective, he states that its outbreak leads 'to the loss of expatriate remittances from Kuwait'. In an ironic upside, however, 'the broadcast of the war on CNN, available only to those TVs with a dish antenna, proves a great boost to sales of satellite TV dish antennas in Kittur' (354–5). From domestic servants to struggling teachers to itinerant labourers and street hawkers, Adiga's Kittur is littered with those who have invariably fallen through the cracks of postliberalization India. In another entry, for instance, the cost exacted by 'super-modernity' and 'progress' is a decimated ecosystem: 'The Sardar Patel Iron Man of India Stadium opens in Bajpe. The construction of houses in the neighbourhood proceeds rapidly, and by the year's end the old forest is almost entirely gone' (354). *Between the Assassinations* offers a powerful reminder that, for every victor there will be a victim, for every beneficiary there will be a fall guy and for every profit made someone, somewhere pays an even higher price. Its readers, Indian or otherwise, are compelled to set these regional events against a much broader socioeconomic backdrop. As such, it provides an intriguing counterpoint to his Booker Prize–winning novel.

Towards the close of *The White Tiger*, its first person narrator, Balram Halwai, describes his attempts to try and capture Bangalore's peculiar timbre amidst the din of postliberalization India:

> I tried to hear Bangalore's voice, just as I had heard Delhi's.
>
> I went down M. G. Road and sat down at the Café Coffee Day [...]. I had a pen and a piece of paper with me, and I wrote down everything I overheard.
>
> *I completed that computer program in two and a half minutes.*
>
> *An American today offered me four hundred thousand dollars for my start-up and I told him, 'That's not enough!'*
>
> *Is Hewlett-Packard a better company than IBM?*
>
> Everything in the city, it seemed, came down to one thing.
>
> Outsourcing. Which meant doing things in India for Americans over the phone. Everything flowed from it – real estate, wealth, power, sex. So I would have to join this outsourcing thing, one way or another. (297–8)[20]

This rich section obliges the reader to reflect on the deliberate design of a novel that, while dramatically centred around chauffeur Balram's murder of his businessman master Mr Ashok, is, from start to finish, preoccupied with the processes, pitfalls and politics of globalization. While many have expressed considerable reservations about *The White Tiger*, more sympathetic commentators have focused on how Adiga explores the effects and affects of macroeconomic systems from the perspectives of those at once a part of and apart from them. Thus, the keyword 'outsourcing', which recurs throughout, provides a framework within which to situate a more nuanced discussion of *The White Tiger*'s reception in terms of postliberalization Indian novels in English and the politics of literary prizes more specifically.[21]

In the above, Balram collects scraps of conversation within the generic, coffee-shop hub that, borrowing from James Clifford, can be seen as a defining chronotope of contemporary, globalized culture.[22] Alongside direct references to the Hewlett-Packards and IBMs stalking the information superhighway, allusions to the computer programming–related compression of time and space captures a defining aspect of what Stan Smith calls this 'most volatile of signifiers'.[23] As such, Adiga's use of 'flowed' can be read alongside Appadurai's notion of 'financescapes':

> It is useful to speak [...] of financescapes, as the disposition of global capital is now *a more mysterious, rapid, and difficult landscape* to follow than ever before, as currency markets, national stock exchanges, and commodity speculations move megamonies through national turnstiles at blinding speed, with vast, absolute implications for small differences in percentage points and time units.[24]

Similarly, in Adiga's passage, where telecommunications seemingly replace human interaction, the tangible realities of 'real estate, wealth, power, sex' become mysteriously virtual. One interpretation of *The White Tiger* is that it attempts to provide a name, face and narrative voice to those swept along in outsourcing's anonymous flow. This corresponds with perhaps the most interesting self-reflexive feature of this excerpt. Balram, literally and figuratively, holds onto pen and paper. While seemingly insignificant, there is the sense that, particularly when set against a backdrop of various *scapes* dominated by the acronyms and brands of increasingly faceless corporations, the act of putting pen to paper has a kind of material, resistant urgency.[25] This in turn could be interpreted as a metatextual reflection by Adiga on the ways in which literature might be seen as writing against the globalized grain.

Thus far, I have focused on Adiga's work in relation to some of the overarching geopolitical and socioeconomic questions it poses and tackles. Yet, this must be set against a more in-depth exploration of how it has been received, by whom and the manner in which this feeds into wider issues surrounding the business of literary prizes. If 'outsourcing' preoccupies Adiga's journalistic and fictional output, greater scrutiny of the comparable keyword 'voice' and how the author tries and/or does not try hard enough to capture it, will open up debates concerning loaded notions such as 'authenticity', 'audience' and 'the real India'. Writing in the *Boston Review*, Amitava Kumar describes how, on encountering *The White Tiger*, his early enthusiasm turned to a disillusionment eventually bordering on dismay. It is the profound disconnection between Adiga's fictional representation and the world in which Kumar grew up that he finds most disconcerting. Strikingly, he highlights Adiga's deficiencies as literary ventriloquism: 'Halwai's voice sounds like a *curious mix* of an American teen and a middle-aged Indian essayist. I find Adiga's villains utterly cartoonish, like the characters in Bollywood melodrama. However, it is his presentation of ordinary people that seems not only trite but also offensive'.[26]

This barbed critique raises fundamental questions about the text, its readership and reception. To what extent do notoriously problematic questions of authenticity preoccupy *The White Tiger*'s Anglo-American audience compared with its Indian one? How do such texts, circulating within genuinely transnational discourses and markets, satisfy the demands of such a disparate readership? Or is it rather the case that they are not produced for a domestic market at all but in order to satisfy the insatiable appetite for the postcolonial exotic and/or grotesque nurtured in the West? An analysis of Kumar's particular rhetoric proves rewarding in this regard. Rather problematically, he conflates what he sees as Adiga's offensive perspective with that of his first person narrator: 'This is at the heart of the book's bad faith. The first-person narration disguises a cynical anthropology. [...] It is an "India for Dummies" that proves quite adept at finding the vilest impulse in nearly every human being it represents. [...] Reviews of the book in mainstream publications, including the *Economist*, present it as a glimpse into the "real India". Whose India is real; Adiga's, or mine?'[27] By placing 'real India' in inverted commas, thus supplementing the notion that his reality and Adiga's are at loggerheads, Kumar confronts his reader, Indian or otherwise, with questions that refuse to go away. If, like Spivak's, they seem ultimately irresolvable, a discursive juxtaposition will at least suggest how and why Adiga's work has provoked such divided responses among readers.

While it is hardly surprising that someone intimately involved with the novel's editing would be more ebullient in the afterglow of the 2008 Booker announcement, Ravi Marchandani's comment provides a stark counterpoint to Kumar's.[28] If he fails the literary objectivity test, the Booker panel chair couches his praise rather differently. For Michael Portillo, '[*The White Tiger*] changed my view of certain things – like what is the real India and what is the nature of poverty'.[29] As a former politician, such high-profile occasions provide tantalizing opportunities to shift into rhetorical overdrive. Yet, his reliance on nebulous notions of 'the real India' and 'the nature of poverty' can be set alongside that of 'voice'. That the 'real' slips and slides between Portillo's and Kumar's statements reminds us that Adiga's preoccupation with globalization and its fallout cannot be divorced from discussion of his work's reception. The email conceit governing the text, for instance, suggests it is written for a transnational audience, in the lingua franca of global hegemony, about socioeconomic processes and programs that problematize notions of self-enclosed nations. Indeed, that *The White Tiger* has provoked such different responses among popular and critical readers *across* geopolitical borders is perhaps an indication of the effectiveness with which it more broadly counters the flattening of difference so integral to the globalizing project.

If the perspectives of Portillo and Kumar seem a little extreme, a recent intervention might prove more instructive. In 'English Spoken Here', Chandrahas Choudhury speaks of the vapidity of the 'global novel [that] often seems to sacrifice the particularities of Indian experience for a watered-down idiom that can speak to readers across the globe'.[30] He continues by reflecting on the differential reception of such texts within and beyond India: 'What readers around the world frequently find instructive, fresh, and moving about Indian novels available to them in English, is often experienced by Indian readers as dull, clichéd, and superficial.' At first glance, these juxtapositions appear entirely appropriate to discussions about *The White Tiger*, particularly when considering its Booker triumph against its failure to 'make the short list for the Vodafone Crossword Book Award, [India's] most prestigious prize for novels in English'.[31] If this forestalls the possibility and/or desirability of literary value judgments, Choudhury's conclusion is more enabling.

Rather than appealing to the problematic concept of 'authenticity', Choudhury argues a 'better measure to judge the Indian novel in English should perhaps be 'the specific' [...]. It is in the details presented and the others left out, that any novel reveals the quality of its engagement with life and the presumptions it makes about its audience.'[32] Building on this, I argue the specificity of Adiga's novel refracts globalization's processes for the very reason that, to reappropriate Kumar's phrase, it is a 'curious mixture' of a book. That economic and literary commentators rely on similar rhetoric to characterize both postliberalization India and the novel is revealing in many ways. In the O'Hara citation above, for instance, globalization is defined as a process riven with 'internal contradictions'. This is the same sense that pervades many commentaries on *The White Tiger*'s problematic 'voice'. It is precisely because Adiga's is a strange, often disorientating mess of a book that it gives the most penetrating insight into a certain aspect of postliberalization India that, for good or bad, throws notions of the 'authentic' or 'real' into disarray. What more potent symbol could you have of the reach of globalization's tentacles than a Hindu shrine located next to an IBM plant near a McDonald's? For a world where 'curious', 'contradictory' and 'confused' are the most appropriate adjectives, perhaps Adiga's tension-riddled work offers a more illuminating window onto this peculiar hyper-reality.[33]

In 'America', Allen Ginsberg declares, 'It occurs to me that I am America.'[34] While Ginsberg was ideologically and poetically committed to battling 'Mammon', there are both formal and thematic links with Adiga's novel. 'America' captures the rambunctious contradictions of a late Eisenhower-era US, with its Cold War neuroses and subversive beatniks lurking behind white picket fences. Similarly, Balram, riven to the core with the paradoxes of his nation-space, might just as justifiably state, 'It occurs to me that I am India.' As the reader perseveres, it becomes increasingly clear why Adiga opts for an antihero figurehead in his debut novel. *The White Tiger* morphs into an extended reflection on *degrees* of criminality, complicity and impropriety, effectively transposing the preoccupations of Ginsberg's poem some fifty years earlier. Readers are invited to set Ashok's grisly murder against a broader backdrop of systemic corruption and violence, latent and manifest. This allows Adiga to gesture towards weightier and, when speculating about how India's bureaucratic elite might have received the text, more disconcerting questions before revealing how Balram earns the murderer tag: 'If I were making a country, I'd get the sewage pipes first, then the democracy, then I'd go about giving pamphlets and statues of Gandhi to other people, but what do I know? I'm just a murderer!' (96).

If such gestures appear overdetermined, Adiga's prose is arguably most effective when, as with *Between the Assassinations*' chronology, he pares it down. The following shows his ability to capture scenes synonymous with the Indian metropolis held in globalization's grip:

> When I drive down Hosur Main Road, when I turn into Electronics City Phase 1 and see the companies go past, I can't tell you how exciting it is to me. General Electric, Dell, Siemens – they're all here in Bangalore. And so many more on their way. There is construction everywhere […]. The entire city is masked in smoke, smog, powder, cement dust. It is under a veil. When the veil is lifted, what will Bangalore be like?
>
> Maybe it will be a disaster: slums, sewage, shopping malls, traffic jams, policemen. But you never know. It may turn out to be a decent city, where humans can live like humans and animals can live like animals. A new Bangalore for a new India. And then I can say that, in my own way, I helped to make New Bangalore […].

Haven't I succeeded in the struggle that every poor man here should be making – the struggle not to take the lashes your father took, not to end up in a mound of indistinguishable bodies that will rot in the black mud of Mother Ganga? True, there was the matter of murder – which is a wrong thing to do, no question about it. It has darkened my soul. All the skin-whitening creams sold in the markets of India won't clean my hands again.

But isn't it likely that everyone who counts in *this world*, including our prime minister (including *you*, Mr Jiabao), has killed someone or other on their way to the top? Kill enough people and they will put up bronze statues to you near Parliament House in Delhi – but that is glory, and not what I am after. All I wanted was the chance to be a man – and for that, one murder was enough. (317–18) [Emphasis added][35]

Coming at the end of *The White Tiger*, this showcases those devices that characterize the urgency of Adiga's poetics and politics throughout. It also anticipates the playful reconfiguration-cum-interrogation of the touristic gaze that will define *Between the Assassinations*. If corporate insignia and the prospect of more to come initially dazzle Balram, Adiga's staccato sentences are accompanied by images capturing the fallout from construction. These lead to suitably opaque ones concerning the ambiguities of revelation and concealment, surface appearance and reality. References to 'veils' and 'masking' thus work against the grain of globalization's branding as universal panacea, as well as that of the fallacious 'real India'. Thus, one of the passage's most striking rhetorical features is its reliance upon questions with few, if any, definitive answers. In terms of the critical controversy discussed above, this seems entirely appropriate. As Balram oscillates between attraction and revulsion, the reader is reminded that *The White Tiger* is very much concerned with Bangalore in relation to postliberalization as a *process*.[36] With a gesture towards taxonomies of human bodies, Adiga returns to one of his essential concerns. From shopping malls to apartment blocks that house masters in air-conditioned penthouses and servants in cockroach-infested basements, such spaces are designed to concretize the realities of social exclusion (rather than inclusion) as lived beyond their walls.[37] From an Agamben-inflected concern with the blurring of distinctions between human and animal life, Adiga returns to Balram's 'I', thereby broadening his critique into the ecological realm.[38] By imagining Mother Ganga as the angel of death rather than the giver of life, he echoes earlier allusions to the literal and figurative pollution of India's iconic water source and tourist attraction by the waste products of globalized industries.[39]

The White Tiger's focus on Bangalore as a paradoxical paradigm in this 'glocalized' setting is thus fitting. As Basu notes, it is an urban space where the curious mixtures of globalization as lived reality rather than boardroom fantasy are played out:

> [Bangalore's] large dotcom hoardings, the cyber cafes, the sleek restaurants offering cuisines ranging from Coorgi to French, and the pubs lining the road are impressive.
> But equally impressive is the rapidity with which all this disappears [...]. Within miles of cruising west the modern buildings give way to modest tenements. Another hour or two of driving and the landscape changes to open fields [...]. The simple huts and hovels of the poor are a reminder of the sameness of India – a sameness dominated, even now, by poverty.[40]

While spectres of 'poverty tourism' hang heavy over such descriptions, Basu's observations provide an interesting supplement to *The White Tiger*, which, from its smallest detail through to its broadest geopolitical and socioeconomic speculations, is concerned with exposition as a means of exploration of those 'curious mixtures' that many see as defining the order of things in postliberalization India. The gesture towards the cult of skin-whitening products in the above citation offers a case in point.

Here and elsewhere, Adiga alludes to the massive industry (cosmetic and commercial) behind commodity fetishes in order to pass comment on the disjuncture between exterior artifice and underlying reality. Indeed, skin-whitening cream appears to be a more ominous metonym for the way in which the globalization lobby relies upon this kind of glossy projection to maintain its hegemonic grip. On another level, however, Adiga uses it as a parodic intertextual reference, recasting Balram's murder and subsequent cosmetic musings in relation to Lady Macbeth's futile attempts to cleanse her hands of the blood of innocents. This lays foundations for the final section, which again obliges the reader to reflect on degrees of complicity and violence, shifting from Balram's crime to more covert activities taking place behind those closed doors of the country's elite. From Siemens factory to Delhi's Parliament House, *The White Tiger* explores specific spaces in conjunction with globalization and its (dis)contents, and thus the disjuncture between appearance and reality.

As such, the novel self-consciously plays with notions of 'connectedness', 'interconnectedness' and 'disconnectedness' that pepper discussions of the postliberalization era.[41] When reflecting on metropolitan architecture, for instance, Balram again ponders how its spatial design enshrines those inequities of power and prestige beyond. 'Interconnected' therefore emerges as the most resonant term: 'I don't know how buildings are designed in your country, but in India every apartment block, every house, every hotel is built with a servants' quarters – sometimes at the back, and sometimes [...] underground – a warren of interconnected rooms where all the drivers, cooks, sweepers, maids, and chefs of the apartment block can rest, sleep, and wait' (129–30). For Adiga, whether talking about individual buildings, urban spaces, national or transnational communities, you simply cannot have one without the other.

Such sections can be read as reconfigurations of *The White Tiger*'s earlier meditations on lightness and darkness, which Kumar, among others, finds most troubling. With slightly more nuanced probing, however, they can be seen alongside debates concerning the politics of literary prizes, as well as the global dissemination and reception of such texts. In the novel's opening pages, Adiga plays with that most tried and, arguably, tired of colonial and postcolonial tropes – 'darkness'. It establishes the 'two Indias in one' concern. Yet, in light of the above, I argue it corresponds with broader globalization concerns: 'Like all good Bangalore stories, mine begins far away from Bangalore. You see, I am in the Light now, but I was born and raised in Darkness. [...] A place in India, at least a third of the country, a fertile place [...]. India is two countries in one [...]. The ocean brings light to my country. Every place on the map of India near the ocean is well-off. But the river brings darkness to India – the black river' (14).

Adiga shifts the reader's focus from darkness associated with a peculiar space to that of the literally and figuratively more fluid river system. One could imagine that, were *Heart of Darkness* to be reproduced in a twenty-first-century context, it, like *The White Tiger*, would focus on how rivers, be it the Nile or the Ganges, are simultaneously arteries that pump lifeblood to and through their respective areas as they also carry the waste products of multinational corporations that in turn poison those same veins. This in itself can be seen as a variation on Adiga's preoccupation with exposure as a means of altering perception.

Towards the end of *The White Tiger*, an ironic comment is passed on the extent to which, while little pieces of America are replicated within the brightly lit malls dominating the urban skyline, the tourist gaze is oriented around the idea that Indian culture can be reified and thus possessed:

> Now, Mr Premier, every day thousands of foreigners fly into my country for enlightenment. They go to the Himalayas, or to Benaras, or to Bodh Gaya. They get into weird poses of yoga, smoke hashish, shag a sadhu or two, and think they're getting enlightened.
> Ha!
> If it is enlightenment you have come to India for, you people, forget the Ganga – forget the ashrams – go straight to the National Zoo in the heart of New Delhi. (275)

This gestures towards Balram's self-mythologization, as he projects himself as the exceptional white tiger, set against the backdrop of a more conventional human zoo. In light of discussions concerning the book's prize-winning credentials and reception, the notion of the tourist-cum-consumer, flying into India with preconceived notions and a prescriptive itinerary to be checked off during their stay, holds greater significance. This nod towards the containment of culture can be linked to those broader debates about the postcolonial exotic, the expectations of transnational readers and the complexities and complicities of the business of literary awards themselves. As the epigraphs from Huggan and Brennan suggest, those texts that are, however problematically, grouped under the slippery heading 'postcolonial' are susceptible to the ossifying branding that beckons the reader as tourist. The covers that scream 'Booker winner', for instance, must be seen in relation to the circulation of postcolonial literature that takes place within a much broader, globalized network of discourses on consumption. As Brouillette argues, 'it is not too much to say that the image of the market reader, like the image of the ignorant and obnoxious tourist, is one inevitable product of postcolonial guilt [...]. It might be useful to think of postcoloniality's conscience as fundamentally touristic'.[42] Like Choudhury, however, Brouillette's caveats are essential: 'The suggestion that postcolonial literature, as it circulates in the Anglo-American marketplace, exists only as evidence of Western fetishization of the rest of human experience, or that *reception* of postcolonial texts is always or only a kind of market colonization, *ignores* a number of factors. Attention to the material organization of the current literary marketplace does not reveal a single market, but rather a fragmenting and proliferating set of niche audiences, which are admittedly united by a set of general rules dictated by the major transnational corporations.'[43]

For texts such as *The White Tiger*, the very debates that attend their production, dissemination and consumption must be seen, in their specificity, as rather more curious mixtures than certain commentators appear willing to admit. In closing, I offer a final analysis of an ironic description of the Ganges, arguing that it can be productively read in light of many of the issues I have touched upon throughout this chapter.

Seen through the less-than-discerning eyes of those caricatured tourists 'who come each year to take photographs of naked sadhus at Hardwar or Benaras', the river appears one of 'emancipation' (15). Shift perspective to Balram and this is immediately undercut by the kind of scene airbrushed from picture postcards: 'No! – Mr Jiabao, I urge you not to dip in the Ganga, unless you want your mouth full of faeces, straw, soggy parts of human bodies, buffalo carrion, and seven kinds of industrial acid' (12). The figurative distance separating the Booker Prize–winning vinegar of Rushdie's pickles and the corrosive acid of Adiga's multinational corporations is not insignificant. In relation to arguments attending the cult of literary prizes, it also suggests we may need to reorient discourses concerning the 'postcolonial exotic'. If heated debates persist as to whether the award of literary prizes is either an emancipatory or restrictive strategy, perhaps the answer is to be found somewhere in between. As I have suggested throughout, the 'curious mixture' of preoccupations and voices that define Adiga's work continues to provoke strong reactions from readers both domestic and international. Yet, in a global context where difference and/or dissidence is under constant siege from the politics and processes of standardization, there are times when such 'curious mixtures' demand the most rigorous of defences.

Notes and References

1 Graham Huggan, *The Postcolonial Exotic: Marketing the Margins* (London: Routledge, 2001).
2 Timothy Brennan, *At Home in the World: Cosmopolitanism Now* (Cambridge, MA: Harvard University Press, 1997).
3 Aravind Adiga, *The White Tiger* (London: Atlantic Books, 2008). All references to this edition will appear in parentheses after the bibliographical information.
4 Huggan explores tensions between the glossy discourse of the Booker Prize and its more troubled/troubling past: 'A discrepancy certainly exists between the Booker's postcolonial winners and the company's high colonial background in the Caribbean sugar trade.' (Huggan, *The Postcolonial Exotic*, xii.)
5 In 'Disjuncture and Difference in the Global Cultural Economy', Appadurai proposes 'an elementary framework […] to look at the relationship among five dimensions of global cultural flows […]. a). *ethnoscapes*, b). *mediascapes*, c). *technoscapes*, d). *financescapes*, and e). *ideoscapes*. The suffix -*scape* allows us to point to the fluid, irregular shapes that characterize international capital as deeply as they do international clothing styles.' (*The Anthropology of Globalization: A Reader*, ed. Jonathan Xavier Inda and Renato Rosaldo (Oxford: Blackwell Publishers, 2008), 51–2.)
6 See Mark Brown, 'Booker Longlist Pits Fiction's Finest Against First Kiss-and-Tell Chimp', *Guardian*, 28 July 2009. Online: http://www.guardian.co.uk/books/2009/jul/28/booker-prize-longlist-me-cheeta (accessed 24 September 2010).
7 Sarah Brouillette, *Postcolonial Writers in the Global Literary Marketplace* (Hampshire: Palgrave Macmillan, 2007), 19.
8 Ibid., 20–21.
9 As the following suggests, using terms such as 'industry' and/or 'business' in relation to literary prizes seems entirely appropriate: '[*The White Tiger*] helped propel Atlantic to a 21% growth in year-on-year sales through Nielsen BookScan for 2008, up to £4.9m. The trend has continued into 2009; its January sales are up 70% on 2008.' (Tom Tivnan, 'Rising Tide', *Bookseller*, 12 March 2009. Online: https://www.futurebook.net/profile/rising-tide.html (accessed March 2010).)
10 In 'The American Scene', John Sutherland draws certain distinctions between literary prizes on either side of the pond: 'The Booker is […] as nostalgically imperial as the statue of Wellington at the Guildhall, under which the winner is announced: only contenders from the home country and the old commonwealth need apply (an exception being made for Eire; no one is sure why). […] American prizes are as different as America itself.' (*New Statesman*, 14 November 2005. Online: http://www.newstatesman.com/node/152019 (accessed 16 August 2012).)
11 As Theo Tait maintains, 'In [Kelman's] essays, he sees himself as a post-colonial writer, and regards African and Caribbean writers as his peers. In an "occupied country" like

12 'Noni had picked a sad account of police brutality during the Naxalite movement by Mahashveta Devi, translated by Spivak who, she had recently read with interest in the *Indian Express*, was made cutting edge by a sari and Combat boots wardrobe.' (Kiran Desai, *The Inheritance of Loss* (London: Penguin, 2006), 218.)
13 See 'Can the Subaltern Speak?' in *Marxism and The Interpretation of Culture*, ed. Cary Nelson and Lawrence Grossberg (Urbana: University of Illinois Press, 1988), 271–313.
14 As Amitava Kumar suggests in 'Bad News: Authenticity and the South Asian Political Novel', Adiga's exposure to such socioeconomic inequity has had a profound impact on his fiction: 'After university [Adiga] returned to India, where for three years he worked as TIME's correspondent before quitting to write fiction. Adiga told me that his novel is the fruit of his labors as a reporter in India. He traveled to various parts of the country, including places whose backwardness shocked his sensibility. *The White Tiger* is his rebuke of the cheerful, and false, notion of a new, transformed India.' (*Boston Review*, November/December 2008. Online: http://bostonreview.net/BR33.6/kumar.php (accessed 16 August 2012).)
15 Gayatri Chakravorty Spivak, *A Critique of Postcolonial Reason: Toward a History of the Vanishing Present* (Cambridge, MA: Harvard University Press, 1999), 306–11.
16 Desai also plays with these CNN/BBC tensions (*The Inheritance of Loss*, 85).
17 P. A. O'Hara, 'The Contradictory Dynamics of Globalization', in *Globalization and the Third World: A Study of Negative Consequences*, ed. B. N. Ghosh & Halil M. Guven (Hampshire: Palgrave Macmillan, 2006), 18 [italics added].
18 Rajan Harshe, 'The Challenges of Globalization and India: Some Critical Reflections', *Globalization and the South Asian State*, ed. B. Ramesh Babu (New Delhi: South Asian Publishers, 1998), 28.
19 Aravind Adiga, *Between the Assassinations* (London: Atlantic Books, 2009). All references to this edition will appear in parentheses.
20 For a potted history of Bangalore, see Smriti Srinivas, *Landscapes of Urban Memory: The Sacred and the Civic in India's High-Tech City* (Minneapolis: University of Minnesota Press, 2001), 237.
21 'What is widely misunderstood in India and in the West, where there is mounting opposition to outsourcing, is that the real problem is not globalization but the inexorable march of technology.' (Kaushik Basu, *The Retreat of Democracy and Other Itinerant Essays on Globalization, Economics and India* (Ranikhet: Permanent Black, Orient Longman, 2007), 94.)
22 Borrowing from Bakhtin, Clifford's chronotope is a 'setting or scene organizing time and space in representable whole form. [...] [It] comes to resemble as much a site of travel encounter as of residence; it is less like a tent in a village or a controlled laboratory or a site of initiation and inhabitation, and more like a hotel lobby, urban café, ship, or bus.' (James Clifford, *Routes: Travel and Translation in the Late Twentieth Century* (Cambridge, MA: Harvard University Press, 1997), 25.)

It is notable that coffee franchises have expanded their sphere of interest into literary prizes. Consider the Costa Book Awards, for example (http://www.costabookawards.com).
23 Stan Smith, ed., *Globalisation and Its Discontents: Writing the Global Culture* (Cambridge: D. S. Brewer, 2006), 2.

(Above continues from previous page:)
Scotland, he has written, "the intellectual life of working-class people is colonised …". Not least, he thinks, this is done through literature, which is controlled by a "coterie" of London-based people who are "very close to power".' ('In His Own Words', *Guardian*, 12 April 2008. Online: www.guardian.co.uk/books/2008/apr/12/featuresreviews.guardianreview22 (accessed June 2010).)

24 Appadurai, *The Anthropology of Globalization*, 53 [italics added].
25 Adiga's novel is, rather tenuously, imagined as a prolonged email between Balram Halwai – boss@whitetiger-technologydrivers.com – and Wen Jiabao.
26 Amitava Kumar, 'Bad News: Authenticity and the South Asian political novel', *Boston Review*, November/December 2008 [italics added].
27 Ibid., 41.
28 For an indication of the seismic impact a Booker Prize win can have on sales, see N. Anand and Brittany C. Jones, 'Tournament Rituals, Category Dynamics, and Field Configuration: The Case of the Booker Prize', *Journal of Management Studies* 45, no. 6 (September 2008): 1036–60.
29 Ibid.
30 Chandrahas Choudhury 'English Spoken Here: How Globalization is Changing the Indian Novel', *Foreign Policy* (November/December 2009): 96–7.
31 Ibid., 96.
32 Ibid., 98.
33 Consider, for example, John Berger's statement: 'I'm tempted to say that the world has never been more confused. Yet this would be untrue. The world has never had to face such global confusion.' (Foreword to Arundhati Roy, *The Algebra of Infinite Justice* (London: Flamingo, 2002), xxii.)
34 Allen Ginsberg, 'America' in *The Penguin Book of American Verse*, ed. Geoffrey Moore (London: Penguin, 1989), 478–81.
35 As Srinivas maintains, 'Some of the most interesting writing on cities and their networks is fictional and includes novels exploring family history, medical mysteries, and the taut relationships between sexuality and politics, to mention a few themes.' (*Landscapes of Urban Memory*, xxi.)
36 See John Weiss, *Industrialisation and Globalisation: Theory and Evidence from Developing Countries* (London: Routledge, 2002), 140.
37 Srinivas' work is once more useful in this context: 'What I remember about these two periods, however, was that despite the presence of multiple life-worlds in the city, they intersected in some types of public spaces – for instance, in the main shopping districts, cinema halls, colleges, offices, parks, and cricket stadiums, many of them creations of the developmental state.' (*Landscapes of Urban Memory*, xxiii.)
38 Giorgio Agamben, *Homo Sacer: Sovereign Power and Bare Life*, trans. Daniel Heller-Roazen (California: Stanford University Press, 1998).
39 This in turn anticipates a key section from the Salt Market Village story in *Between the Assassinations*: 'As he walked down the twisting streets [with] fatigued day-labourers sleeping in the shade, and with thick, still, glistening pools of effluent, he was reminded of that *strange mixture* of the strikingly beautiful *and* the filthy which is the nature of every Indian village – and the simultaneous desire to admire *and* to castigate that had been inspired in him from the time of his first visits' (330) [emphasis added].
40 Basu, *The Retreat of Democracy*, 241.
41 As Upendra Kachru notes, 'Whether it is Friedman's flat world or Columbus's round world, this global *interconnectedness*, which we call globalization, with its geopolitical fallouts, is the single most significant trend of our day.' (*Extreme Turbulence: India at the Crossroads* (Delhi: HarperCollins, 2007), 89 [emphasis added].)
42 Brouillette, *Postcolonial Writers in the Global Literary Marketplace*, 21–5.
43 Ibid., 24 [emphasis added].

Chapter Seven

'THE MULTINATIONAL'S SONG': THE GLOBAL RECEPTION OF M. G. VASSANJI

Laura Moss

On his author website, M. G. Vassanji makes his own multinational status clear: 'If pressed, Vassanji considers himself African Asian Canadian; attempts to pigeonhole him along communal (religious) or other lines, however, he considers narrow-minded, malicious, and oppressive.'[1] One of the vanguard of writers from the South Asian diaspora in Canada, Vassanji is indisputably at the core of contemporary Canadian writing.[2] Having won the Commonwealth Writers' Prize (Africa) and twice the Giller Award (one of Canada's most prestigious literary prizes), and having been awarded the Order of Canada in recognition of his literary service to the country, it is fruitful to ponder why Vassanji's work has been so successful with a Canadian audience, in university settings and for a public readership, and with global readers alike.

Vassanji has without question reached the status of a major author. In addition to his awards, he has been reviewed in newspapers and magazines around the world and been interviewed by high-profile talk show hosts on radio and television. His fiction is studied in universities and high schools and read in book clubs and coffee shops. I suggest that Vassanji's negotiation of the complexities of 'Indo', 'African' and 'Canadian' identities in his fiction and nonfiction (set in India, Kenya, Tanzania and Canada) as well as in his own editorial and critical work, contribute to the ever-fluctuating conversations in public discourse about globalization, migration and flexible conceptions of home and national affiliation. It is precisely Vassanji's quiet refusal to be boxed in by expectation of nationality – or of genre, I might add – that echoes the increasing desire of global subjects to think laterally about identity and place, and that he and his publishers have harnessed in marketing the simultaneity of Vassanji as an African, South Asian, Canadian writer.

Critic Simon Gikandi begins his entry for Vassanji in the *Columbia Guide to East African Literature in English Since 1945* with a statement of difficulty: 'The novelist M. G. Vassanji is hard to categorize because of his hybrid background.'[3] Nearly every promotional piece (including the author's own webpage) and nearly every review of Vassanji's work trots out his international credentials: born in Kenya, educated in Tanzania and the USA at the University of Pennsylvania and Massachusetts Institute of Technology (MIT) where he earned a PhD in theoretical nuclear physics, Vassanji moved to Canada in 1978 to take up a postdoctoral fellowship with Atomic Energy of Canada and later to become a research associate at the University of Toronto (1980–89). With the success of his first novel, he left his work as a physicist and became a full-time writer. He has since lived in Toronto with his family and published six novels – *The Gunny Sack* (1989), *No New Land* (1990), *The Book of Secrets* (1993), *Amriika* (2000), *The In-Between World of Vikram Lall* (2003) and *The Assassin's Song* (2007) – two books of short stories – *Uhuru Street* (1990) and *When She Was Queen* (2005) – a memoir – *A Place Within: Rediscovering India* (2008) – and a biography of the writer *Mordecai Richler* (2009) for the Penguin Extraordinary Canadians series.[4] Vassanji's complex of biographical information situates his fiction and nonfiction in an international framework. He may have won national awards and been lauded by Canada and in Africa but he is unequivocally a transnational figure who explores the complexities of global movements and local histories.

What is not often mentioned in Vassanji's promotional material is his role as an editor and critic and, as a result, how instrumental he has been over the past thirty years in building a strong and recognizable South Asian Canadian writing community. Vassanji arrived in Canada at a time when many first-generation Canadians were vociferously arguing for the need to open up Canadian literature (and Canadian culture) to more minority voices and stories. He and several like-minded scholars, critics and writers joined forces to start the *Toronto South Asian Review* (TSAR) in 1981 (published since 1993 as the *Toronto Review of Contemporary Writing Abroad*). The journal's mission is to 'make accessible to a wide audience literature that traces some part of its inheritance and meaning in the culture, traditions and history of the Indian subcontinent'.[5] The binding trace of inheritance is key here as a means to link artists from India, Africa and the Caribbean with those already in North America.

In 1985, TSAR expanded to become a press as well as a journal and launched its inaugural collection of essays, *A Meeting of Streams: South Asian-Canadian Literature*, edited by the editor of the TSAR journal and the new editor of the press, M. G. Vassanji. Critic Arun Mukherjee notes that *A Meeting of Streams* is 'the first time one comes across the idea of a grouping of writers defined by their ethnicity' in English Canadian writing.[6] Mukherjee compares writing in English by South Asian writers to the longer tradition of writing joined together by ethnicity and language such as Icelandic Canadian Literature. She continues to note that over the course of the next decade, there was a proliferation of works that 'freely categorizes Canadian authors according to their ethnic or racial origins' (24).

On the blurb for *A Meeting of Streams*, Vassanji's collection itself declares a need for 'a concerted and many-sided look at the literature' of writers of South Asian origin. The critical essays highlight not only the very *existence*, which at the time was crucial to emphasize, but also the *significance* and *merit* of a range of literature from a variety of South Asian communities in Canada as they negotiate the local and historical specificities of that writing. In noting the potentially essentializing implications of the term 'South Asian', Mukherjee cites Vassanji's own wrestling, in 1993 shortly before the journal name change, with the label he helped to popularize: 'I have never sensed a passion behind that label 'South Asian' – no political front, not even a loosely defined conscious aesthetic or the probing for one: it seemed to be simply a very convenient and the least discomfiting umbrella to fit under.'[7] The point that Mukherjee makes, through Vassanji, is that 'the South Asian Canadian community does not have a monolithic perspective, and nor do its writers' but, Mukherjee adds, there is a tentative sense of a shared history that joins writers on the same platform (38). The umbrella term that Vassanji and TSAR strategically employed effectively helped to create a critical mass of readers and critics invested in the field within Canada. TSAR has since opened its mandate to now focus on fiction, nonfiction and poetry of 'New Canadian and World Writing'. One may note that the website for TSAR highlights the current inclusivity of the press in its governing statement: 'TSAR Publications is devoted to publishing and promoting "new" Canadian writing. We consider for publication writers of any origin whose work in some way is inspired by the diversity of our world (specifically Canada) and the interaction and sharing of cultures.'[8]

Acting as editor of both the journal and press for many years, Vassanji was a significant part of these intellectual and entrepreneurial groups and, concomitantly, had substantial impact on the cultural and critical frameworks that have proceeded to define his own literary reception within Canada. As with his strategic grouping with TSAR, Vassanji's early writing about Canada seems also to have been somewhat strategically motivated. His first work set in Canada, *No New Land*, follows the Lalani family in Don Mills, a suburb of Toronto, as they respond to an accusation of sexual assault by the father. This quiet, and at times deeply ironic, novel is about family, alienation, religion, self-doubt and often failed attempts at intergenerational communication. It is also Vassanji's least successful novel, as it follows a rather formulaic engagement with 'immigrant issues'. Subsequent work is less overtly concerned with marking a place for the quotidian stories of East Africans in Canada. In the 2005 collection of short stories set partially in Toronto, *When She Was Queen*, Vassanji takes on a similar set of themes but this time is more nuanced in his execution. While the majority of Vassanji's fiction travels between North America, East Africa and India, his work persists in drawing on thematic concerns that appeal in Canada: liminality, negotiating multiple identities, multiculturalism, immigration, citizenship and historicity among them.[9]

As the 1990s progressed, the prevailing critical trend in Canadian criticism shifted from reading the novels of new Canadians set outside Canada as mainly supplemental to national imperatives to recognizing them as central to Canadian literature. Groups like TSAR helped instigate change to reflect the significant transformations in the larger Canadian society. The shift in attitudes to literary works clearly mirrors the reconfiguration of demographics in Canada and alterations in attitudes about Canadian constitutive identities over the past forty years. According to Statistics Canada, on the 2006 Canadian Census, people reported more than 200 ethnic origins and, since 1991, over fifty per cent of newcomers to Canada have hailed from Asia (Statistics Canada's categorization), including South Asia. In contrast, in 1971, Asians accounted for 12 per cent of newcomers.[10] In cultural terms, Vassanji's increased visibility and popularization, signalled by the winning of national and international acclaim, is often cited as exemplary in illustrating the dismantling of separate categories such as 'multicultural' or 'ethnic' to a reconfigured 'mainstream' Canadian literature. However, this was not always the case. When *The Book of Secrets* was first awarded the Giller Prize and when Rohinton Mistry's *A Fine Balance* won the same award the following year (1995), there were grumblings in the national media about whether novels that were set in Africa and India should be considered eligible for an award honouring the best of *Canadian* writing. Now, a decade and a half later, when much of the finest (and most financially successful and globally well-received) fiction written by Canadians tells stories about elsewhere and is written by first-generation Canadians, such a criticism could no longer even find its feet or, hopefully, be given press.

Still, Vassanji continues to be concerned with the relationship between his own writing and the expectations of Canadian audiences. In his 2006 editorial for the journal *Canadian Literature*, 'Am I a Canadian Writer?', Vassanji asks this question of himself as a way of answering other second-person self-interrogations: 'Whom do you write for? Who is your audience?'[11] In addressing these basic questions, Vassanji has voiced his desire to move beyond what he sees as the expectations of 'Canadianness', arguing that 'we all know the Prairie-grandmother novel; the growing-up-in-Newfoundland-or-Nova-Scotia, walking-along-the-beach-with-an-ancestor novel; the World

War I novel; the cool-thirtysomething or -fortysomething Vancouverite novel'.[12] His method, echoing the trend with most contemporary Canadian authors, is to write novels without resorting to these well-worn types or geographically determined genres. Instead, he suggests remapping Canadian literary landscapes to include Kenya, Cambodia, India and Rwanda: 'the idea I am putting forward is that new Canadians bring their stories with them, and these stories then become Canadian stories' (12).

For the Vassanji of 2006, the Canadian stories are malleable enough to encounter the mass migrations of people from around the world. They also withstand explorations of personal history and cultural memory in the countries of origin of their writers. It is useful to note that throughout Canadian literary history many writers have approached the nation in such open terms. The difference in the contemporary framework is that writing about people and places outside Canada is no longer viewed as an adjunct to central Canadian writing. Now, Madeleine Thien's *Certainty* (2006), David Chariandy's *Soucouyant* (2007), Anita Rau Badami's *Can You Hear the Nightbird Call* (2007), and Dionne Brand's *What We All Long For* (2005) join Vassanji's *The In-Between World of Vikram Lall*, for instance, as prominent examples of Canadian novels that span histories, generations and countries and tell Canadian stories – in Burma, Trinidad, India, Vietnam and Kenya, as well as in Canada.

The North America of Vassanji's adulthood is present in his fiction as characters wander on the snowy banks of Lake Ontario in *The In-Between World of Vikram Lall* or participate in anti-Vietnam protests in Massachusetts in *Amriika*. Still, as Gikandi notes, Vassanji's fiction is consistent in its exploration of the themes he began to explore in *The Gunny Sack*, particularly 'the struggle by Indians in Africa, and later North America, to come to terms with their multiple histories of displacement while rebuilding their communities in exile'.[13] Vassanji is particularly adept at narrating the legacy of displacement and it is this trajectory that seems particularly appealing to international readers.

With the promotion of his multiple personal trajectories, Vassanji is read as an African writer who immigrated to Canada and who, because of his heritage, fit into the diasporic framework of South Asia. As if to emphasize his Canadianness and the international appeal of his work on India, the reviews quoted for *A Place Within* and *Assassin's Song* on the Penguin India webpage are from the *Globe and Mail* and *Quill & Quire*, published in Toronto. In Canada, this means that Vassanji is regularly included in the same breath as Mistry (born in India), Neil Bissoondath (born in Trinidad) and Michael Ondaatje (born in Sri Lanka), some of the most central and successful contemporary Canadian writers.[14]

The critics, and those at TSAR, are not alone in linking Vassanji to other South Asian writers. His publishers have also taken full advantage of the group affiliation, as he has often been marketed alongside writers from India, Sri Lanka and Pakistan, as well as Africa and Canada. I suggest that such canny associational marketing comes out of both the South Asian Canadian literary community's strategic affiliation and out of publishers' recognition of group appeal in a popularized postcolonial climate.

Vassanji's rise to literary stardom coincides with the rise in academia of postcolonial theory and an international post-Rushdie hunger for historical revisionist writing in postcolonial contexts. The cover of *The Gunny Sack* makes this link explicit, calling it 'Africa's answer to *Midnight's Children*'. While he does not *chutnify* history in the novel, Vassanji does reinscribe East African history to showcase a multigeneration genealogical Indian presence.[15] As such, he engages in the popular act of rewriting history to include the stories of those not previously included in national epics. Glossing his own motivation to write *The In-Between World of Vikram Lall*, Vassanji explains that the novel is intended to address a gap in knowledge: 'Books set in Kenya, especially those made into movies or TV serials for Masterpiece Theatre, glorifying the English aristocracy in Kenya, hardly mention the presence of Indians, who played an important role in the growth of Nairobi, the building of the railway, and the politics of the country. Their dilemma was that they were neither white nor black; and they were both Asian and African.'[16] Such an intention to narrate, and thus complicate, the histories of Indians in Africa is carried through several of his novels.

In his first novel, and in *A Book of Secrets* and *The In-Between World of Vikram Lall*, Vassanji carefully ties together several generations of Indian family stories in East Africa through material objects (a gunny sack, a colonial diary, books and money) and reminiscences of mercantile methodologies and displaced cultural memories. As a review in *India Today*, cited on his publisher's website, rather hyperbolically notes, 'Using the gunny sack as a metaphor for memory, Vassanji has written a great book that captures the essence of an immigrant people.'[17] He narrates the impact of colonialism on African subjects, Indian merchants and labourers, as he follows the presence and afterlife of British and German imperialism. In *The In-Between World of Vikram Lall*, he also traces the individual legacy of the struggle for independence in Kenya, particularly the Mau Mau uprising, through the eyes of small children as they grow into a world of love, violence, corruption and greed. Vassanji does not write of the countries of his birth or his early education with nostalgia but rather with a critical awareness of the implications of collective history on individual lives. In academic circles, I suspect that Vassanji has also benefitted from the popularization of theories from India and Africa as cutting edge in subaltern studies, postcolonial studies (and subsequently diaspora studies) and globalization studies.[18]

But even before postcolonial theory became a standard part of North American university curricula, the study of world literature written in English (WLWE) and Commonwealth literatures helped to bring a selection of the history of Anglo-Indian writing to the attention of non-Indian audiences. That broad-based comparative study tended to focus on a small handful of writers from each Commonwealth community: Raja Rao, R. K. Narayan, Rabindranath Tagore and Anita Desai, most predominantly from India. Similarly, African writing was represented in the work of a few: Chinua Achebe, Amos Tutuola, Wole Soyinka, Ngugi wa Thiong'o and Okot p'Bitek. Over the decades, the field has transitioned from Commonwealth studies to diaspora studies or from a fixed geographically framed paradigm to one based on the concept of movement. Such a transformation of critical frameworks has occurred in response to the realities of migration and the resulting multiple constituencies of readers and of writers such as Vassanji, at once African and Indian and Canadian. Earlier categories and theories assuming a fixed nationality are simply no longer productive. Increased global movement has also lead to increased visibility of diasporic writers.

With greater visibility, the desire to read work from the South Asian diaspora in North America goes well beyond the specialized university classroom. There is clearly now an international audience hungry for work from the African and Indian diasporas. Vassanji's multinational publishing houses have harnessed this hunger. It is difficult to say just how much publishers have influenced the trend towards diaspora studies but there is little doubt that they have capitalized on the international desire for writing that touches on multiple locations and multiple histories. Freer global movement of texts and international distribution has led to a greater worldwide accessibility of fiction published in countries like Canada and India as well. However, with multinational publishing conglomerates controlling the major publishing houses (with the Bertelsmann Group controlling Doubleday, Random House, Knopf and Pantheon, for instance) there has also been increased pressure placed on small, independent presses. It appears that the impact of this corporatization of publishers has been felt by younger, less-established writers than Vassanji. Over the course of his career, Vassanji has consistently chosen to publish with the large companies (as well as TSAR): Canadian (Doubleday, McClelland & Stewart, Penguin), Indian (Penguin, HarperCollins), American (Knopf, Picador) and British (Heinemann, Canongate). These publishers have been instrumental in showcasing his work as prize worthy in the local and global markets and in nominating his work for international and national awards. But it still remains a question how much input or control the publishers have on the kinds of novels that the writers they have under contract produce and exactly what market they are trying to tap. Still, the ubiquity and power of Vassanji's particular publishers ensure that his work will be advertised, promoted, sold and read around the world.

It is an interesting offshoot of the long history of globalization and multigenerational diasporic migrations that Vassanji had an Indian publisher – Penguin India – well before he had stepped foot on Indian soil. Indeed, it was the popularity of *The Gunny Sack* (first published in the Heinemann African Writers Series) that first got Vassanji invited to India. Over a decade after he marked himself as a member of the South Asian community in Canada, Vassanji travelled to the land of his grandparents' birth, two generations removed from the land he grew up thinking of as a 'distant homeland'. It is a remarkable coincidence that the time commonly marked as the watershed for postliberalization in India roughly corresponds with Vassanji's first visit to the country (1993). His impressions of India from his initial pilgrimage, and from many subsequent visits, are detailed in his memoir *A Place Within: Rediscovering India*. The memoir tells not only his own story but also outlines an outsider/insider perspective on Indian history of the last two decades. While Vassanji is careful to distance himself from pronouncing on the specifics of the volatile politics of India, particularly the 1993 riots in Bombay, he does not refrain from commentary or judgement on events and individuals. He also tracks, in an unabashedly subjective fashion, his impressions of the impact of liberalization on India over the course of his visits. Again, I turn to the fascinating act of self-presentation on Vassanji's website – 'Some Personal Notes on the Books' – where he provides metacommentary on *A Place Within*. He waxes eloquent about his motivations: 'India provokes response and this book is mine. My visits to temple, mosque, church, or synagogue, a beautiful monument or a willfully neglected ruin, an area devastated by mob violence or a friend's house or club, a venerated author or a humble *mukhi*, from the southernmost tip of Kanya Kumari to the misty heights of Shimla, from the viceroys' residence to a Kali temple were all driven by my attempts to understand myself culturally and historically'.[19] In this search, he encounters a country in a state of flux (for him it is sometimes a terrifying and at other times invigorating flux). He also finds that he is at home there. And yet he is also at home elsewhere: in Toronto, in Dar Es Salaam. Home is flexible. In a Canadian interview about *A Place Within*, when Vassanji is asked if he feels caught between two worlds, he answers promptly in the negative: 'I went there and I was just Indian. I grew up speaking Indian languages and that helped disguise myself. What I thought was a distant homeland, I realized was very much a part of me. I feel Indian. I also feel African. I feel Canadian. If I was younger I'd feel angst, you know, who am I? But at this age, many countries, it doesn't matter.'[20] This is where Vassanji, who finds the boxing in of categories abhorrent, is at his most convincing. The assertion that 'it doesn't matter' does not make him postnational but, rather, multinational. While he spent his earlier years creating umbrella categories, he is now an unapologetically multinational figure who can be three things at once with no strategic appellations. When literature emerges from such appealing simultaneity, particularly when it is as well written as Vassanji's work, it is also bound to be well received globally.

Notes and References

1. M. G. Vassanji, 'Biography'. Online: http://www.mgvassanji.com/Biography.htm (accessed 5 January 2013).
2. I use the large umbrella term (as employed by Vassanji) to include Michael Ondaatje, Rohinton Mistry, Himani Bannerji, Zulfikar Ghose, Uma Parameswaran, Suwanda H. J. Sugunasiri, Shauna Singh Baldwin, Anita Rau Badami, Arun Mukherjee, Ashok Mathur, David Chariandy, Neil Bissoondath, Cyril Dabydeen, Arnold Itwaru, Harold Sonny Ladoo, Sam Selvon, and Shani Mootoo, among many others.
3. Simon Gikandi and Evan Mwangi, *The Columbia Guide to East African Literature in English Since 1945* (New York: Columbia University Press 2007), 172.
4. M. G. Vassanji, 'Some Personal Notes on the Books', December 2009. Online: http://www.mgvassanji.com/PersonalNotes1.htm (accessed 15 June 2010).
5. Quoted in Arun Mukherjee, *Postcolonialism: My Living* (Toronto: TSAR, 1998), 30.
6. Ibid., 24.
7. Ibid., 6.
8. TSAR Books, 'Welcome to TSAR Publications'. Online: http://www.tsarbooks.com (accessed 12 June 2010).
9. Importantly, as I am arguing the centrality of Vassanji's work for contemporary Canadian literature, others have argued about his significance in the framework of African literatures. Vassanji is often included in overviews of East African literature, as with Gikandi's *Columbia Guide*. In *Literature of Africa*, G. D. Killam argues that he 'has established himself through his publication of six novels […] as a major African writer' and proclaims that 'Vassanji is the finest authentic voice of Asian Africans.' (G. D. Killam, *The Literature of Africa* (Santa Barbara: Greenwood Publishing Group, 2004), 28.)
10. Statistics Canada, 'Ethnic Diversity and Immigration' (Chart 13.1: Recent Immigrants to Canada, by region of origin), 7 September 2007. Online: http://www41.statcan.gc.ca/2007/30000/ceb30000_000-eng.htm (accessed 14 May 2010).
11. M. G. Vassanji, 'Am I a Canadian Writer?', *Canadian Literature* 190 (Autumn 2006): 7.
12. Ibid., 8.
13. Gikandi and Mwangi, *East African Literature*, 173.
14. See, for instance, Martin Genetsch, *The Texture of Identity: The Fiction of MG Vassanji, Neil Bissoondath, and Rohinton Mistry* (Toronto: TSAR, 2007).
15. In an interview with Allan Gregg, Vassanji notes that 'the term Hindu is a modern term so for me having lived away and not also being part of the politics, the modern politics of hatred that has existed since 1947, I prefer the term Indian to Hindu or Muslim'. (TV Ontario, 29 March 2009. Online: http://www.youtube.com/watch?v=a0sCN8jz2Rk (accessed 15 June 2010).)
16. M. G. Vassanji, 'More Personal Notes on the Books'. Online: http://www.mgvassanji.com/PersonalNotes2.htm (accessed 4 January 2013).

17 *India Today*, review of *The Gunny Sack*, quoted on Penguin India website. Online: http://www.penguinbooksindia.com/en/content/gunny-sack (accessed 14 June 2010).
18 In North America, the success of critics like C. D. Narasimhaiah, Homi Bhabha, Gayatri Spivak, Harish Trivedi, Partha Chatterjee and Meenakshi Mukherjee has been instrumental in mainstreaming postcolonial theory.
19 Vassanji, 'Some Personal Notes on the Books'.
20 Vassanji, interview by Allan Gregg.

Chapter Eight

'SHREDS OF INDIANNESS': IDENTITY AND REPRESENTATION IN MANJU KAPUR'S *THE IMMIGRANT*

Letizia Alterno

In *The Immigrant* (2008), Manju Kapur sets out a complex network of multiple relationships that affect its protagonists not only as human beings, but also as political subjects and societal members. As the title indicates, these individuals find themselves in the process of naturalizing their migration experiences in a world of increasing global interconnectedness. Indeed, Nina and Ananda's experiences, two Indian-born citizens permanently moving (albeit in different times) to another Western country, are shaped by at least two major institutional and cultural apparatuses: India and Canada. I want to suggest here that Manju Kapur's novel participates in discourses of globalization and cosmopolitanism by making the complexity of the immigration experience and its multiple ambivalences the crucial focus of her story. Addressing the influence and significance of Western and Indian societal and cultural structures on the protagonists' selves, I shall argue that the locus of a private, political and societal shift in identity, as well as the ambivalence of this construct, is explored through the polyphonic function of fluctuating models, such as the immigrant venture and the experience of marriage. Kapur invites the reader to consider that both 'global', and to an extent essentialized, models need redefining as they are no longer adequate for describing the protagonists' sociopolitical realities in a postliberalization Indian context and in diaspora.

The contemporariness of Kapur's analysis is inline with ongoing debates on diasporic subjects caught in the processes of migration, cultural transition, adaptation and identity and gender across national contexts. All of Kapur's novels published to date probe into the difficulties of dealing with a respectful loyalty to family and the social environment expected of middle-class Indian women, while managing their conflicting tendencies to live a modern life with modern values in postliberalization India or in diaspora. The conflict between domesticity and the outer space, tradition and modernity profoundly affects her characters.

Placed in the cosmopolitan spaces of global cities, *The Immigrant*'s protagonists are located in direct confrontation with global political forces such as the politics of migration. Talking about refugee migration in *Means Without End: Notes on Politics* (2000), Giorgio Agamben's examination of the political status of modern refugees can be useful for a better understanding of the immigrant characters in this novel. Though Agamben addresses a different kind of migration from the examples suggested in the novel, like Kapur, he lays emphasis on the recurring presence of immigrants in contemporary globalized societies. More significantly, his main argument centres on the representation of the immigrant as a disruptive category, which is the novel's main concern:

> If the refugee represents such a disquieting element in the order of the nation-state, this is so primarily because, by breaking the identity between the human and the citizen and that between nativity and nationality, it brings the originary fiction of sovereignty to crisis. [...] Inasmuch as the refugee, an apparently marginal figure, unhinges the old trinity of state-nation-territory, it deserves instead to be regarded as the central figure of our political history.[1]

What concerns Agamben here is indeed the disruptiveness of the refugee as a temporary, nonpermanent, category within the nation-state order. What concerns Kapur in *The Immigrant* is to bring the originary fiction of a 'true' Indian or a 'true' Canadian identity – as well as the fiction of a 'true' marriage – to crisis. Moving fluidly across national and cultural boundaries, Kapur's immigrants Nina and Ananda also seem to act as disruptive elements to rigid categories of nationality and citizenship, mainly through their respective – and conflicting – processes of naturalization. Kapur's choice to give them (principally Nina) a voice seems to challenge the host society's view of their status as immigrants as a threat to the nation. The novel is primarily concerned with one of the ongoing effects of globalization upon the political subject: a process of identity questioning and cultural reformulation that gives rise to Kapur's protagonists' marital union as well as their final separation. In a globalized reality such as theirs, Nina and Ananda should be defined more appropriately as 'denizens', namely permanent, noncitizen residents in a country that is different from their country of origin, a neologism firstly suggested by Tomas Hammar in 1990 in his book *Democracy and the Nation State*. Kapur's selection of Canada as a long-standing, global, culturally plural society is not surprising. Canada's contemporary status as a multicultural society was legally formalised in the late 1980s, mainly through the Canadian Multiculturalism Act (1988), which aims not only to recognize and promote multiculturalism as reflecting the cultural and racial diversity of Canadian society, but also to preserve their cultural heritage. Yet, since the storyline develops during the late 1960s and 1970s, the Canadian context she is suggesting is preparatory to a series of changes in immigration admission policy in the 1980s, when the country had a major influx of immigrants from Asia. What is remarkable of Kapur's style is the way through which readers of *The Immigrant* are enabled to witness the protagonists' itinerary of a culturally globalized adaptation process, defined by psychologists as 'acculturation'.

Without entering the sociopsychological minutiae of the acculturation process (under critical scrutiny since the early 1930s), it is useful to point out, for a better understanding of the forms of cultural pluralism proposed in *The Immigrant*, that acculturation develops, broadly, through a three-step process involving *contact, reciprocal influence* and *change*.[2] Determined by the political events outlined in the novel, the story develops around the period preceding Indian liberalization. Significant events include the defeat of Indira Gandhi and the Congress in the 1977 general election, which later saw the birth of the Janata Party, the first non-Congress party in power with Morarji Desai as prime minister from 1977 to 1979, and the ultimate collapse of this ministry, followed by Charan Singh's election as prime minister from 1979 to the beginning of 1980. The same year would see Indira Gandhi's return to power (though the novel's storyline halts at the inflation crisis preceding her looming re-election). In the novel, the third-person narrative voice privileges Nina's story of cultural and societal acclimatization, which becomes a leitmotif in the novel, recurrently evoked by the expression, 'When in Rome do what the Romans do'.

It is through Nina's voice that her psychological progress and experiences are recounted. In psychosociological jargon, the process of 'acculturation' refers to 'the changes an individual experiences as a result of being in contact with other cultures, or participating in the acculturation that one's cultural or ethnic group is undergoing'.[3] In Nina and Ananda's cases, *contact* is established through the cultural influence of two global, imagined communities: the Indian and the Canadian societies. The weight of these cultures upon their sense of individuality and freedom is crucially made clear throughout the novel. On the one hand, Ananda refers for moral direction to the *Bhagavad-Gita* his Indian family has left him, the teachings of which he also seems to indirectly question: 'Do your duty, never think of the consequences; life is full of suffering – that he liked'.[4] On the other hand, Nina criticizes her social upbringing based on some old-fashioned, pre-liberalization Indian cultural values transmitted by her mother: 'Her mother was such a vehicle of patriarchy, why was her concern for her daughter always expressed through worry about Ananda's well-being?' (243). The novel shows an attempt to detach itself from representations of gender – particularly female gender – that remain anchored to both nationalism and patriarchy. In both cases, experiences of cultural discomfort and resistance result from both choices of challenging and accepting aspects of their cultural upbringing. In this novel Indian masculinity too is observed and scrutinized. Towards the end of the novel, Ananda's self-questioning shows regret towards his decision of following his family's desires:

> Ananda kept his own stress close to his heart. He had chosen according to his family's wishes, but in doing so had experienced a fresh set of difficulties. And how would he not? He was not the boy they had planned for, he was as much someone else as he could possibly be. (328)

While Ananda has followed his family tradition and agreed to an arranged marriage, he has also detached himself considerably from this Indian tradition, embracing other Western cultural values. Similarly, though Nina has refused to blindly adopt some of the stigmatized women's roles sanctioned by Indian cultural tradition (contrarily, she is thirty and unmarried, and earns her own life as a teacher of English Literature in an elite college), her anxieties ultimately arise from her acceptance of an arranged marriage suggested by her mother that has devastating consequences. In this picture, the multicultural Canadian world is also the country of opportunity, one that has provided her with a sense of freedom from such constrictions, as 'to a certain extent this country freed emotional needs from the yoke of matrimony and social sanction' (329).

    The textual evidence above provides an indication of the *reciprocal influence* that the two acculturating groups – the Indian and the Canadian – have on each other. Ananda and Nina are represented as subjects acting in a globalized context and interacting with 'new' traditions as it were, as well as accepting changes in the original patterns of their cultural group. The question arises though as how much change occurs in the lives of Canadians interacting with them. The changes affecting what sociologists indicate as 'the dominant groups' (the Canadians in this case, as they constitute the majority compared to the Indian immigrant minority culture) are not fully developed in the novel. We are mainly given access to the lives of Ananda, Nina and their slender family community in Canada, whereas only occasionally and succinctly does Kapur venture about the other side of this relationship. Among the Canadian affected individuals are the women activists Nina befriends for a short period of time in the novel, and yet we are not given a clear indication of how much, how little or if at all Nina's influence has played a role in their lives. If this is the author's deliberate attempt to indicate that, manifestly, this group's detachment from Nina's cultural contribution reinforces colonialist-type strategies of cultural authority (suggesting that only the immigrant side needs to adapt to dominant culture) or if this is a writer's failed attempt to expand on this relationship's reciprocal influences cannot be clearly assessed. Sociologist studies show however that reciprocal influence also involves changes in the dominant groups, specifying that '"dominance" is not considered a necessary prerequisite for acculturation to take place'.[5] Moreover as David Sam and John Berry show in *The Cambridge Handbook of Acculturation Psychology*: 'The larger the cultural distance between groups the more difficult it is to experience mutual sympathy.'[6]

In the novel, the third constituent of the acculturation process, *change*, plays a dominant role in the definition of its main characters' sense of cultural identity and freedom. Change involves for Nina not only the very act of joining the diasporic flux by her territorial move from India to Canada, but a shift in social status, from a single woman and established teacher to an unemployed (albeit temporarily) housewife, as well as a shift from a more socially restrained to a more liberated sexual identity. Marriage and migration in a globalized context become synonyms for change in the novel, and Kapur is careful to delineate the most significant aspects of Nina's shifting, unstable sense of identity and its inevitable transformations through marriage (another form of migration in the novel).

The very experience of physical migration in a globalized world – the official moment of border crossing, her entry to Canada as an immigrant from India clutching her passport apprehensively – is indicative of the profound pain Nina will experience later in the story. In contrast to Abdulrazak Gurnah's choice to privilege the experience of Mr Shaaban's forced immigration in his 2001 novel *By the Sea*, Kapur does not make this experience the central focus of her novel, preferring to concentrate on the process of global migration as a complex stage of acculturation. Kapur's deliberate use and recording of Nina's language fully registers the enormity and flux of globalization within the novel's form. After suffering a series of intimidating and disguisedly aggressive questions challenging her 'decent, respectable, god fearing and worthy' self, Kapur effectively makes Nina vent her discontent with the unfair treatment through an imaginary short written note to her husband:

Dear Ananda
This is not your country. You are deceived, and you have deceived me. You made it out to be a liberal haven where everybody loved you. This woman is looking for a reason to get rid of me. I am the wrong colour, I come from the wrong place. See me in this airport, of all the passengers the only one not allowed to sail through immigration, made me feel like an illegal alien. See, see, see.
Love Nina. (106–7)

While discrediting socially enforced representations of the West as the home of liberal democracy, Kapur establishes Nina's experience of immigration control – one of the cultural effects of globalization – as one of denial, rejection, illegality, judgement and alienation. She is also careful to highlight (in clever counter-Orientalist fashion) the nonsanitized moments that this experience entails for a nondominant migrant like Nina: 'Numbly she walks down the corridor. She feels soiled, accused of trying to take something not rightfully hers' (107). In remarkably Fanonian style, the experience also makes Nina realize *the fact of her blackness* through the look of the 'white-other' (it is not coincidental that in the above note Nina also asks her husband to 'see' her):

> What assimilation when your body stamped you an outsider?
> Never, for a moment, in all her years at home, had she to think about who or what she was. She had belonged. Only now was she beginning to realise how much that meant. (154)

Brusquely, Nina is forced to recognize that *she is a migrant 'other'*. Later, she will realize that 'she is an immigrant for life' (122), 'a floating resident' as she describes herself at the end of the novel. Her coming to terms with this alienating effect of diaspora is similar to the way in which Menaka Raman, an Indian immigrant to contemporary Britain, alludes to her experience of migration in her personal account *Immigrant*:

> I am migrant.
> I'm migrant.
> Im-migrant.
> Immigrant.
> I like to think that this is how the word immigrant was created. It seems kinder. It takes the harshness and edge off a word that can so easily sound abusive. It makes me feel like a bird that has temporarily flown the nest, meaning to return home one day. Albeit a rather foolish bird that has confused the concept of migration, leaving a warm land for one that is decidedly not.[7]

Contrarily to Raman though, Nina's sense of belonging will increasingly lose its permanence and acquire more diverse and global connotations of cultural and geographical multiplicity, until the moment when 'anywhere could be home' (330). Kapur's political engagement with questions of cultural migration becomes manifest through the first signs of Nina's resistant attitude towards blind acceptance of her unjust and categorical treatment as an unwelcomed guest (even if her psychological refusal is never overtly expressed in words to the immigration officer):

> Rage fills her. Why were people so silent about the humiliation they faced in the West? She was a teacher at a university, yet this woman,

probably high school pass, can imprison her in a cell-like room, scare her and condemn her. Though she was addressed as ma'am, no respect is conveyed. (106)

Things adjust only little by little in the novel. At first, while half-enjoying her Indian Oberoy honeymoon, 'Nina had not realised the adjustment process her mother had spoken of so long and so lovingly would begin the moment she married' (98). As discussed above, among the unexpected changes that the marital transition initiates is a social one: 'She never anticipated though the respect that came with marriage, *a tiny shift of focus*, and there it was; Nina Sharma, an accepted member of society, married, bound for the Western big time' (99; emphasis mine). At this point of the story, Nina does not fully realize how transformational a process migration – territorial, social and marital – will be for her. Gradually, her sense of adjustment, as reinforced by her mother's advice ('[…] things take time. In the end patience and love achieve their rewards. A woman's duty is to understand this' (130)), conflicts with her changing identity as an immigrant: 'As immigrants fly across oceans they shed their old clothing, because clothes maketh the man and new ones help ease the transition. […] Those women who are not used to wearing Western clothes find themselves in a dilemma. If they focus on integration, convenience and conformity they have to sacrifice habit, style and self-perception. The choice is hard, and in Nina's case it took months to wear down her resistance' (150).

Like old clothing loosening down, her expectations about marriage also start deteriorating. Apart from 'the state of permanent sexual frustration she was in' (178), she slowly realizes that 'having a husband should not have meant such lonely desperation' (179). Discomfort, dissatisfaction, disorientation and desperate loneliness accompany most of her mature married days as no 'words of promise' could 'convey how much stress she would undergo while assaulted by changes, changes so thorough that she felt rootless, branchless, just a body floating upon the cold surface of this particular piece of earth' (176). That is, until she starts discovering new possibilities of cultural and gender freedom through the readings of Simone de Beauvoir's *The Second Sex* and Germaine Greer's *The Female Eunuch* suggested by 'the women's group that encouraged her to be angry and assertive' (330), however faulty and nonapplicable to her Indian cultural background they might be:

> Right now she was looking for an answer as to why she was the way she was.
> A woman, an Indian, an immigrant.
> Which came first?
> Her female self, according to Beauvoir. (218)

Significantly, sexuality becomes a means of self-exploration only outside the conventional bond of marriage. Both Nina and Ananda rediscover themselves through extramarital affairs with two white lovers that are ultimately never revealed, sincerely and openly, in the novel. In this globalized context, Nina's liberated identity starts to be defined as 'Canadian' once she experiences sexual liberation (as well as the tragic experience of rape) through her love affair with Russian library colleague Anton and social independence after being awarded a grant to become a degree-owning, state-approved librarian. As David Sam and John Berry argue, '[i]mmigrants are not a passive factor in acculturation.'[8] Nina herself proleptically recognizes that 'for an immigrant changed situations meant changed priorities' (245). Kapur's thematic concerns link in with contemporary discourses that centre on globalization and questions on immigration politics and seem to acknowledge the fact that 'nations' immigration policies and their cultural majorities influence the form and the success of immigrants' acculturation'.[9] *The Immigrant* testifies to an increasingly multicultural and cosmopolitan world, a 'continent full of people escaping unhappy pasts. She too was heading towards fresh territories, a different set of circumstances, a floating resident of the Western world' (330). Here Kapur finds a way – through difference – to link Nina's immigration with other (such as Menaka's) similar experiences. They are part of those groups of newcomers that, according to Sam and Berry, 'are making the Western world culturally more diverse and "de-Westernizing" it to some degree'.[10]

'Pull up your shallow roots and move', Nina encourages immigrants (330). Those 'shreds of Indianness transported across oceans', the few Indian cultural companions in Canada that had previously alleviated Ananda and Nina's loneliness, did not mean much to their overall immigrant experience after all, compared to their renewed experiences of marriage and acculturation (35). For Ananda, 'marriage had been the most significant step in the remaking of his old self. There was no one to appreciate the irony of this. After he married everything changed, his mind, his heart, his penis. In this change his wife had been left behind. It was not her fault. It was the situation' (328–9). For Nina, in the end, temporariness 'was the ultimate immigrant experience', as the last page of the novel indicates: 'Not that any one thing was steady enough to attach yourself to for the rest of your life, but that you found different ways to belong, ways not necessarily lasting, but ones that made your journey less lonely for a while. When something failed it was a signal to move on. For an immigrant there was no going back' (330).

To conclude, *The Immigrant* – a novel produced and received globally in a postliberalization context – reinforces the impossibility of categorizing socially and culturally established constructs as identity and marriage. Rather than representing fixed categories aimed at reinforcing a nation- or patriarchy-bounded cultural imaginary, Kapur's protagonists appear constantly as shifting territories of ambivalence and multiplicity in the novel. As denizens of the world, Nina and Ananda's experiences of geographical, social and identity shifts ultimately reinforce the novel's most succinct and final acknowledgment that their arranged marriage 'had not, after all, been the perfect solution' (182).

Notes and References

1 Giorgio Agamben, *Means Without End: Notes on Politics* (Minneapolis: Minnesota University Press, 2000), 20–21.
2 David L. Sam and John W. Berry, *The Cambridge Handbook of Acculturation Psychology* (Cambridge: Cambridge University Press, 2006), 14.
3 Ibid., 14.
4 Manju Kapur, *The Immigrant* (London: Faber & Faber, 2009). All quotations from this novel refer to this edition and are indicated parenthetically in the text.
5 Sam and Berry, *Acculturation Psychology*, 15.
6 Ibid., 178.
7 Various authors, *From There to Here: Sixteen True Tales of Immigration to Britain* (London: Penguin, 2007), 3. In *The Immigrant*, apart from alluding to natural migratory movements when discussing migration, Nina significantly uses the same imagery (home/warmth) when referring to India: 'So different from home. There when the sun shines, it means warm in winters and bloody hot in summers. Here, alas, it means no such thing' (269).
8 Sam and Berry, *Acculturation Psychology*, 178.
9 Ibid.
10 Ibid.

Chapter Nine

INSIDE 'THE TEMPLE OF MODERN DESIRE': RECOLLECTING AND RELOCATING BOMBAY

Maria Ridda

Preparing the Ground

An article published in the *Economist* in 2005 announced that 'at times of great change, nations inevitably become introspective. In India's case, one recent consequence of a rapidly growing and globalizing economy has been an outpouring of books with titles like 'Remaking India', 'Shaping India of our Dreams', 'The Great Indian Dream', 'Rising Elephant' and 'Rethinking India'. Among the authors who have managed to outline the fast-changing nature of the Indian nation-state are Suketu Mehta and Vikram Chandra, whose popularity is attributed to their ability to 'transcend the interests of the English-speaking elite'.[1] The authors of *Maximum City* (2004) and *Sacred Games* (2006), Suketu Mehta and Vikram Chandra respectively, have enjoyed increasing popularity in the West, especially among the members of the South Asian diaspora. As the article points out, Mehta's text in particular has managed to reach wider audiences due to its ability to present 'a remarkable documentary of life in India's largest city, now known as Mumbai'.[2] Presenting what has been defined a realistic portrayal of the Indian city, the book received a major literary award in 2005: the Kiriyama Prize, given for those texts that encourage a greater understanding of the nations of the Pacific Rim and South Asia; and it is soon to be made into a film by UK director Danny Boyle, who spoke of how Mehta's book provided him with a lucid insight into the city of Mumbai for his Oscar-winner film *Slumdog Millionaire*.[3]

Maximum City has received widespread acclamation for its hybrid portrayal of Mumbai, satisfying both Western audiences and South Asian diasporic groups. In this essay, I will demonstrate how Bollywood cinema functions as a visual archive for the representation of Bombay in diasporic fiction. I will also explain that contemporary Hindi cinema, due to its emphasis on India as a global superpower, forges a link between Western audiences and South Asian diasporas. As it seeks to recreate an idea of modernization that fits with wider conceptions of what constitutes economic globalization, Bollywood satisfies both diasporic and UK- and US-based audiences: the former who can connect with the homeland and embrace the cultural rhetoric of India as a modern superpower, the latter who find a familiar territory in the representation of Western modernity. In this essay I will include a brief rationale of the significance of Bollywood cinema for South Asian diasporic audiences, employing *Maximum City* and *Sacred Games* as examples of the ways in which the Hindi movie functions within fiction.

In relation to *Maximum City*, Mehta discusses the impact of Bollywood cinema on his process of self-awareness, by positing the issue of identity within his writing. The article in which the author discloses these views constitutes a perfect corollary of *Maximum City*, where Mehta simultaneously sketches the decor of the book and reflects on how the Hindi movie configures itself as a palimpsest for the formation of his identity: 'Why do I love Bollywood movies? To an Indian, that's like asking why we love our mothers; we don't have a choice.'[4]

Mehta establishes a connection between the representation of India in his writing and his intimate knowledge of Bollywood cinema: 'My personal history of Bollywood is entwined with my personal history of Bombay […]. Bombay is a city whose contrasts are so extreme that only movies that make no claim to represent reality could do justice to it.'[5]

What is important is that the *incipit* of this quote, 'My personal history of Bollywood', is followed by the clause 'personal history of Bombay', an unexpected reversal of propositions in which one would expect that the intimate knowledge of the city is fostered by Bollywood films, rather than the former deriving somewhat preconceptually from the latter. An analogous line of argument is pursued by Chandra, who discusses the filmic archive of Bollywood cinema in relation to the multilayered representation of India/Mumbai in his recent novel *Sacred Games* (2006): '[Film] has quite profoundly influenced the way I tend to think and imagine. It was a large part of my imagining of this book.'[6] What emerges from these perspectives is the connection between the representation of reality proposed in cinema and its impact upon a medium of respective visual value, fictionality. Both authors agree on the primacy of collective belonging fostered by Bollywood.

The representations that their texts provide, shaped on the predicament that 'Bombay is just like New York',[7] have enabled the authors to reach a wide audience in the West. UK and US readerships find in these texts familiar images related to the representation of a modernity they know. The familiarity that they instigate in Western readers constitutes the objectification of diasporic desires, as will be demonstrated in the next section. At the same time, Mehta and Chandra also view the city from its darkest corners, an image that tends to defamiliarize Western audiences. In reference to *Maximum City*, the *Economist* highlights this ambivalent attitude: 'This is not the city of bankers, stockbrokers and call-centre workers that many business visitors encounter. Rather the book delves into the interlocking worlds of communal violence, politics, gangsterism, commercial sex, film-making and even religious renunciation.'[8]

By stating that the text 'delves into the interlocking worlds' of 'communal violence', 'film making' and 'religious renunciation', the article also points out that the representation of the city is constructed in opposition to a world familiar to most readers ('the city of bankers […] that many business visitors encounter'). This world, unknown to the majority of UK- and US-based audiences, also satisfies their desire for 'exoticism' (as will be discussed in the final part of this essay).

In the following sections, I will discuss the role of contemporary Bollywood cinema in *Maximum City* and *Sacred Games*. I will explain how both texts employ cinematic tropes to connect to the image of the homeland as a modern superpower. In the third section, I will focus on the actual significance of the Hindi movie for the specific texts analysed and for the South Asian diaspora in general. As will be demonstrated, *Maximum City* and *Sacred Games* use the tropes of contemporary Bollywood cinema in a self-referential way to concretize an image of the homeland, which tends to defamiliarize other readerships.

Bombay as a Temple of Modern Desire

Vijay Mishra defines cinemas as 'temples of modern desire'.[9] This insight provides a basic understanding of the status and magnitude of contemporary Bollywood cinema. Locating films in the sphere of spirituality and holiness, Mishra argues that they materialize 'collective desires'.[10] He compares the religious rituals performed in a temple to the act of watching a Bollywood movie, where the 'oneiric' iconography posits itself as the correlative object of the individual's desire.[11] The individual is conceived as part of the wider collectivity, in that films restage shared interests and inherent values. Despite the polysemic and amorphous features of Bollywood cinema, Mishra observes that one of the major components of its textuality resides in the enactment of the discordant dialectic between tradition and modernity, where the latter 'is disavowed even if it is endorsed'.[12] Mishra maintains that contemporary Bollywood cinema articulates the dynamics of the contradictory process of India's modernization. I want to reprise these arguments and apply them to the representation of India in South Asian diasporic texts.

Bollywood cinema further expands the representation of contingency by furnishing a rich intertextual filmic archive exuding 'collective desire'. Framing my argument within the directions indicated by Mishra, I will analyse the space of Mumbai in conjunction with the concept of modernization. If contemporary Bollywood cinema fosters the creation of a 'pan-Indian' existence shaped by the idea of 'India as a temple of modern desire', how do South Asian diasporic texts incorporate this predominant ethos, which simultaneously appeals to UK and US audiences?

Before proceeding to address the implications related to this interrogative, I will elucidate the diasporic status of these texts, as their narratives are predominantly concerned with an extremely located and realistic representation of contemporary Mumbai. For instance, the choice to locate *Maximum City* within the scenario of South Asian diasporic texts could be challenged, given its denomination as a nonfictional account of Bombay. The tone of the incipit itself reminds one of the documentary accuracy of travel guides, furnishing information on the exact location of the city and its history, alongside a brief description of its status as a nodal point of transnational exchanges.

The initial section of the text entitled 'Power' functions as a prologue to the rest of the narrative, by sketching the specific spatio-temporal coordinates of the city. It covers a period of about nine years, starting with the 1992 riots and terminating in 2001 at the end of the author's journey. In this section, each incident of particular resonance is scrutinized. The 1992 riots, which tore the city apart, are presented as part of a continuum based on the sequential logic of cause and effect. Everything so far seems to direct us to the journalistic and historical quality of this narrative. However, even if we take into account the factual character of *Maximum City*, it is possible to formulate the hypothesis that the text responds to a narrative plot of 'translation' and 'transmission', shaped by an individual account of events.

The factual validity that the *incipit* of the text attempts to proclaim is immediately undermined by a number of personal interjections: 'God help us. I left Bombay in 1977 and came back twenty-one years later […]. Twenty-one years: enough time for a human being to be born, get an education, be eligible to drink.'[13]

Such intrusions alongside the necessity to reinscribe the author's diasporic sensibility within the space of the text undermine the status of *Maximum City* as a nonfictional account of the city. The assumption that factual accuracy is a comparatively difficult task to achieve through the written medium is further supported by the urgency to forge and shape identity, the necessity to 'transmit and translate' the author's exilic sensibility.

Analogously, *Sacred Games*, whose protagonist is the Bombayite gangster Ganesh Gaitonde, is concerned with the rewriting of multiple diasporic selves.

The *fabula* or story, constructed through the bipartite and complementary narratives of Sartaj Singh, a police inspector, and Ganesh Gaitonde, covers approximately fifty years. The linearity of the text is complicated by the accounts furnished by secondary characters assuming the connotation of Greek chorus–like figures, equally displaced, directing the narrative into retrospective versions of history and events: the sanguinary happenings following and preceding Partition told by Sartaj's mother; the events concerning the undercover police operations narrated by the intelligence officer K. D. Yadav; the inquests into the threat of a nuclear bomb as documented by the government secret service agent Anjali Mathur. The plot, however, maintains the façade of a traditional account, reminiscent of detective fiction, in which the ascent to success, the defeat and the final death of the gangster occur within a very realistic and traditional denouement employing the timeless tropes of birth, life and death.

Of all the characters, Ganesh Gaitonde exhibits the most peculiar attempt to reconstruct his 'self' in the act of 'telling' and reinscribing his identity through a fictionalization of his existence. Being forced to leave Bombay and conduct a deracinated existence with some members of his organization on a boat off the coast of Thailand, Gaitonde relies on the past and the memories of his city. Only the physical and mental distance from his homeland prompts in the character a clarity of vision. Gaitonde is constantly troubled by the urge to find his identity, the necessity to conceptualize 'home'.

If the city in both texts responds to the restaging of an exilic sensibility, how does it articulate the ongoing dialogue between displacement and the desire to connect to a 'pan-Indian' sense of belonging? In attempting to answer the question posed at the beginning of this section, where I defined Bollywood cinema as a temple of modern desire, I will demonstrate how the representation of the city in the two texts utilizes contemporary filmic intertexts to express a will to enter 'into some generic taxonomy' of belonging.[14] Global belonging, as I will subsequently argue, also posits itself as the common point of appreciation of both UK and US audiences and diasporic groups.

The examples I will employ are two films by Karan Johar, *Kuch Kuch Hota Hai* and *Kal Ho Naa Ho*.[15] Mehta mentions *Kuch Kuch Hota Hai* as the most exemplary objectification of 'what people want to see'. He describes it as 'a wonderfully entertaining film […]. There are no villains in it. It is a big Punjabi puppy love film about college romance, the middle-class Indian's Halcyon days.'[16] Karan Johar, director and screenwriter of *Kuch Kuch Hota Hai* belongs to the new generation of Bollywood directors concerned with the representation of India's alignment with global culture. In particular, his films incorporate diasporic narratives of nonresident Indians, contributing to the iconographic status of the country as the crux of global and transnational exchanges. *Kuch Kuch Hota Hai* is the story of a romantic love triangle set in Bombay. Paradigmatic scenes open the film, with the two protagonists Rahul and the tomboy Anjali attending St Xavier College in Bombay. Despite being set entirely in India, the film incorporates diasporic tropes. The specific decor of the initial scene is permeated with iconographic representations of Western life, immediately detectable in the clothes all the students wear: loose denim trousers, Gap T-shirts and baseball caps with hardly any sign of Indian clothing. The majority of students engage in Westernized spare-time activities in the courtyard of a college reminiscent of the classic Hollywood representation of American school life. As in the US stereotype, students are divided into the respective factions of the popular, beautiful and fashionable versus the studious and unfashionable, spending their time listening to music, dancing and mimicking cheerleading routines. It is significant that the idyllic romance between Rahul and Anjali commences on the pretext of a number of basketball matches where the two play against each other, this being an obvious allusion to their flirting. However, the love story is complicated by the arrival of the principal's daughter, Tina, just returned from Oxford. She is portrayed as a sophisticated and erudite woman, wearing 'Westernised clothes in a sexualised sense'.[17] As Manas Ray observes, Tina embodies the stylish and urbanized middle-class diaspora, capable of negotiating and synthesizing both cultures.[18] For instance, she speaks English and wears miniskirts and low-cut tops, but she is also able to sing Hindu religious hymns celebrating India's ancestral traditions. What emerges from this brief description of the plot is that the West is not portrayed as a fractural element, but it is very much part of India; it has been internalized.[19]

This tendency is further detectable in the second film by Karan Johar, *Kal Ho Naa Ho*, entirely set in New York. The surreal scenario of mid- and downtown Manhattan constitutes the setting of another love triangle between Naina Catherine Kapur, a fashionable young woman living with her family, Rohit, a student and impresario administering his parents' successful business and Aman, a wealthy and altruistic man hiding a secret. The opening scenes of the film are set in an unnamed neighbourhood of New York where the spectator is introduced to Naina's household, troubled by her father's recent suicide. The house, inhabited by her mother, Jennifer, a younger brother, an (allegedly) adopted sister, a grandmother and two aunts, posits itself as the incarnation of the transnational and eclectic character of their homeland, where the *desi* community both celebrates and endorses India's process of modernization. In the domestic space, different religious orientations are tolerated, a composite variety of food is consumed and Western clothing is replaced by traditional Indian *sarees* and *salwar kameez* only on special occasions. Unsurprisingly, the same area where Naina and Aman live is predominantly inhabited by South Asian families, all joyfully performing their Indianness in the form of an affiliation with their motherland as 'a temple of modern desire'.

One of the most illustrative scenes of the film is set in Jennifer's restaurant, where a further song and dance sequence performed by all the members of the family and friends functions to reinforce a 'pan-Indian' sense of belonging. On the verge of bankruptcy, the restaurant is rescued with the help of all the friends and family, working together to renovate it, singing in unison: 'Let's speak in one voice [...]. May those who clash with us fall apart.' The scene closes with Aman's booming words, 'We must get India to New York', while lowering the American flag and raising triumphantly the Indian one. Indeed, *Kal Ho Naa Ho* may as well be set in Bombay as *Kuch Kuch Hota Hai*, with its incorporation of the West into the East, while still preserving a distinctive sense of affiliation with the homeland. In an interview with Pankaj Mishra, Karan Johar observes that it is possible to be 'Indian' in every part of the globe.[20]

Jigna Desai argues that the incremental treatment of diasporic tropes in Bollywood cinema coincides with the endorsement of India's economic liberalization, an ongoing process which started in the '80s and reached its peak in the '90s: 'The ideal diaspora is one that responds to the hail of the homeland with its economic and technological investments.'[21] Therefore, the iconic image that the nation-state wants to propagate is one where the West is now an integral part of India, itself the aegis of modernity. Unsurprisingly, as Ray notices, films such as *Kuch Kuch Hota Hai* 'create a virtual West within the bounds of India'.[22] Films then reflect the discourse created by the nation-state, where 'the West has been internalised into the country to the extent that it does not even have to announce that it is the West'.[23] If this applies explicitly to *Kuch Kuch Hota Hai*, set in a modernized India, it also concerns Johar's third film, entirely produced and set between New York and Chicago. For instance, *Kal Ho Naa Ho* portrays Indian characters and life, even if in a dislocated context. In other words, if the spectator locates the décor of the film in New York, it is only because this is suggested by the long-panned camera shots focusing on the stylized iconography of the city (the Chrysler Building, the Brooklyn Bridge, Times Square).

The internalization of the West 'within the bounds of India' is what underpins the portrayal of Mumbai in both *Maximum City* and *Sacred Games*. This discourse permeates the majority of the descriptions of the city in Mehta's text, where Bombay constantly dreams of the West':[24] 'it is an imitation of a Western city', and it is the place where 'the first world lives smack in the centre of the third'.[25] The incremental transnational character of Bombay is demonstrated by the influence that global media-laden culture exerts on the urban space. In both texts the city strives to create a virtual 'West within the bounds of India'.[26]

Urban space incorporates filmic intertexts deriving from contemporary Bollywood cinema, itself contributing to a vast repertoire of narratives connecting viewers around the world. In *Sacred Games*, Sartaj Singh sees billboards advertising computer classes and sponsoring Bollywood stars:[27] 'A perfectly round moon dodged behind buildings and darted out between billboards for next week's Shah Rukh Khan release, a grand love story.'[28]

What emerges from these observations is the indivisible connection between the characterization of the city provided by the text and the intertextual cinematic archives shaping the way in which Bombay is reconceptualized. The reference to Shah Rukh Khan constitutes a valuable pointer to analyse the subtext of both *Sacred Games* and *Maximum City*, and as such it requires further contextualization.

The 'star system' of Bollywood celebrities both directs and constitutes the narratives of Bombay cinema itself.[29] Research on the trends of the contemporary Hindi movie shows that the most popular hero is the one who expounds the discourse of the nation-state as a temple of 'modern desire'. Rajinder Kumar Dudrah identifies this hero with Shah Rukh Khan, the icon of contemporary Bollywood cinema who 'makes possible the desires, fantasies and anxieties of urban/diasporic India as an identity through his performances'.[30] The leading actor of both *Kuch Kuch Hota Hai* and *Kal Ho Naa Ho*, Shah Rukh Khan has gradually established himself as a pop icon, 'in tandem with the circulation of Bollywood in the moment of globalisation'.[31] Anne Ciecko argues that stars are interfacing with the exponential growth of capital possibilities offered by global multinationals through advertising, through their appearances at world cinema festivals and their circulation 'as cultural icons on the Internet'.[32]

In *Sacred Games*, what is significant is the gradual transformation Gaitonde undertakes in accordance with the shifting image of the Bollywood movie star. For instance, Ganesh Gaitonde becomes a hypermobile character: he conducts his illegal operations on the Internet and is involved in the production, advertising and exhibition of a Bollywood movie. In parallel with the contemporary Hindi film and its incorporation of diasporic themes, Gaitonde learns about audiences' expectations through the weekly *India Abroad*, a magazine published for South Asians in the diaspora. Moreover, the film entitled *International Darmaka* is shot in different locations: 'in Bombay, London, Lausanne, Munich, Tallinn and Seville'.[33] The film is broadcast on cable and satellite TV in order to reach wider audiences around the world.[34]

In a further conflation of cinema and literature as 'temples of modern desires', *International Darmaka* restages and fictionalizes the global status Gaitonde progressively acquires as a popular international gangster. Film and reality become so inextricably interrelated that it is difficult to separate Gaitonde the character from his filmic persona. It is indicative that at some point, he undergoes plastic surgery 'to build' his new identity: 'I […] felt the urge to renew myself because of the coming age. A new world needs a new man.'³⁵ The gangster's progressive transformation into a fashionable pop icon alongside the decor in which he moves presents a version of India in which the 'West has been internalised'.³⁶

In Chandra's text, the portrayal of a 'virtual West' coincides with the advent of new technologies, gradually 'encumbering' the space of the city. While at the beginning of the novel Gaitonde watches videos and listens to the song sequences of films on cassettes, he gradually becomes acquainted with modern technologies.³⁷ Cassettes are promptly replaced by CDs, videos by DVDs, to be subsequently substituted by cable TV.³⁸ In *Maximum City*, technologies are referred to as 'objects' through which 'the world outside is [increasingly] crowding the world inside'.³⁹

In reference to the expansion of new media and technologies in India, Sangita Gopal argues that the transition from one medium to another, including the circulation of filmic intertexts through the Internet, coincides with the country's endorsement of economic liberalization sanctioned by the victory of the BJP in the 1998 general election. The years between 1998 and 2004 were marked by a free market economic policy of nonintervention, resulting in the liberalization of trade and foreign investment with major privatizations of influential government corporations. The country's alignment with the global economy was sanctioned by the exponential increase of help the state offered to the rising information technology industry.

This backdrop is what, according to Mishra, makes contemporary Bollywood cinema 'a temple of modern desire'. This is also the reason why South Asian diasporic fictions, incorporating the ethos of hypermobility, instigate familiarity among UK and US audiences who can recognize the universal templates of globalization in the representation of cities situated in the economic South: 'the city of bankers, stockbrokers and call-centre workers that many business visitors encounter'.⁴⁰

However, it is possible to argue that if the desires of the 'national groups that make up the South Asian diaspora' are framed by a wish to articulate global belonging, differences are then flattened with 'Bombay being just like New York'.⁴¹ This leads to a question: how do diasporic texts articulate a unique representation of the homeland without aligning themselves with the predominant rhetoric of economic globalization?

Recollecting Bombay

In response to the interrogative posed in the previous section, I will ground my argument in the theoretical backdrop furnished by Vijay Mishra, in which he defines South Asian diasporic films as 'authentic artifacts'.⁴²

Throughout his study on Bollywood cinema, Mishra applies Walter Benjamin's theorizations contained in 'The Work of Art in the Age of Mechanical Reproduction'. In this seminal essay written in 1936, Benjamin discusses the transformation of the work of art with the advent of new technologies of distribution and replication. Before the appearance of photography/cinema, the work of art used to retain specificity – authenticity in terms of a unique relationship between the creator and the object of creation. The artwork preceding 'modernity' was placed in a fixed context, out of which it was believed not to exist; it was believed to retain auratic status. Benjamin imbues this aura with religious connotations by equating it with a sacred ritual, where art reveals itself in its specificity as if in a moment of intuition/epiphany.

The aura of the artwork disappears with the advent of the synchronic and serialized reproductions, bringing a democratization of art that, deprived of its obscurantism, is now accessible to all. This process shifts the emphasis from production to reception, where the latter configures itself as the moment in which the audience becomes actively involved in the interpretation/decoding of the artwork. In these terms, the object of creation assumes politicized connotations in that it becomes an instrument in the hands of the collectivity, the expression of a democratization of culture and society. Framing this theory within the context of Bollywood cinema, Mishra argues that since the colonial occupation it has continued to embody a democratization/collectivization of culture, devoid of elitist connotations.[43] This is strengthened all the more in the digital age, which allows even greater access for even more people as well as the opportunity to reform and reshape (or 'mash') the artistic content itself.

However, in a tenuous reframing of this argument, Mishra observes that Indian diasporic cinema articulates a different kind of discourse. Here the desire to reconnect to the homeland results in the creation of India as an artefact retaining 'auratic' status. In these films, the artefacts are presented as kitsch: 'the impure replica of the impossible-to-attain originality'.[44] The cinematic principle of kitsch, by drawing 'attention to its impurity and artificiality', provokes in the spectators the same kind of identification at work in any piece of art produced 'in the age of mechanical reproduction'.[45] Indeed, it is precisely because of this *kitschiness* that South Asian diasporic viewers cannot entirely suture the distance between the 'here' (film) and 'there' (spectator). In other words, diasporic cinema consciously 'collects' Bollywood intertexts to create a distance from the rhetoric of global affiliation.

As Benjamin explains, the widening accessibility of art abolishes the cultic value in which it has been immersed so far, transforming the beholder into an owner or collector. Hannah Arendt believes that collecting 'redeems' things from their merely materialistic function by investing them with social 'genuineness'.[46] In this way, art is entirely in the hands of the spectator/collector, who reproduces his/her unique narrative/gaze.

By expanding this argument, I want to argue that diasporic texts articulate the same dialogue with Bollywood cinema: they utilize Bollywood intertexts as artifacts to circumvent the same kind of 'identificatory' process at work in the homeland, while simultaneously reproducing a counterhegemonic narrative of the diaspora, shaped by an individual 'recollection' of the homeland.

This is demonstrated in both *Maximum City* and *Sacred Games*, where cinematic intertexts constitute the palimpsest upon which space is recreated. Both texts seem to function as contemporary Bollywood movies – defined as 'loose compounds of various elements' like action, crime, love, song-and-dance sequences – with the complex apparatus of the 'star system' contributing to the internal and external unification of the narrative tropes.[47] Contemporary Bollywood films are also 'urban and increasingly global in [their] settings' which adds to their attraction to Western audiences.[48]

In parallel with what happens in contemporary Bollywood cinema, both texts are structured as loose narrative compounds. They present 'action' in the form of a quest/journey: in *Maximum City* it is the discovery of Bombay that leads the narrator through a series of encounters and incidents; in *Sacred Games*, action assumes the shape of an inquest with the detective Sartaj Singh investigating the death of Ganesh Gaitonde.

The detective/crime thread is also restaged in Mehta's text where the narrator's encounters with the underworld are meticulously described as independent and fictionalized narrative units. This trope, informing the overall narrative of *Sacred Games*, is further dissected into independent short stories or episodes reminiscent of classic detective fiction. Apart from the microtext of the police inspector (Singh) chasing the criminal (Gaitonde), there exist a conspicuous number of self-contained narrative units utilizing similar motifs.

Love also constitutes an independent narrative compound in both texts. In *Maximum City*, this is detectable in the encounter between the author and the dancer Monalisa. The controversial relationship between the two seems to echo a number of cinematic intertexts of melodramatic reminiscence, where the triangle element is aptly resolved by the moral rectitude of the male hero. In *Sacred Games*, the love 'thread' is represented by the relationship between the inspector Sartaj Singh and Mary Mascarenas alongside Gaitonde's romance with the actress Zoya Mirza.

Songs similarly punctuate the narration of events. In Mehta's text, these songs belong to the cinematic archive of Bollywood. In *Sacred Games*, both Sartaj Singh and Ganesh Gaitonde sing and 'perform' song and dance sequences, as evidenced by the association of scene/motif with a memorable melody.

Dancing and acting as the leading characters of a Hindi movie, Mary and Sartaj also reinforce the fundamental role that the 'star system' plays both in India and abroad. Stars of Bollywood cinema circulate and build their own public and fictional personas through a number of magazines.

Forging a public image through the pages of the newspapers constitutes a recurrent trope in the entire narrative of *Sacred Games*. This informs the character of Ganesh Gaitonde, particularly. People are eager to know about his life and attempt to build his persona from information released in the newspapers. As specified in the previous section, the gangster constitutes a contrapuntal image of the contemporary movie celebrity Shah Rukh Khan, the new commodified hero. Throughout the narrative, Gaitonde compares himself to an actor/celebrity performing a role: 'I had seen scenes from my own life in two dozen films, sometimes exaggerated and sometimes reduced, but still true. I was filmi, and I was real.'[49]

In this passage, Gaitonde's awareness of his identity as performance generates a suture between his fictional/public persona and his real existence. This creates a troubled self-examination, where the character is attempting to connect/identify with his media-laden image while simultaneously trying to forge his individual narrative. In other words, Gaitonde partakes in the ambivalent process described above as both spectator of and actor in an imitation of a Hindi movie. The utilization of Bollywood intertexts as 'commodities' invested with social and emotional value provides an oppositional view of the homeland as a global superpower. While the representation of the city as a nodal and transnational point constitutes a familiar territory for UK and US audiences, the self-referentiality of Bollywood intertexts within diasporic fiction highlights its artificiality. As a consequence, the constructedness of filmic intertexts creates distance among South Asian diasporas and defamiliarization for Western readers.

Conclusion

In *Maximum City*, and in *Sacred Games* in particular, the contemporary Hindi movie constitutes a palimpsest upon which the authors superimpose their narratives. However, it is precisely because of this crafted use of Bollywood cinema that the text announces its use as an 'authentic' artefact. Diasporic narratives, in attitude akin to that of the collector, appropriate and assemble the tropes of Indian cinema by 'redeeming' them from their own materiality.[50] The text therefore articulates a 'creative' reinscription of Bollywood cinema, paying homage to the pivotal role it plays among diasporas. As Mary Gillespie observes, Bollywood cinema exerts an immense fascination on both the diaspora and wider audiences because it represents the 'real India'.[51] Even if it does not embody the 'real (immigrant communities)', it restages the values South Asian diasporas should aspire to. At the same time, the contemporary Hindi movie's incorporation within the diasporic text furnishes UK and US audiences with 'ready-made' versions of exoticism through the lens of familiarity. For example, talking of the popularity of *Sacred Games*, an article in *New Statesman* points out, 'Now Vikram Chandra, in a book that reportedly took seven years to write and won him a $1m advance in the US, seeks to capture the whole boiling stew of Mumbai and its criminal underworld in one giant, 900-page narrative.'[52]

Here the popular reception of the novel is described in a fashion that appropriates the equally popular tropes of Bollywood cinema with its 'boiling stew of Mumbai and its criminal underworld'. Analogously, the self-referentiality of filmic intertexts functions to create familiarity among the members of the South Asian diasporas, while instigating exoticism in Western readers.

Gita Rajan and Shailja Sharma maintain that the increasing popularity of postcolonial Indian writing in the West (and in particular the US) is closely intertwined with the fulfilled expectations of an audience eager for exoticism. Rather than attributing to the term a negative connotation, they regard it instead as a synonym for unfamiliarity and foreignness. Since postcolonial fictions play out the contradictory dynamics of the familiar and unfamiliar so appealing to the American audience, the popularity of Mehta's and Chandra's texts can be attributed to their ability to instigate unfamiliarity, prompting a new refutation of concepts such as foreignness and assimilation. This depiction of the 'dark corners of the metropolis – the slums teeming with desperate village migrants, the underworld full of criminals and violent nationalists' allows UK and US readers to compare and contrast Bombay with the Western city with which they are familiar.[53]

Notes and References

1 'Not Losing Hope', *Economist* (US Edition), 7 April 2005. Online: http://www.economist.com/node/3839714 (accessed 14 January 2013).
2 Ibid.
3 Sudha Menon, 'After "Slumdog", Danny Boyle set to film "Maximum City"', *Live Mint*, 30 May 2009. Online: http://www.livemint.com/2009/05/30014715/After-8216Slumdog8217-D.html (accessed April 20 2010).
4 Suketu Mehta, 'Bollywood Confidential', *New York Times Sunday Magazine*, 14 November 2004. Online: http://www.nytimes.com/2004/11/14/movies/14BOLLYWOOD.html (accessed March 20 2010).
5 Ibid.
6 Vikram Chandra in Ginny Wiehardt, 'An Interview with Vikram Chandra', *About.com: Fiction Writing*. Online: http://fictionwriting.about.com/od/interviews/a/chandra_2.htm (accessed 24 September 2010).

7 Suketu Mehta, *Maximum City* (London: Review, 2005), 8.
8 'Not Losing Hope', *Economist*.
9 Vijay Mishra, *Bollywood Cinema: Temples of Desire* (New York and London: Routledge, 2002), 1.
10 Ibid.
11 Ibid.
12 Ibid., 4.
13 Mehta, *Maximum City*, 3.
14 Vijay Mishra, *The Literature of the Indian Diaspora: Theorizing the Diasporic Imaginary* (London and New York: Routledge, 2007), 185.
15 The first film was directed by Johar and the second was scripted by him but directed by Advani.
16 Mehta, *Maximum City*, 408.
17 Manas Ray, 'Chalo Jahoji: Bollywood in the Tracks of Indenture to Globalization', in *City Flicks*, ed. by P. Kaarsholm (London, New York and Kolkata: Seagull Books, 2007), 169.
18 Ibid.
19 Ibid., 168.
20 Pankaj Mishra, *Temptations of the West: How to be Modern in India, Pakistan and Beyond* (London: Picador, 2006), 171.
21 J. Desai, *Beyond Bollywood: The Cultural Politics of South Asian Diasporic Film* (London and New York: Routledge, 2004), 193.
22 Ray, 'Chalo Jahoji', 168.
23 Ibid.
24 Paraphrased from Mehta, *Maximum City*: 'The Bombayite might dream of the West', 34.
25 Mehta, *Maximum City*, 26, 38.
26 Ray, 'Chalo Jahoji', 168.
27 Vikram Chandra, *Sacred Games* (London: Faber & Faber, 2006), 422.
28 Ibid., 434.
29 Rajinder Dudrah, *Sociology Goes to the Movies* (New Delhi and London: Sage, 2006), 87.
30 Ibid.
31 Ibid., 86.
32 A. Ciecko, quoted in Dudrah, ibid.
33 Chandra, *Sacred Games*, 686.
34 Ibid., 666.
35 Ibid., 734.
36 Desai, *Beyond Bollywood*, 168.
37 Chandra, *Sacred Games*, 114.
38 Ibid, 558, 664.
39 Mehta, *Maximum City*, 589.
40 'Not Losing Hope', *Economist*.
41 Mehta, *Maximum City*, 7.
42 Mishra, *Bollywood Cinema*, 241.
43 Ibid., 13.
44 Ibid., 242.
45 Ibid.
46 Ibid.
47 Ray, 'Chalo Jahoji', 158.
48 Ibid., 165.

49 Chandra, *Sacred Games*, 800.
50 Hannah Arendt, introduction to Walter Benjamin, *Illuminations* (Glasgow: Fontana, 1977), 47.
51 Mary Gillespie, quoted by Mishra in *Bollywood Cinema*, 269.
52 Andrew Holgate 'Lost in the City', *New Statesman*, 4 September 2006.
53 Rachel Shea, 'New in Paperback', *Washington Post*, 6 November 2005.

Chapter Ten

TABISH KHAIR: MARKETING COMPULSIONS AND ARTISTIC INTEGRITY

Om Prakash Dwivedi

Tabish Khair started his literary career with the widely acclaimed critical book, *Babu Fictions: Alienation in Contemporary Indian English Novels* (Oxford University Press, 2001), which has proved to be a valuable addition to Indian English criticism. Very soon, Khair shifted over to writing poetry and novels, but sadly his position as a poet/novelist is still to be acknowledged in the literary world. This is largely due to the fact that he lives and writes in Denmark and not in London. Charles Lock points to this predominant exoticism of London's presence among Indian writers, that 'London has long been the place where every Indian writer (in English) aspires to be published; Britain is a place where middle-class Indians have long felt at home. That Khair had been living in Denmark for some years before he ever went to Britain is a deviation from the conventional path that distinguishes him from other Indian writers, and that gives his work an unusual shape, in terms of both theme and audience.'[1] This comment ostensibly maps the continuity of colonialism in the postcolonial period, which necessitates that Indian writing *has* to be written from the centre or the colonies where the Whites have been to as rulers, like the US, Canada or Australia. In order to be considered visible and successful, an Indian writer must speak from the centre and not from the erstwhile colonies. This clearly is the politics of Indian English literature – they need to speak from the origin of their masters, they need to belong to elsewhere (popularly known as 'diaspora') and withdraw from India. Here I must add that the focus of this paper, though, is not this; rather it seeks to make a brief study of Khair's fictional oeuvre. The paper also aims at exploring the overt themes in Khair's writings and his critical reception in the English-speaking world.

Tabish Khair (1966–) was born in a Muslim family in Ranchi (formerly in Bihar, now the capital of Jharkhand) and grew up in Gaya, a small town in Bihar, popularly known as the site where Gautam, the founder of Buddhism, attained enlightenment. Tabish's grandfather studied for his medical degree at the Prince of Wales Medical College in Patna in the 1880s. Tabish earned his undergraduate degree in history, sociology and English from Gaya College and a master's in English from the local Magadh University.

Khair's first collection of poems, *My World* (Rupa, 1994), was favourably reviewed by eminent poets and critics like Keki N. Daruwalla, Adil Jussawalla, Vilas Sarang and Shiv K. Kumar: in one of his emails to me, Khair recalls being encouraged by the reviews, as he had no contacts whatsoever with the main poetry circles of the big cities of India until then.

Khair's *An Angel in Pyjamas* (HarperCollins, 1995) was described by *India Today* as 'the calling card of a writer with the power to fascinate'.[2] Soon Khair left for Copenhagen, Denmark, to do his doctorate, and his thesis was published as *Babu Fictions: Alienation in Indian English Novels*.

Khair also published a collection of poems, *Where Parallel Lines Meet* (Penguin, 2000), for which he won the prestigious All India Poetry Prize. He considers his poetry and fiction published before 2000 to be mostly the work of a young poet struggling to find his voice.

Picador published Khair's second novel, *The Bus Stopped*, in 2004. It has since been translated into French and Italian. Along with novels by Hari Kunzru and Nadeem Aslam, it was shortlisted for the Encore Award in the UK. Khair has also coedited various books and journals, including a casebook of essays on Amitav Ghosh (Permanent Black, 2005) and *Other Routes* (Signal Books, 2005), an anthology of pre-1900 Asian and African travel writing, with a foreword by Amitav Ghosh.

Khair's third novel, *Filming: A Love Story* (Picador, 2007), came out to huge critical acclaim. It was shortlisted for the Vodafone Crossword award in India and was listed by Khushwant Singh among his best 20 novels published by an Indian or a writer of Indian origin since 1947. A Danish translation was published in 2009 and other translations are forthcoming. Khair has also published an illustrated storybook for 5- to 7-year-old children, *The Glum Peacock* (Zubaan Books, 2008), listed by *Time Out* as one of the 50 best reads for children.

Later came *The Gothic, Postcolonialism and Otherness* (Palgrave, 2009), a collection of essays that deals with the theme of 'otherness' as witnessed in the study of gothic novels and its relevance in the context of postcolonial societies. In 2010 Khair published his latest novel *The Thing About Thugs* and a collection of poems, *Man of Glass* (both from HarperCollins). Currently, the writer lives in Aarhus (Denmark) with his two children.

The first novel to be written by Khair was *An Angel in Pyjamas* (1995). It is partly written as a kind of spoof of magical realism. It presents two seemingly independent streams of stories: one in Phansa, the fictional town of Khair's novels, and the other in Delhi. The story in Phansa is centred on a half-baked and small-town 'love story' that clearly evokes R. K. Narayan; however, Phansa is a harder, more strife-torn town in 1980s North India than Narayan's Malgudi, and the situations in Phansa are riven by religious, class and provincial conflicts. The other segment – in Delhi – revolves around the reappearance of the Urdu poet, Asadullah Khan Ghalib, who is looking for the halo of an angel that has fallen to earth, and an unemployed Sikh youth, who is finally arrested and tortured as a Sikh terrorist. This part is a clear tongue-in-cheek take on magical realism, as in Salman Rushdie. The two streams of narrative do converge in the end – a feature that Khair has employed to powerful effect in his later novels – but, primarily, the novel is a humorous, ironic attempt to trace out North Indian contemporary realities in the light of the two dominant streams of Indian English fictive narration, as symbolized by Narayan and Rushdie. Pankaj Mishra describes the novel thus: 'In his first, startlingly prescient novel Tabish Khair not only described the roots of religious extremism. He also explored, with much humour and irony, the lives lived on the borderlines of the small town and metropolis – the ambiguous region where India's many conflicts of class and religion are played out.'[3]

Khair's second novel, *The Bus Stopped* (2004), proved to be a greater success than his earlier work. It is a novel that deals on the one hand with the notion of home as a site of identity and memory, and on the other the explicit theme of diasporic sensibility. The escape from self or from the homeland sometimes becomes so strikingly painful that one feels almost like a nowhere man. In postcolonial novels, home is one of the important ingredients of identity construction/destruction. Time and again, Khair writes about these schizophrenic movements in *Filming*. His nostalgia for *desh* (homeland) becomes apparent when one reads *The Bus Stopped*. The home itself in this novel is mobile: 'I have found and lost, lost and found my houses too. I make my home on buses and aeroplanes, in hotels and rented apartments' (198).[4]

It seems that Khair's journey from India to Denmark might have prompted him to write this journey-filled novel. His past continues to haunt him in his present and the readers can get an explicit sense of it while reading *The Bus Stopped*. Khair is the kind of writer who spins his narrative in such a crafty manner that sometimes it becomes difficult for his readers to comprehend. The narrative structure of *The Bus Stopped* is different from the structure of *An Angel in Pyjamas*, but this is because Khair changes his style according to the demand of the story.

In *The Bus Stopped*, the rude driver Mangal Singh, who seems to be the leading character of the novel, is the one who drives the vehicle and makes it possible for the people to travel across time and space, from Gaya to Phansa, escaping from their personal histories. His presence can be witnessed throughout the novel. For Singh, this travelling is but one of the means to overcome his failed dreams and aspirations. Singh is a bitter man, a failed novelist, but an observant one who 'sees life in still small images, almost frozen' (12). He has a broken marriage and his beautiful cousin Sunita is now married to the owner of the bus company for which he works. We have a paradoxical figure in Singh. Being a failed man himself, he does not shy away from carrying the travellers to their desired destinations in order to fulfil their purpose and dreams. When he whistles to announce the scheduled departure of the bus, people hear 'a sound that cuts across the dawn, the field and the houses like a bird in flight' (14), and the bus becomes the agent that transports and transforms various people and their destinies and identities. The bus also features a conductor, Shankar, who often enters into altercations with Singh; he regards Singh as: 'rapacious, a womaniser, a drunkard' (149). Both differ in their personal opinions but the commonality that unites them is that they both live miserable lives.

Sex is also one of the overt themes in this novel. Zeenat, a servant, is one of the passengers on the bus travelling from Gaya to Phansa. The novelist gives a flashback of a sexual encounter in which Zeenat seduces the young Irfan, who lives in the neighbourhood where she works. This entire sexual encounter is disclosed to the readers during the bus journey. It so happens that one day Irfan visits her neighbourhood and comes across Zeenat sitting near the staircase. He tries hard to overlook her, but falls in to her seductive trap:

> Standing in the slanted darkness of her doorway, she pressed closer to me. I grew bolder and cupped her breast. It was then that I felt her pulling away at the strings of my pyjamas. The act was unexpected. It was too much: it went beyond the bounds of what I had allowed myself to imagine. It brought up echoes of my parents' voices. It brought up an image I had caught from the rooftop and never understood: the old rickshaw puller leaving her room one evening, looking around himself as if he had stolen something.
>
> I tried to pull her hand away with my left hand, the right one still cupped around a shapely breast. But she laughed, a short, dismissive laugh, considering it a game or a youth's initial reticence, and easily pinning my obstructing arm with one hand, she pulled open my pyjamas and started fondling my penis. Her touch was rough and soft at the same time, it was incredibly lovely and frighteningly knowing. Her smell was as palpable as her touch. You are ready, she said with some surprise. (109–10)

The bus itself is full of myriad of troubled stories. Chottu, the servant of an elderly woman living alone in the Kanchenjunga Apartments in Patna, abhors the idea of being educated by this elderly woman so much so that he ends up murdering her, and the immediate escape he finds is to catch the Gaya to Phansa bus.

The image of journeying is not only central to this novel but becomes one of the overt leitmotifs. It speaks of journeys and also exposes its inherent consequences in an almost universalist fashion. In so doing, it uncovers the different perspectives of a single journey in an increasingly globalized world. Asserting on the dynamism of travel, Justin D. Edwards rightly states that it enables 'one to understand the importance of "reinterpreting" and, if necessary, "reinventing" himself by exploring ethnicities, national identities and cultural differences'.[5] It stands true in the present-day context where travel *is* ostensibly a natural process of transition and transformation. Travel, then, has the inherent efficacy to place people either in ignominy or to make them feel euphoric. In this novel, Khair meticulously churns out a single journey, and in this very act of travelling, he inevitably succumbs to the temptations of returning.

Khair's next novel, *Filming: A Love Story* (2007), uncovers interweaving different voices, different perspectives, and is full of seemingly complexities in terms of plot and themes. The novel is replete with plenty of characters, each character playing a different role; it is very much in the form of a film. But it is these complexities that make the novel a real pleasure for its readers and make them feel as if they are watching a movie that contains many subplots. The action takes place between the 1920s and the 1940s, but the narration of the novel continues to oscillate back and forth. The uniqueness of the novel lies in the fact that, instead of giving numbers to chapters, Khair offers us different reels that project the knee-deep problems of human life. The novel projects seven reels *in toto*: each dramatising specific emotions or sentiments in the form of different *rasas*. A *rasa* (Sanskrit for 'juice' or 'essence') denotes an essential mental state and is the dominant emotional theme of a work of art or the primary feeling that is evoked in the person that views, reads or hears such a work.[6] Whereas a reel of film is wrought with dreams, fantasies and illusions, Khair's reels are presentations of bitter and sweet realities. What is particularly important to register in this novel is the intricate artistic manner in which the writer probes and shows how a reel intersects the real and how easily the real becomes the reel in fiction. We get a clear-cut glimpse of Khair's perfectionism in the narration of one of the other major characters, Batin: 'It is difficult, young man, for me to recount just one story, for each leads to another. You know when I was your age I used to believe that stories had a beginning and an end. Now I know that they only have hooks, many hooks, and each hook is caught up by another hook' (220).[7]

The narration of *Filming* starts in 1929 and immediately we see a physically fragile Harihar, his wife Durga and their young son Ashok travelling on a bullock cart. Travel has become a necessity for this financially distraught family: Harihar and his family screen silent movies to rural audiences in order to earn their livelihood. Harihar dreams of producing a film on his own someday but his miseries seem to perpetually eclipse his dreams. Durga, a prostitute by profession, takes up acting after a series of discreet discussions in the garb of prostitution with her regular customer, Harihar. They start sharing their desires with each other and soon they elope to live with each other elsewhere.

The main theme that underlines the entire novel is of homeliness and homelessness. It is 'about mobility, about how people move from place to place, time to time, name to name; and it is about barbed wire, how we are entangled in the barbed wire of history' (70).

Right at the start of the novel, Harihar and his family are seen moving to Anjangarh where they plan to organize another film show. Here, they meet the local landlord's son Chotte Thakur, who permits them to stage a show in the *maidan* near his *haveli*. Thakur, too, is a failed man, as his father denies him the permission to pursue his career in music and dancing, and hence his artistic ambitions remain unfulfilled. Very soon, their show, which is originally meant for the public, turns into a private affair, as Durga dances regularly at late nights along with Thakur. The situation becomes more complicated when Thakur starts spending time with Harihar: both barter their knowledge on films and music, and consequently develop a strong bond. To further worsen Durga's condition, Malikini, the lady of the house, showers her motherly love over Ashok. Previously an outsider, Ashok now becomes the cynosure of Malikini's eye, so much so that a deal is struck in which Hari signs Ashok away to Thakur's family in return for funding his own film, *Aakhri Raat*.

Quite rightly, Khair brings out a doubled notion of home, where a person with 'no home, no address' cannot be trusted and concurrently, 'people who have too many faces and too many voices do not have a home' (119). The condition of living a nomadic life resonates throughout the novel. Even little Ashok wants a 'home like the homes he saw. The homes he sometimes entered, and invariably left. [...] There was no space for him in other people's homes' (100–101). Finally, when he moves to the *haveli*, he realizes the sense of security that comes with this word 'home'. The novel problematizes the sense of (un)belonging, which becomes manifest in the constant geographical and identity shifts of characters.

In addition to the above-mentioned themes, the novel also offers commentary on India's churning out as a nation after the strikingly painful partition in *Filming*. In so doing, Khair follows the Rushdian way and successfully mingles fiction with history. Due to Partition, the situation is now chaotic and people are finding it hard to change their locations and loyalties. Saleem, an actor who is in love with Durga, is one such Muslim figure who opts to remain in India and continue working in Harihar's studio, but this communal chemistry is obfuscated in an attack hurled upon the studio by Hindu fundamentalists on the same day that Gandhi is assassinated. Khair is rhetorical in his portrait of Partition: 'One day we discovered that time was vitrescent and the fused light of our dream struck the prism of 1947 and refracted into the orange and yellow of Hinduism, the green of Islam, the red of violence, the blue of a disappointed hope, and into the indigo and violet of subtle, unredeemable differences' (168). Khair probably wants to point out that sometimes construction of home itself can come through mass destruction, as it is in the events that follow the Partition; one might be able to get a home but this homeliness undoubtedly comes through homelessness and massacre. This, of course, is quite evident in the present-day postcolonial world where identity construction quite often ironically comes through fragmentation.

Khair, it needs to be asserted, is one of the major talents to emerge from the liberalized India. The process of liberalization started in India back in 1991 and yielded great results and an unbelievable impact on India's economy. India has now become a rapidly growing economy in the world due to its unprecedented Gross Domestic Product growth rate. Quite expectedly, a booming economy also provided a platform for Indian writers to showcase their creative talents to the entire world. Unlike the Indian English writers (i.e. writers who live in India and write) who wrote prior to liberalization without achieving any phenomenal success, postliberalization writers have become strikingly visible, thanks to the rapid transformation brought about by globalization. It also meant a growing economy coupled with the changing lifestyles of Indians who now came in touch with multinational companies and their products. It also brought about a revolution in the media sector and consequently Indian English writers appeared in newspapers and other print media regularly, which made their visibility more pronounced. Liberalization introduced India to the big international publishing houses and led to the rise of bookshop chains, which expanded and magnified the field for Indian English writing. One thing that still worries me, however, is the kind of role played by these publishing houses. Indian writers have started appealing to international audiences, but it is still the diasporic authors who steal the show as publishing houses are more inclined towards this latter group due to their locations and their *preferred* writing techniques. I refer to this technique because it is a bitter truth that diasporic sensibility has become a hot-selling commodity in postcolonial literature. Publishers are more interested in publishing the kinds of works that appeal to international audiences; writers, too, are aware of how the cookie crumbles in today's publishing world and consequently write on such carefully selected topics. In return, writers are bestowed upon with sterling honours and handsome royalties, and globalization has truly impacted the genre of fiction writing. But the reason for Khair's continual refusal to be enveloped within the rubric of a diasporic author is a simple and logical one. One of his articles, which he wrote in reply to a trenchant criticism that categorized him as a diasporic author, substantiates this fact: 'When I published my first novel, *An Angel in Pyjamas*, some years ago, an Indian critic took me to task for being a "diasporic Indian" who had written a typically "clever" novel. It was a strange mode of criticism, made even more so by the fact that I had lived in a very small Indian town for most of my life, emigrating only a few months prior to the publication of my novel, while the critic lived in one of those big Indian cities from which places like my home town tend to be invisible.'[8] It is the very ambiguity of globalization that has made literature a commodity rather than simply an art; it increases the visibility of writers who are settled in or writing from the centre, while at the same time subdues into darkness less privileged writers belonging to elsewhere. Ironically, it is not the quality of the book, but marketability and the amount of hype and money it generates that are the parameters of its success.

There is no greater impact of liberalization on Khair's writing, perhaps because he left India in 1996. In one of our email exchanges, Khair acknowledged that liberalization did not make much of a difference to him at the personal level. In the same email, he also registered his concerns at the ways in which those who make profit from it generally cancel out the rights and privileges of people who suffer due to this liberalization and globalization. His concerns outlined in the email highlight his style of writing. He is not the kind of author who twists his style to meet the demands of the publishing industry – especially those that are always inclined towards publishing fiction with postcolonial themes. His strength lies in the fact that, unlike other postcolonial authors, he does not present exotic Orientalism, but instead provides an alternative to his reader to think over the very idea of humanity. All three of his novels legitimize this statement. He seems always fascinated to get engaged with these discourses that tend to decimate the very idea of humanity in this increasingly globalized world. In so doing, he emerges as a liberalist (or, to be more accurate, a humanist) and for this very reason he always refuses to bracket his works under the rubrics of colonialism/postcolonialism studies.

Unlike other media-savvy, high-profile writers, Khair is not a household name, but this has more to do with his location than literary skills. Still he has his share of positive critical responses in the literary world. His books have been reviewed in many international journals and magazines. The *Hindu* comments thus on *The Bus Stopped*: 'Khair manages to carry off his tale, or rather tales, with something close to aplomb [...]. He manages to be funny and irreverent, serious and compassionate in turn.'[9] The *Independent* comments thus: 'A lyrical journey through small-town India'.[10] *Outlook* states, 'On the surface about a bus journey, *The Bus Stopped* is a novel that reflects deeply into the nature and circumstances of human nobility in our modern, unforgiving world.'[11] The *Guardian* echoes these thoughts: 'The journey allows stories to emerge with immediacy and leisure, with abrupt shafts of humour.'[12] All these reviews and comments inevitably magnify the stature of Khair as a novelist, especially as the reviews mainly come from the West, again an implicit tendency of Indian English literature since its very inception to try to earn an official sanction and promotion from the West to be sold in the global market.

Filming also made a mark in both the Indian as well as Western print magazines. The *Times Literary Supplement* comments that it is 'an absorbing novel which is distinguished by its ambition, its structural inventiveness and its highly evocative prose.'[13] The review of *Filming* in the *Independent* only affirms the sheer brilliance of this novel, that it is 'superb [...]. Elegantly structured and taut with understated passion. *Filming* is a brilliant recreation of the lost world of early cinema and the continuing tragedy of religious hatred.'[14]

To conclude, Tabish Khair is a major talent in the field of Indian writing in English, with a distinctive voice. Unlike other Indian diaspora writers, Khair's uniqueness lies in the fact that he possesses a clear understanding of his Indian culture and roots, largely because he spent the first thirty years of his life in India and has first-hand acquaintance with the ethos of small-town India. Another remarkable feature of his novels is his authentic representation of characters, particularly from the lower strata of society. By 'authentic representation', I mean that the characters are created by Khair out of his own experience while living in India. I would probably associate this to his upbringing in Gaya, where Khair spent his childhood and youth. With his uncanny knack for the sound, sight and smell of the 'real' India, it is only a matter of time when Khair attains his status as a major force to reckon with in the 'fiction market'.

Notes and References

1 This point has been further clarified in my forthcoming book, *Tabish Khair: A Critical Assessment* (London and Kolkata: Roman Books, 2013).
2 Quoted from the inside cover of Tabish Khair, *An Angel in Pyjamas* (Delhi: HarperCollins, 1995).
3 Ibid.
4 Tabish Khair, *The Bus Stopped* (London: Picador, 2004). Subsequent references to this text are given in the body of the paper itself.
5 Justin D. Edwards, *Postcolonial Literature: A Reader's Guide to Essential Criticism* (Basingstoke: Palgrave Macmillan, 2008), 83.
6 Museum of Learning, 'Nava Rasas'. Online: http://www.museumstuff.com/learn/topics/Nava_rasas (accessed 20 May 2010).

7 Tabish Khair, *Filming: A Love Story* (London: Picador, 2007). Subsequent references to this text are given in the body of the paper itself.
8 Tabish Khair, 'Whose Identity is it Anyway?', *Guardian*, 12 November 2005. Online: http://www.guardian.co.uk/books/2005/nov/12/featuresreviews.guardianreview1 (accessed 8 March 2012).
9 Shiv S. Kumar, 'When Lives Intersect', *Hindu*, 2 May 2004. Online: http://www.hindu.com/lr/2004/05/02/stories/2004050200180300.htm (accessed 25 June 2011).
10 Alev Adil, 'The Bus Stopped by Tabish Khair', review in the *Independent*, 24 May 2004. Online: http://www.uni-saarland.de/fileadmin/user_upload/Professoren/fr43_ProfGhoshSchellhorn/Tas_Datenbank/South_Asia___Diasporas/Khair_The_Independent.pdf (accessed 21 January 2013).
11 Siddhartha Deb, 'Memory on Wheels', *Outlook*, 3 May 2004. Online: http://www.outlookindia.com/article.aspx?223760 (accessed 25 June 2011).
12 Isobel Montgomery and David Jays, 'Whales, Tales and the Funny Side of a Hijacking', *Guardian*, 16 April 2005. Online: http://www.guardian.co.uk/books/2005/apr/16/featuresreviews.guardianreview22 (accessed 21 December 2010).
13 Peter Parker, 'Bioscope-wallah', *Times Literary Supplement*, 3 August 2007, 18.
14 Chandak Sengupta, '*Filming: A Love Story* by Tabish Khair', *Independent*, 29 June 2007. Online: http://www.independent.co.uk/arts-entertainment/books/reviews/filming-a-love-story-by-tabish-khair-455065.html (accessed 25 June 2011).

Chapter Eleven

ROHINTON MISTRY AND THE CANLIT IMPERATIVE

Patricia Gruben

'When you shall these unlucky deeds relate, speak of me as I am; nothing extenuate, nor set down aught in malice: tell them that in Toronto once there lived a Parsi boy as best he could. Set you down this; and say, besides, that for some it was good and for some it was bad, but for me life in the land of milk and honey was just a pain in the posterior.'

Rohinton Mistry, 'Squatter'[1]

The work of Indo-Canadian novelist Rohinton Mistry focuses on the personal struggles of individuals within society, largely within the Parsi community in which Mistry grew up in midcentury Bombay. His writing has been compared more frequently to Dickens, Balzac, Tolstoy and other nineteenth-century European realists than to the more contemporary, postmodern idiom of South Asian writers like Salman Rushdie and Vikram Chandra. Mistry's transparent style, combined with great psychological insight into character, supports his popularity throughout the English-speaking world and his numerous international awards. However, the critical reception of his work in India and North America reflects complex aesthetic, political and theoretical debates among his serious readers. Particularly in Canada, scholarly work on Mistry's fiction is the site of an ongoing discussion about postcolonial issues and Canadian identity politics, as well as trends in literary criticism and the government funding policies that support it.

Mistry was born into a Parsi family in Bombay in 1952. After receiving a degree in mathematics and economics from the University of Bombay, he emigrated to Canada, married and took a job in a Toronto bank. Ten years later he enrolled in a course of English and philosophy at the University of Toronto and began publishing short fiction. *'Swimming Lessons' and Other Stories from Firozsha Baag* appeared in 1987 and brought him national recognition in Canada. His first novel, *Such a Long Journey* (1991), extended his reputation internationally, winning the Canadian Governor General's Award for fiction and the Commonwealth Writers' Award for best book of the year, and receiving a nomination for the Booker Prize. It was adapted into a much-admired film directed by Canadian Sturla Gunnarsson with a screenplay by another Bombayite Parsi, Sooni Taraporevala.

A Fine Balance was published in 1995; it won the Giller Prize and the Commonwealth Writers' Prize as well as another Booker nomination, and was the first of only two Canadian novels ever to be selected for Oprah's Book Club. *Family Matters* (2002), is Mistry's most recent novel and again made the shortlist for the renamed Man Booker prize. *The Scream*, a short story, was released in 2009 as a special edition illustrated by Tony Urquart to benefit World Literacy of Canada. On the heels of his appearance on Oprah Winfrey's talk show in late 2001, Mistry was in the news for cancelling his US publicity tour for *Family Matters*, fed up with the racial profiling that thwarted his travels in the wake of September 11.[2] Otherwise he lives quietly in Brampton, north of Toronto, and grants few interviews.

The Parsi community of Mumbai is the setting for virtually all of Mistry's published work except for *A Fine Balance*, which encompasses a broader cross section of Indian society. The Parsis are a tiny minority in India, but particularly visible through their philanthropy and artistic accomplishment. Since the Zoroastrian Parsis arrived in Gujarat in the tenth century, they have taken pains to maintain their identity with distinctive religious practices, a refusal to accept converts and the excommunication of those who marry outside the faith. They came into their own during the colonial era, when opportunities arose to work with the British as bankers, traders and industrialists. Parsis have also been prominent in literature, theatre and film. With Indian independence in 1947 and the ensuing communal tensions, they have felt increasingly threatened, though not specifically targeted. This anxiety, along with ambition for educational and business opportunities, is responsible for the disproportionately large Parsi diaspora, particularly focused on other Commonwealth countries. The 2001 census counted 70,000 Parsis in India; it is predicted that by 2020 only 23,000 will be left.[3]

Mistry, along with Bapsi Sidhwa, Sooni Taraporevala and Dina Mehta, has introduced Parsi culture to English-speaking readers around the world. His first published work, *Firozsha Baag*, is a collection of short stories set in a Parsi apartment complex in South Bombay. The stories overlap and intertwine; a protagonist of one tale will show up as minor character in another. Most are written in the third person yet are inflected with the distinctive biases, blind spots and aspirations of their subjects, which are amplified or contradicted in later stories. Four of the stories – 'The Ghost of Firozsha Baag', 'Of White Hairs and Cricket', 'Lend Me Your Light' and 'Swimming Lessons' – are told in the first person. The latter three are narrated by young Kersi Boyce as he grows up in the apartment block and, at age 19, emigrates to Toronto. As his age and activities roughly parallel Mistry's own, it is tempting to see him as an alter ego, particularly since in 'Swimming Lessons' he emerges as a writer of short stories about Firozsha Baag.

Such a Long Journey (1991) is set in an apartment block much like Firozsha Baag in 1971. The focus here is on the family of bank worker Gustad Noble, his wife Dilnavaz and three children. His eldest son, Sohrab, has been accepted at the Indian Institute of Technology, a matter of great pride, but Sohrab tells his father that he wants to study literature instead. Gustad's disappointment stems partly from his own sense of social decline since the loss of his father's business during his childhood. When Sohrab moves out after a heated argument, Gustad must learn to let go. His loyalty and judgement are tested on another plane when Jimmy Bilimoria, an old friend who has vanished from his life, suddenly returns and asks him to deliver cash from his bank for an unexplained and perilous political intrigue. The novel juggles Gustad's family concerns with his commitment to friendship and moral responsibility.

Such a Long Journey launched Mistry's preoccupation with setting the personal problems of individuals and families against larger political conflicts that they do not understand, though they keenly feel the impact. Political crisis was the foundation for his next novel. At more than seven hundred pages, *A Fine Balance* is Mistry's longest work to date and the one with the broadest reach. Through its four main characters from diverse backgrounds living together in a tiny flat, the novel explores the personal tragedies resulting from the convergence of ageless social conflicts under Indira Gandhi's Emergency of 1975–77. These four are Dina, a Parsi widow running a small wholesale dress-making business out of her apartment; Ishvar and Omprakash, a low-caste uncle and nephew from a distant village who work for her as tailors; and Maneck, a student from Northern India whom Dina takes in as a boarder. Each endures a personal crisis exacerbated by the intrigues and mismanagement of Indira Gandhi's government and the individuals who enact her chaotic policies.

Again in *Family Matters* (2002), Mistry frames a family's interpersonal tensions within larger political and economic concerns. Nariman, an elderly professor with Parkinson's, is foisted off by his stepchildren into the far smaller apartment of his younger daughter Roxana, causing tensions in her marriage. Her husband Yezad in turn must confront a larger world in which his job and his life are threatened when his employer becomes involved with politics.

As a popular contemporary novelist, a South Asian and a diasporic Canadian, Mistry has been the subject of a broad range of interpretations in several monographs as well as numerous book chapters and articles. Critics and scholars have variously described him as a psychological realist, a satirist, a postcolonial subject and a representative of multicultural CanLit tropologies.

A large body of journalistic and scholarly writing concentrates on Mistry's psychological insights and social concerns in the tradition of the nineteenth-century European novel. John Updike in the *New Yorker* called him Tolstoyan. Pico Iyer in the *New York Review* likened him to Victor Hugo and Thomas Hardy. In the *London Review of Books*, Frank Kermode cited Dickens, Stendhal and Arnold Bennett. Mistry himself set an epigraph from Balzac at the start of *A Fine Balance*: 'Rest assured: this tragedy is not a fiction. All is true.' The book jacket of *A Fine Balance* called it '*the* India novel, the novel readers have been waiting for since E. M. Forster.'[4]

A notable exception to these accolades came from Australian feminist writer Germaine Greer. On BBC television in 1996 she said of *A Fine Balance*, which had just received the Commonwealth Writers' Prize and been shortlisted for the Booker: 'I absolutely hate it. ... I just don't recognize this dismal, dreary city. It's a Canadian book about India. What could be worse?'[5] One can only speculate about the sensitivities of a British Australian toward the vexed question of diasporic identity. At the same time, Indian critics have complained that Indian novelists who write in English, like Mistry, are privileged both internationally and 'at home' over writers who work in Indian languages.[6]

Popular reaction to Mistry's work in North America has focused on the verisimilitude and depth of his settings and characters, and his depiction of an unfamiliar culture. In an interview with Mistry on her talk show in 2002, Oprah Winfrey expressed an oddly narcissistic response to *A Fine Balance*, telling the panellists who had chosen the book as its first Canadian title: 'When I started reading this book, ... I felt a little bit of shame that I knew so little. Like September 11 for me, it just knocked me out of my little bubble of my life and put me in a whole other place.'[7]

Robert L. Ross of the University of Texas asks if Mistry's wide readership stems from curiosity about the Parsis, particularly their unusual funereal practices. He concludes that this cannot be the only reason, because Mistry is more popular than fellow Parsi novelist Bapsi Sidhwa. Can it then be that an 'exposé of political corruption and tyranny during Indira Gandhi's tenure still hold that much interest?' No, 'the tempest that is Indian politics [...] probably fails to intrigue most readers of Mistry's work.'[8] Ross concludes that Mistry reaches people because 'he transforms the historical situations and the reality of Indian life into a metaphor that shows how the individual reacts to widespread corruption [...] and how people respond to the endless forms of tyranny that government and society inflict.'[9] This 'academic' gloss seems as inflected by American cultural politics as that of Oprah and her audience. Several Indian scholars have elaborated on the dominant social realist reading of Mistry's work by concentrating on his depiction of contemporary Indian society. In a review of *Family Matters*, Karma Sawka writes:

> While the story of taking care of our aging and dying elders is a worldwide issue, the minutiae of this family's daily life is distinctly Indian. Bombay's train system, arranged marriages, unending corruption of government, religious discrimination, exploding pressure-cookers full of curry, Catholics vs. non-Catholics in a cricket match, pollution and jewel toned saris, extremists whose goal it is to abolish Valentine's day and attack Muslims, children escaping into an Enid Blyton book to fantasize about the sort of British that aren't even in England [...] the beauty and the agony of India act almost as another character in the story.[10]

Bindu Malieckal notes the sense of displacement and irrelevance felt by many of the Parsi characters in *Firozsha Baag* as a reflection of their uncertain status as a tiny minority in postcolonial India. Nilufer E. Bharucha, an authority on Mistry and a fellow Parsi, describes the Parsis as 'an assimilative people who have over the centuries perfected the difficult art of being both global and local at one and the same time – something the rest of the world is beginning to talk about only very recently.'[11] Yet Bharucha criticizes *A Fine Balance* as the least accurate of Mistry's novels because as a Parsi he does not truly understand the caste system.

Thus the perception of Mistry's work as realist predominates in both popular and scholarly writing, in both India and the West. Still, some contemporary critics work against the grain in their reading, finding moments of irony, self-reflexivity and farce as evidence that he is not working entirely within the realist aesthetic. They find influences of oral storytelling traditions as well as the colonial subaltern's appreciation of irony as a tool for political critique. Though no one has gone so far as to call Mistry a postmodernist, it is indeed possible to find moments of circular and interrupted narratives, self-reflexivity, satire and quotation in his work. One example is the self-referential joke mentioned earlier in reference to 'Swimming Lessons', the final story in *Tales from Firozsha Baag*. 'Swimming Lessons' is set mainly in Toronto and narrated in the first person by Mistry's alter ego Kersi Boyce, who has himself just written a collection of stories and sent them home to his parents. The parents' reaction on reading these stories is interspersed with the chronicle of Kersi's isolated life in a Toronto apartment building. From the conversation between mother and father, we learn that Kersi's stories are the very ones that we've been reading earlier in the book; their comments reflect Mistry's gentle mockery of his own critics, particularly those who wonder why he almost never writes about his adopted country:

> My hope is, Father said, that there will be some story based on his Canadian experience, that way we will know something about our son's life there, if not through his letters then in his stories; so far they are all about Parsis and Bombay, and the one with a little bit about Toronto, where the man perches on top of the toilet, is shameful and disgusting, although it is funny at times and did make me laugh, I have to admit, but where does he get such an imagination from, what is the point of such a fantasy [...].[12]

After Kersi's mother replies that his childhood in Bombay must be the most meaningful part of his life, Father says that, according to 'one theory I read somewhere, it may or may not be true [...] he is writing of these things because they are far enough in the past for him to deal with objectively, he is able to achieve what critics call artistic distance, without emotions interfering; and what do you mean emotions, said Mother, you are saying he does not feel anything for his characters, how can he write so beautifully about so many sad things without any feelings in his heart?'[13]

   Another notable aberration from the realist mode is the strange rhetorical outburst in 'Lend Me Your Light', again narrated by Kersi. Here he describes his experience of riding a commuter train in Bombay in the style of a sixteenth-century morality play:

> The drama began when the train, Reality, rolled into the station. It was overcrowded because everyone wanted to get on it: Virtue, Apathy, Corruption, all of them. Someone, probably Poverty, dropped his plastic lunch bag amidst the stampede, nudged on by Fate. Then Reality rolled out of the station with a gnashing and clanking of its metal, leaving in its wake the New Reality. And someone else, probably Hunger, matter-of-factly pick up Poverty's mangled lunch, dusted off a chapati which had slipped out of the trampled bag, and went his way.[14]

Mistry sometimes engages in over-the-top satire, particularly aimed at government bureaucracy or corruption. In another early short story, 'Squatter', the long-suffering Sarosh (who has renamed himself Sid in Canada) asks for help from the Canadian 'Multicultural Department' to solve his one remaining obstacle to complete acculturation: learning to sit instead of squatting on the toilet. He is offered a solar-powered artificial sphincter that can be sewn into his body and operated with a handheld transmitter, allowing him to evacuate at will: 'And you must understand what that means. You will never be able to live a normal life again. You will be permanently different from your family and friends because of this basic internal modification. In fact, in this country or that, it will set you apart from your fellow countrymen. So you must consider the whole thing most carefully.'[15]

These youthful experiments with style have diminished in Mistry's later writing. Still, his frequent use of irony remains, particularly in the bitter chronicles of the ravages of Indira Gandhi's Emergency in *A Fine Balance*. Describing the thoughts of a policeman while brutally conscripting beggars for a work camp, he writes:

> Never again would he deal with this fellow. Whining and whimpering non-stop, like a whipped dog. If it weren't a question of paying for his daughter's sitar lessons, he would chuck these overtime assignments without a second thought. Not only did he have to deal with scum like the Facilitator; the late nights also kept him from rising before dawn and putting in an hour of yoga as he used to. No wonder he was so short-tempered these days, he reflected. And suffering all this stomach acidity? But what choice? It was his duty to improve his child's marriage prospects.[16]

Irony, as Linda Hutcheon points out, is the weapon of the observer; it 'allows speakers to work within a dominant tradition but also to challenge it.'[17]

Peter Morey questions the common perception of *A Fine Balance* as realist. While admitting that the novel's dominant form is tragedy, he notes that it is also farcical in places, often mocking the self-serving machinations of those in power and the Kafkaesque contradictions of the Emergency itself. 'Indeed, the surface of the novel, characterized by the fine detail that brings the text to life, is everywhere marked by eruptions of the symbolic, the satirical, the allegorical and the carnivalesque: thereby indicating that Mistry is here developing a more stylized and syncretic way of representing the world than the conventional critical view, which sees him simply as a realist writer, would allow.'[18]

Morey goes on to argue that Mistry engages in a 'postcolonial subversion of power by pinpointing its excesses and absurdities' and continues this subversion in the very form of the narration, describing the Emergency as an arena 'where distinctions between performers and spectators have been obliterated and all participate in the carnivalistic life.'[19] He particularly notes the funeral procession of a mutilated beggar that slows traffic and eventually ingests not only a motley cross section of Indian society, but a sympathetic police escort as well. However, Morey neglects to note the similarity in ironic social critique to such nineteenth-century novels as Dickens's *Bleak House*, in which a lawsuit spanning generations spins out in an equally Kafkaesque style without a trace of 'postcolonial' context.

For many British and North American academics, *all* literature of the diaspora is post-colonial and therefore a literature of resistance. Homi Bhabha (another Bombay Parsi) describes diasporic writing as a projection of personal and cultural anxiety:

> As Freud writes, anxiety, like ontopology,[20] is an archaic, atavistic 'cathexis of longing … a defensive reaction to the felt loss (or displacement) of the object' […]. Anxiety keeps visible and present both the moment of birth as a trace and the displaced state and in that sense constitutes a transition where strangeness and contradiction cannot be negated and must be continually negotiated and worked through. Anxiety is a culture's longing for place and its borderline existence, its objectlessness that does not lack an objective, the mediatory moment between a culture's ontopology and its displacement, the tryst between the phantasm of rootedness and the memory of dissemination.[21]

Indeed this 'anxiety of displacement' does appear overtly in the short stories in *Firozsha Baag*, most noticeably in 'Squatter' and 'Swimming Lessons'. Canadian scholar Caroline Herbert draws on 'Radhakrishnan's notion of diasporic "double duty" – of accountability to, rather than irresponsible detachment from, the homeland […]. Mistry offers representations of migrants whose attempts to distance themselves from local and national politics are revealed as impossible and irresponsible […]. Mistry's representations reveal an anxiety over his position as a migrant writer, and his work seems to mobilize writing as a means of avoiding a problematically apolitical detachment from India.'[22]

Ajay Heble notes that Nariman, the narrator of 'Squatter', intends his story to be a moral lesson about staying true to one's roots; yet Nariman contradicts his own advice by introducing new English words to his young listeners, driving a Mercedes Benz, styling his moustache after Clark Gable and whistling the 'Colonel Bogey March' from *Bridge on the River Kwai*. For Heble, these details 'remind us that post-colonial identity is always already a hybridized formation […]. Rather than simply proceeding on the basis of an opposition between the new world (as a source of alienation) and the old world (as the only authentic source of values), Mistry interrogates the relationship between diverse cultural groups and dismantles traditional structures of authority which privilege an essential cultural purity.'[23]

The Parsi scholar Nilufer E. Barucha complains that 'Euro-Americans [in particular] tend to lump together all writers from former colonies […] and consider their discourse in the light of postcolonial theory'.[24] She finds this both reductive and particularly misleading in the case of Parsi writers, since colonialism actually raised the status of their community. The anxiety of the Parsi immigrant to England or Canada is arguably no greater than that of his cousin who stays behind fearing communal conflicts, the encroachment of polluting influences and rapid depopulation. The postcolonial model is challenged on another front by Laura Moss, who writes, 'If a text does not fit the profile of postcolonial resistance, as realist texts seldom do, it is generally considered incapable of subversion.'[25] She wryly notes that some critics are too focused on the subaltern prototype to acknowledge that Mistry's primary targets are not the legacy of the long-departed British, but the caste system and communal conflicts of indigenous India.

Canadian scholars of diasporic literature are in a double bind. Not only must they confront the bugaboo of postcolonial theory in relation to Mistry (and specifically, to Mistry as chronicler of Parsi culture), they must also come to terms with defining Canadian literature itself. Canada, itself a former colony, is a country of thirty-five million that did not repatriate its own constitution until 1982 and still considers the Queen of England to be its head of state; yet it lies contiguous to the US, which has ten times its population and incalculably greater influence on the world. Thus English Canadians suffer from the identity crisis of not knowing whether they are colonizers or colonized. Lacking significant resistance to the British domination of three centuries, Canada lacked the overweening 'promised land' mythology of the American 'melting pot'. The current nonwhite population in its three major cities, Toronto, Montreal and Vancouver, including significant South Asian representation, approaches a majority; the Canadian government has responded to this with a government policy supporting multiculturalism rather than assimilation. Nonwhite ethnicity is an advantage in the disbursement of arts council funding, with both a tacit undercurrent of affirmative action and special programs explicitly targeting artists of aboriginal and ethnically diverse origin. This wave laps against a shaky beachhead of white Canadian identity, which has always perceived itself as 'other' in relation to British colonialism, American cultural dominance and even its own inhospitable climate.

At the same time, literary scholarship has shifted from the formal and theoretical approaches of the '70s and '80s (in parallel with scholarship in film) to a more sociological approach, supported by the international interest in postcolonial critique. In Canada, the sociological trend in the humanities is accompanied (some would say driven) by changes in government-sponsored funding bodies. The Social Sciences and Humanities Research Council, the main granting body for academic studies of literature, has moved markedly toward a sociological approach in its funding patterns in the past decade. Smaro

Kamboureli notes that 'CanLit is marked by a precariousness suggestive, in part, of the nation-state's politics of remembering and forgetting, on the one hand, and the positivism with which Canadian literature has been supported and exported by government agencies, on the other […]. If the state posits Canada as an imagined community, CanLit is both firmly entangled with this national imaginary and capable of resisting it.'[26]

Given the ambiguous identity of both Canadian citizenry and CanLit, it is not surprising that these paradoxes and conflicts of interest are reflected in the Canadian writing about CanLit and Mistry's work in particular. Though Mistry has lived in Canada for almost forty years, he rarely writes from the immigrant's point of view. He refers to Canada (usually obliquely) as 'away', from the point of view of those who remain behind. Only his early short stories 'Squatter' and 'Swimming Lessons' deal substantively with questions of exile and alienation. The anomaly of a diasporic writer who barely addresses diasporic conflicts poses a dilemma in Canadian writing about his work.

Nevertheless, Canadian critical and scholarly writing about Mistry tends to focus on his place as a diasporic writer; consequently, his short stories receive disproportionate attention. References to Canada are teased out and analysed. Debate about Mistry's identity as a Canadian reflects a larger anxiety about what it means to be Canadian in the first place. Canadian critics have focused on issues of hybridity and displacement in the writing of Canada-born writers as well as immigrants, claiming that our unsettled sense of national identity makes us all the more susceptible to the questions of globalization that permeate all contemporary cultures. Mistry himself has said, 'I'm certainly more of a Canadian writer than an Indian writer, because I have no sense of being part of any group or school or generation of Indian writers. But that doesn't really interest me at all. All I try to do is tell a good story.'[27] Smaro Kamboureli writes, 'This elsewhereness inscribed in CanLit intimates that Canada is an unimaginable community, that is, a community constituted in excess of the knowledge of itself, always transitioning.'[28] She cites recent pressures on academics in the humanities in Canada to work on collaborative and interdisciplinary projects, to produce outcomes that have an immediate and obvious impact, to write government grant proposals structured like scientific inquiry, and to adopt 'the rhetoric of knowledge production, corporatization, and global citizenship'.[29] Moving critical studies into a social science framework naturally brings social context into dominance over aesthetic and formal analysis.

Ven Begamudre, another Indo-Canadian writer, quotes Alberto Manguel's observation that the exile has a double task: 'to procure for himself an image of the absent country that will allow him a constant point of reference, and to procure for others an image of that same country that will not lend itself to easy clichés and mere local color'.³⁰ Begamudre writes that Mistry has a special significance for him because 'without meaning to, he gave other writers of our generation permission: not to write about Canada yet be Canadian writers.'³¹

Although Mistry's fiction is obviously concerned with social issues, he forgoes engagement with the race-based identity politics of Canadian writers and artists such as Ashok Mathur, Monika Kin Gagnon and Richard Fung. Mathur notes that writers of colour have evolved since the 1980's from marginality to in dominance, almost seeming to 'to *represent* CanLit in many quarters.'³² At the same time, the literary publishing industry, influenced by the star-making machinery of big-box bookstores and book prizes, has become another corporate empire most interested in maximizing profits: 'To do this, the industry must manufacture not just a particular kind of taste, but a great equalizing taste. That is, the big titles it puts out have to be successful in the big-box stores, the academy and the media in order to move the number of units required to create maximum profits with minimum costs [...]. Certain writers must be pushed to the top, become household names by providing a particular sensibility to the reading public.'³³

Though Mistry rarely writes about Canada, his literary style fits easily into the still-dominant English Canadian realist tradition of Alice Munro, Carol Shields, Margaret Laurence and Margaret Atwood. As a writer whose work portrays a rich, unfamiliar world, is accessible to the general reader and refrains from anti-Western rhetoric, Mistry is a prime candidate for promotion. In anticipation of his appearance on *Oprah*, Vintage printed 700,000 copies of *A Fine Balance* and had sold 542,000 before the show even aired.³⁴

It seems that some interpreters are reaching to situate Mistry as a postcolonial, postmodernist writer, citing passages of carnivalesque excess, political satire and self-reflexivity to bolster the argument for stylistic innovation. Yet these devices are found equally in the nineteenth-century novels of Dickens, Austen and Flaubert. Despite the various uses to which Mistry's fiction has been put by academics, publishers and journalists, the foundation of his reputation and popularity remains his skill as a psychological realist and his ability to combine the personal narratives of ordinary people with the larger social and political struggles surrounding them. Mistry's work, based on the traditions of the psychological novel, can stand on its own among Western readers who are not seeking formal innovation so much as insight into character and society. They may find challenges in Mistry's relentless dissection of the misery brought on by political mismanagement, individual selfishness and physical limitation. Nevertheless, his depiction of humanistic values of family and individual morality still manage to reassure readers navigating a global culture of increasing uncertainty.

Notes and References

1. Rohinton Mistry, *'Swimming Lessons' and Other Stories from Firozsha Baag* (Toronto: McClelland & Stewart, 1987), 177–8.
2. 'Mistry cancels US tour over racial profiling', *Times of India*, 3 November 2002. Online: http://articles.timesofindia.indiatimes.com/2002-11-03/news-interviews/27294154_1_canadians-airports-publisher (accessed 5 January 2013).
3. Nilufer E. Bharucha, *Rohinton Mistry: Ethnic Enclosures and Transcultural Spaces* (Jaipur: Rawat Publications, 2003), 42.
4. Susan Fisher, 'Teaching Rohinton Mistry's *A Fine Balance*: Two Cheers for Universalism?', *Canadian Literature* 190 (Autumn 2006): 182.
5. Robert Ross, 'Seeking and Maintaining Balance: Rohinton Mistry's Fiction', *World Literature Today* 73 (1999): 240.
6. Peter Morey, *Rohinton Mistry* (Manchester University Press, 2004), 18.
7. Oprah's Book Club, '*A Fine Balance* discussion', 24 January 2002. Online: http://www.oprah.com/oprahsbookclub/A-Fine-Balance-Discussion-Highlights/1 (accessed 5 January 2013).
8. Ross, 'Seeking and Maintaining Balance: Rohinton Mistry's Fiction', *World Literature Today* 73 (1999): 239.
9. Ibid., 239–40.
10. Sawka, Karma, review of *Family Matters*, *Mostly Fiction Book Reviews*, 12 December 2002. Online: http://www.mostlyfiction.com/world/mistry.htm (accessed 15 December 2012).
11. Bharucha, *Rohinton Mistry*, 15.
12. Mistry, *Firozsha Baag*, 256.
13. Ibid.
14. Ibid., 195.
15. Ibid., 169.
16. Rohinton Mistry, *A Fine Balance* (Toronto: McClelland & Stewart, 1995), 377.
17. Linda Hutcheon, *Irony's Edge: Theory and Politics of Irony* (New York: Routledge, 1995), 9.
18. Morey, *Rohinton Mistry*, 98.
19. Ibid., 118–19.
20. Derrida's term for 'the specific conjuncture of identity, location and locution that most commonly defines the particularity of an ethnic culture', (Bhaba, 34).
21. Homi Bhabha, 'On the Irremovable Strangeness of Being Different', in 'Four Views on Ethnicity', *PMLA* 113, no. 1 (January 1998): 35.
22. Caroline Herbert, '"Dishonorably Postnational?" The Politics of Migrancy and Cosmopolitanism in Rohinton Mistry's A Fine Balance', *Journal of Commonwealth Literature* 43, no. 11 (2008): 11. Online: http://jcl.sagepub.com/content/43/2/11.full.pdf+html (accessed 16 December 2012).
23. Ajay Heble, 'A Foreign Presence in the Stall: Towards a Poetics of Cultural Hybridity in Rohinton Mistry's Migration Stories', *Canadian Literature* 137 (Summer 1993): 53.
24. Bharucha, *Rohinton Mistry*, 41.
25. Laura Moss, 'Can Rohinton Mistry's Realism Rescue the Novel?' in *Postcolonizing the Commonwealth: Studies in Literature and Culture*, ed. Rowland Smith (Waterloo: Wilfrid Laurier Press, 2000), 158.
26. Smaro Kamboureli, preface to Kamboureli and Roy Miki, eds, *Trans.Can.Lit: Resituating the Study of Canadian Literature* (Waterloo, ON: Wilfrid Laurier University Press, 2007), viii.

27 Stephen Smith, 'Rohinton Mistry: Back in Bombay', *Quill & Quire*, May 2002. Online: http://www.quillandquire.com/authors/profile.cfm?article_id=2369 (accessed 20 October 2010).
28 Kamboureli, *Trans.Can.Lit*, x.
29 Ibid., xi.
30 Ven Begamudre, 'Greetings from Bangalore, Saskatchewan', *Canadian Literature* 132 (Spring 1992): 9.
31 Ibid., 11.
32 Ashok Mathur, 'Transubracination: How Writers of Colour Became CanLit' in *Trans.Can.Lit: Resituating the Study of Canadian Literature*, 146.
33 Ibid., 149–50.
34 Smith, 'Rohinton Mistry: Back in Bombay'.

Chapter Twelve

AMITAV GHOSH: THE INDIAN ARCHITECT OF A POSTNATIONAL UTOPIA

Sajalkumar Bhattacharya

The history of Indian fiction in English goes back a long way in time. Even if we mark 1864 as the starting point of Indian fiction proper (the year of Chattopadhyay's *Rajmohan's Wife*), it is still, as a genre, almost one hundred and fifty years old. In her 'The Anxiety of Indianness', Meenakshi Mukherjee locates the various important milestones in this eventful journey, as well as the variety of challenges faced by its practitioners over the decades. The avowed aim of the first phase of these writers consisted of two definite strands. On the one hand, these writers had to engage themselves in the project of constructing national identity. This construction invariably depended on what Mukherjee describes as 'an erasure of differences within the border and accentuating the difference with what lies outside.'[1] To this effect, in all these novels, a homogenized Indian tradition was deliberately constructed and pitted against an equally unified imaginary West. The Indianness in these works of Indian fiction rested upon the binary between the East and the West. At the same time, this construction of Indianness, both in the early phase and in the phase of nationalism, was not without a sense of anxiety, which came with a constant awareness of just how different the 'alien reader' (to whom these novels were primarily addressed) was. Mukherjee discusses elaborately in her essay how in the early phase these novels had to indulge in elaborate explanatory asides or semantic or lexical shifts, or how the writers had to be constantly on guard to keep English readers in good humour, the implicit anxiety being to uphold the ordinary Indian soldier's loyalty to the Crown. With the rise of nationalism, we had another group of novelists, keen and anxious to consolidate its Indian roots in order to resist the colonial onslaught. This group was using the site of the Indian English novel to reaffirm its faith in nationalism.

The literary landscape changed remarkably in 1980s, when a new category of novelists arrived on the scene. Timothy Brennan, in *Salman Rushdie and the Third World* (1989), describes the group as that of 'Third World Cosmopolitans'. Salman Rushdie was, of course, the pioneer of this group. His *Midnight's Children* (1981) opened up a new era in Indian fiction in English, as it reconfigured the relationship between the individual and the nation. The most striking thing about these writers is that if they have successfully resisted any attempt on the part of their colonial masters to hegemonize their identity, they have equally resisted a similar attempt on the part of the nation to hold them as exclusively their own. The primary achievement of Rushdie and his colleagues has been to render the borders of the nation-state porous, and it is through these pores and fissures that their identity has spilled into a transnational world, an event facilitated by liberalization, which took over the world in the 1990s. Though they continue to be described as *Indian* writers in English (because of their preoccupation with Indian themes, Indian locales and postcolonial issues as well as because of their origin), they are undoubtedly products of cultural hybridity, which has proved, in their case, an advantage 'in negotiating the collisions of language, race and art in the world of disparate people comprising a single, if not united world.'[2] Hence they unmistakably belong to the world. The most successful of these writers include, apart from Rushdie, Bharati Mukherjee, Amitav Ghosh and Upamanyu Chatterjee, to name a few. Far from being victims of diasporic angst, they have found an answer to the *Unheimlichkeit* in a pragmatic acceptance of their transnational citizenship and their fluid identities. Indo-US writer Bharati Mukherjee celebrates this 'fluid identity' in the preface to *Darkness and Other Stories*: 'Instead of seeing my Indianness as a fragile identity to be preserved against obliteration […] I see it now as a set of fluid identities to be celebrated. […] Indianness is now a metaphor, a particular way of comprehending the world.'[3] Thus, to these writers, the transnational condition is essentially liberated from the throes of any restrictive 'shadow lines', as they have confidently secured citizenship of the world.

Amitav Ghosh is of course a classic example of this transnationalism. With eight popular novels already to his credit, he has, of late, ensured his name in the list of the most successful postcolonial Indian writers in English round the globe. One of the most significant voices in Indian literature during the last two decades, Ghosh was initiated to transnationalism at an early age, growing up 'globally' because of his father's transferable job at various locations round the world. Born in Kolkata on 11 July 1956, Ghosh grew up in East Pakistan (Bangladesh), Sri Lanka, Iran and India. His father was a lieutenant colonel who later became a diplomat, working across the borders. Belonging to the privileged upper class, Ghosh had his education in the elite educational institutions in India. After passing out from Doon School in Dehra Dun, he pursued a BA honours course in history at St Stephen's College, Delhi University. Thereafter, he did his MA in sociology from the same university in 1978. In 1982, he received a DPhil in social anthropology from Oxford University (St Edmund's Hall). As part of the research, he spent a considerable time in Egypt doing fieldwork in the village of Lataifa. Ghosh's transnational identity was further consolidated in his professional life. After working for a brief period as a journalist for the *Indian Express*, New Delhi, he entered the teaching profession. He had been a visiting fellow at the Centre for Social Sciences, Trivandrum (1982–83), a visiting professor of anthropology at the University of Virginia (1988), the University of Pennsylvania (1989), the American University in Cairo (1994) and Columbia University (1994–97), and assumed the chair of distinguished professor of comparative literature at Queens College of the City University of New York (1999–2003). Finally, he became the visiting professor in the Department of English at Harvard University. In 2005, however, he left all these jobs in order to concentrate exclusively on literary activities. Thus, while 'place' and 'time' have been equally fluid concepts right from his childhood, his love for anthropology has engaged him in looking at human history as an ongoing, multifaceted project. This love for and specialized training in the subject have been prominent factors in the grooming of Ghosh as a novelist. He is by turn a sociologist, a historian, a teacher, a travel writer, an essayist alive to a range of crucial contemporary issues from terrorism to conservation of nature and can slip in and out of these categories with remarkable aplomb. But behind all these, it is Ghosh the anthropologist that has decisively shaped his focus as a novelist and has engaged him in the task of putting the individual back in the centre of the narrative even while not negating similar attempts of other individuals. In an interview with John C. Hawley in 2004, he categorically reflects, 'My fundamental interest is in people – in individuals and their specific predicaments. If history is of interest to me it is because it provides instances of unusual and extraordinary predicaments.'[4]

Particularly concerned with the South Asian diaspora in the different regions of the world, Ghosh has, therefore, set himself in the task of narrating an anti-Hegelian history of the world incorporating the hitherto left-out narratives of the common individual, the predicament of individuals against the historical backdrop, their attempt to resist the hegemony of the nation through their own stories and their search for their own identity. In his essay 'The Ghosts of Mrs Gandhi', Ghosh observes, 'It is when we think of the world the aesthetic of indifference might bring into being that *we recognize the urgency of remembering the stories we have not written.*'[5] This was in 1995, and in a recent interview with me, Ghosh seems to reiterate the importance of the individual over the nation's history with equal emphasis: 'The same history does not create the same individual, and that is what is interesting about it. History remains at the background, but a hundred different individuals exist living the history in their own ways. An artist aims to bring these different stories to the fore.'[6] The observation unmistakably points to an anthropologist's dedication to 'remembering' stories that otherwise slip from consciousness and from recorded history. Clearly, it is the act of remembering and unravelling existing macronarratives and understanding the ways in which they trap individuals into roles, and the rejection of such roles and such metanarratives while constructing one's own narrative, role and significance that have been Ghosh's prime concern as a novelist of the postcolonial period. Right from *The Circle of Reason* (1986) until *River of Smoke* (2011), most of which are essentially family sagas, Ghosh has primarily remained engaged in the exploration of this issue. And in doing this, he has constantly foregrounded the dubious nature of borders dividing nations and peoples.

'Ghosh's work [...] underlines the novelist's interest in traveling as a metaphor for the human condition' says James Clifford.[7] Ghosh's characters travel ceaselessly, wilfully or under compulsion. Most of his novels are all accounts of human journey, figurative and literal, and most of these journeys are on bodies of water, itself an interesting trope regarding the fluidity of borders. This gives Ghosh the scope to explore the issues of dislocation, migration and cultural cross mingling from a very positive angle. Robin Cohen, in his book *Global Diasporas: An Introduction* (1997), represents the contemporary global migration in quite favourable terms. He iterates that globalization today has been more of a boon than a curse for the diaspora because of its liberating and ameliorative aspects. One advantage of the diasporic migration that Cohen celebrates is the multiple affiliations and associations that globalization offers to compensate for the angst of deterritorialized social identities. It is this ability of transnational adaptation that leads people of the world to break their barriers and enthusiastically participate in the project of fashioning their lives in creative and unorthodox ways, resulting in the creation of new families. Refused an active role in the macronarrative of the nation, they live their micronarrative lives most vibrantly in these newly created family bonds. Denied any political or economic subjecthood, the familial space is their only domain to shape the identity. This is also the case in Ghosh's fictional world, where he notes with wonder how people never refrain from weaving new patterns of life through the creation of new families across time and continents.

Paul Sharrad, in his essay 'Fabricating Community: Local, National and Global in Three Indian Novels', observes that the national and the global are intersecting spaces, just as they are also in opposition. So, Sharrad concludes unequivocally, 'we have to continue to think with, through and beyond the national without simply subscribing to an anti-national hostility or "end of history" post-national globalised triumphalism.'[8] In fact, Ghosh, too, never rules out the validity of the existence of the nation, though he has constantly made us aware of the potential threats in its official maps and borders. In his interview to me in 2009, Ghosh categorically states that he is not against the nation as an institution, nor does he think that the institution will soon suddenly wither. But one of the important achievements of Ghosh as a postcolonial writer has been to draw our attention to the porosity of the nation's borders and the transnational reterritorialization of the diaspora that makes this intersection of the national and global a resourceful space. As home becomes multiple, identity becomes more and more ambiguous, rich and complex. In this connection, Ghosh's unambiguous views on borders are noteworthy. When asked to reflect on his engagement with borders, literal and metaphorical, in his novels and essays, he responds, 'What interested me first about borders was their arbitrariness, their constructedness – the ways in which they are "naturalised" by modern political myth-making. I think this interest arose because of some kind of inborn distrust of anything that appears to be "given" or taken-for-granted.'[9]

It is this stand that sets Ghosh apart as the most important voice in the postliberalization era, and it is the facilitation of a transborder relation that has been Ghosh's engagement throughout his literary career to date. However, it is in his second novel, *The Shadow Lines* (1988), that Ghosh focuses exclusively on the nature of the national border – a typical postcolonial issue that has been claiming his attention more and more ever since. As the macronarrative of the nation is increasingly threatened by the micronarrative of the individual hitherto neglected, the failure of the nation as a restrictive space and its porosity are becoming evident. To explore this porosity and to fill up the fissures that characterize these national histories of South Asia, Ghosh takes up the task of retrieving alternate family histories that would fill up these fissures and face the deep-seated traumas.

The Shadow Lines is essentially a memory novel that weaves together personal lives and public events in India, England and Bangladesh, along with the members of three generations of two families. Some remarkable international events like World War II and the Partition of India and East Pakistan, and a mix of interesting coincidences, create an overlap in the stories, constituting the larger plot. Finally, we are introduced to a great cross-cultural bonding and a new transnational family emerging out of it. On the one hand, one large family, consisting of members with intimate blood relations, breaks up into two distinct units under the traumatic pressure of a political event that engages itself in the dangerous game of imagining borders where there were none; on the other, two families, separated not only by thousands of miles across the globe, but also by language, religion, customs and culture, become so close to each other that ultimately the lines demarcating them reduce to the point of becoming nonexistent. They become 'shadow lines', eventually problematizing the concepts of nation, family and borders. The novel thus narrows down what is going to be Ghosh's concern for the next few years: the power of the imaginative quality and futility of geopolitical borders, the struggle between the official history and the lived story and the role of the familial space in this struggle. Ultimately, we come to understand that the Bartholomew's atlas is no more a dependable guide to the world because 'the solid lines', to quote Meenakshi Mukherjee, 'dividing countries turn into glass, through which it is clearly visible that Chiang Mai in Thailand is spatially closer to Calcutta than New Delhi, Chengdu in China is nearer than Srinagar is.'[10]

Ghosh's project in *The Shadow Lines*, therefore, is to create a postnational utopia that thrives on the mysterious pull across borders. Ghosh explores this mysterious pull between individuals and families who engage themselves in significant, redemptive humane relationships. The empathy that develops between Tresawsen and Mayadevi, Tridib and May, the narrator and May, Jethamoshai and Khalil help them transcend the partitions created by war, communal violence and racism. The importance of this transnational empathy projected by Ghosh can hardly be overestimated in today's world, the integrity of which is constantly being threatened by disruptive and divisive forces. As Murari Prasad observes, 'Ghosh [...] passionately searches for strategies for survival in a violent, hate-filled world of narrow divisions and finds in love the enabling and productive action to tide over separatist propensities of communities and nationality groups.'[11] Thus, *The Shadow Lines* travels a long way from the totalizing narrative of homogenized community as discernible in Raja Rao's *Kanthapura* (1938). Standing in the vortex of violence and murderous rampage, Ghosh reiterates the necessity of the mental creation of transnational family, an effective site for the sustenance of human relationships irrespective of borders. By focusing on a Fanonian 'occult zone where the people live', Ghosh has not only used this novel as an eloquent critique of the colonial hangover and cultural dislocation in the postcolonial era, but also found a satisfactory answer to the postcolonial diasporic angst. And it is precisely this that has made Ghosh's relevance global and his appeal eternal.

In *The Glass Palace* (2002), Ghosh's focus on the mobile contours of home continues. It is primarily the story of an orphan with Herculean tenacity and endurance, by virtue of which he forsakes the past, heals the pain of dislocation and adapts to various homes transnationally. Rajkumar is a true multicultural. He is a reinvented migrant and his story is another of Ghosh's examples of how to address the problem of settling and resettling communities and individuals amidst the confluence of nations and nationalities, who are able to gather in the half-light of foreign tongues 'the signs of approval and acceptance'.[12] While barriers and boundaries seem to define the psyches that attend the making of nations and nationalities in *The Glass Palace*, the author collapses these margins and presents a set of characters who are 'at home' everywhere. In the postcolonial condition, which is primarily defined by an experience of loss and a sense of displacement, it is this ability to relocate to new spaces and adapt to these spaces that gives an edge to Ghosh's characters. They belong to a new group of people unfettered by the burden of 'otherness', and wonderfully blessed with a diasporic hope, equipping them with a rare strength to fight diasporic anxiety.

The remarkable feat that Ghosh seems to achieve in *The Glass Palace* is his jugglery with so many margins, nations and nationalities, and ultimately to collapse all these differences in one home. His position has been neatly summed up by Meenakshi Mukherjee in her essay 'The Anxiety of Indianness', where she has suggested that for Ghosh, 'words like "marginality" and "hybridity" seem irrelevant […] and segmenting the worlds into first and third regions [is] a rather absurd activity.'[13] As a postcolonial novelist, Ghosh has earned for his fictional characters a freedom from the throes of the nation. Rakhee Moral's observation at the end of her essay '*The Glass Palace* as Postcolonial Narrative' is worth noting: 'The postcolonial (in Ghosh's world) is by virtue of this displaced and mobile location then, freed of gender, class and political affiliations as he moves unhindered and unrestricted in his peregrinations across the vast spaces of the worlds and cultures he understands and internalizes.'[14] Ghosh is, therefore, a postcolonial and then a postnational, whose unmistakable focus is on the transnational identity that is forged across all spatial and temporal borders.

However, in *The Shadow Lines*, speaking from a middle-class, educated, metropolitan, privileged background, Ghosh can address only a limited class in the society – a small percentage of educated, English-speaking Indians. Vinita Chandra accuses him, in her essay 'Suppressed Memory and Forgetting: History and Nationalism in *The Shadow Lines*', of his inability to represent any other class in the novel. Ghosh presents different versions of freedom and its importance in the construction of identity through almost all the major characters in the novel – Thamma, Robi, Ila, Tridib and the narrator – but all these versions emanate from the same privileged class position. Chandra points to this limitation in Ghosh: 'The discourse of freedom in the novel is thus restricted within this parameter of privilege which applies to a very small, albeit powerful, percentage of population, and is therefore not able to represent the full import of this issue to the construction of a national identity.'[15]

Ghosh overcomes this most successfully in *The Hungry Tide* (2004). The novel denotes a distinct shift in Ghosh's focus. From his preoccupation with the exploration of the arbitrary and vexing nature of national borders in his earlier novels, he now turns to the personal divisions between individual human beings. Locating the theme of his novel in the remote Sundarbans, Ghosh engages himself in finding the possible clues to the effective communication between two almost antonymous groups of the so-called elitist bourgeois characters and the traumatized, mostly illiterate, marginalized characters inhabiting the region. Finally he resolves this in an ethical vision where he finds this communication possible through the civic opportunities created by the agency of the cosmopolitan individual.[16]

Let us consider the example of Kanai. Kanai is an economically successful man. And commensurate with his achievements is the insularity of the privileged city dweller. His smugness is, after all, paradigmatic of the self-satisfied, self-important, well-educated bourgeois citizen. As his aunt Nilima observes, 'Things have come very easily to [Kanai] so he doesn't know what the world is like for most people.'[17] But placed in a locale where all boundaries are only tentative, Kanai's experiences and meetings with the 'other' begin to work a transformation in him. This initiates in him an examination of the self, the condition that makes Ghosh's ethics possible. We see this process at work in Kanai's denigration of Fokir, a low-caste fisherman. Kanai's abuse stems from his need to assert his class inflected authority and reconstitute his social and cultural norms. When he insults Fokir, Kanai becomes conscious of how entrenched his class and cultural convictions are within him. It is through this experience that his cosmopolitan vision arises, replete with glaring moral truths. He not only grasps the structures of violence and oppression operating within the dominant social order, but in his epiphany Kanai sees the decentring of his identity and values, and the extent of his false bourgeois consciousness. This is replaced with an emancipatory, though humbling, consciousness. Kanai confides to Piya that he is a changed man, in awe of the 'shocking novelty' of the emotions he feels. Such profound feeling inculcates an alternative mode of knowledge, a humanist awakening inherent in Kanai's concluding remarks: 'At Garjontola I learnt how little I know of myself and of the world.'[18]

The novel concludes with a vision of a new cosmopolitan activity. Kanai is publishing Nirmal's notebook, with the aim of reaching international communities of readers and scholars. At the same time, Piya is collaborating with Nilima, a union between the global and the local that promises to empower the subaltern inhabitants of the tide country through Piya's international contacts. As readers, we are urged into thinking towards the possibility of social and political transformation in real life (not only in fiction) through the creation of familial bonds. In the author's note attached at the end, Ghosh refers to the real life counterparts of Nirmal and Nilima: Sri Tushar Kanjilal and Shrimati Bina Kanjilal. He refers to their voluntary activities at Rangabalia (Sundarbans) and speaks very highly of how their efforts have brought about positive changes in the area.

There is, again, a big leap from the intimate, smaller space to the vast, transnational world in *Sea of Poppies* (2008). In this first part of a trilogy conceived on a vast compass of time and space, Ghosh deals with the problems and politics of the diasporic movement in history in such minute detail as has not been attempted earlier. In the process, the *Ibis* becomes a site of new community formation; that is, communities composed of lives unfixed from their cultural moorings.

Paul Gilroy, in his influential work *The Black Atlantic: Modernity and Double Consciousness* (1993), uses the image of the ship to symbolize the formation of new communities among black people located in and moving between Africa, the Caribbean, America and Britain. This ship, according to Gilroy, is 'a living, micro-cultural, micro-political system in motion' that bears witness to the black oppression but, more importantly, the possibility of mingling diverse ideas and cultural practices en route.[19] For Gilroy, these transnational routes provide a better way of thinking about black identities in the present than notions of roots and rootedness. The *Ibis* in *Sea of Poppies* is exactly such a ship, where all cultural, economic and racial borders are rendered porous, giving birth to a new hybridity. In this novel, Ghosh brings together a motley crew of sailors, convicts, migrants and even lovers gathered from as varied corners of the world as one can think of – from the interiors of Bihar and Bengal and other parts of Asia, and even England and the United States – all of whose lives have been intricately linked with opium politics. We have Neelratan, the educated polished Zamindar of Rashkhali estate; Ah Fatt, an opium addict and a convict of Parsi and Chinese descent; Zachary and Paulette, representatives of a class of mixed origin; Sarang Ali, a pirate; and finally the girmitiyas, all put together on the *Ibis*, turning it to a floating cauldron of different histories, geographies, language and culture. As the novel unfolds itself, it merges all the stories of individual pain and suffering into a narrative of hope and movement towards the future.

What, then, is the source of this new energy? It is an indomitable spirit to struggle for life. In the face of new threats, all the characters from different economic statuses, races, cultures and castes, huddle together in a new emotional space where coresidence, rather than blood, determines the family. A new home is possible not out of a sense of loss, but of the ability to transform all hostile conditions of life into a source of positive energy. And even this is not the ultimate conclusion. At the end, Ghosh has only promised us a new beginning with a further mingling of varied cultures; we find four characters embarking on a new life, taking the hybridity formed on the *Ibis* into further motion. And most suggestively, they do not even have their small *putlies* this time. *River of Smoke* (2011), which has already been received by the reading world with great enthusiasm, quite expectedly expands on the theme of border crossing. While in this second part of the trilogy Ghosh has remarkably engaged literature in the task of focusing new light on the history of human civilization, the narrative unmistakably records the eternal human instinct to ignore all boundaries and forge bonds across them. The mystery of lived human experience in Ghosh has, thus, always transcended the artificial borders of nation and race.

The basis of Ghosh's transnationalism has been to use fiction as the melting pot of the local and the global, the immediate and the universal. As a result, Ghosh can reach out to a large readership of varied tastes and cultures – university students to amateur readers, historians and anthropologists from Egypt to Japan and USA to Australia – and all this without diluting the unmistakable Indian flavour of each of his novels. The most interesting thing in this regard is Ghosh's use of varied locales. His novels are anchored to Indian suburbs as well as American airports, Egyptian villages to Burmese palaces, and like their globetrotting creator the characters in his novels travel untiringly from one location to another, shrinking the global world to a global village. Even in *The Hungry Tide*, where the local is restricted to a remote, rural area of the Sundarbans, one can hardly miss the universal issues and eternal note that concerns Ghosh.

The literary world has eagerly acknowledged Ghosh's contribution. Almost every fictional work by Ghosh has received one award or another: the Prix Medicis Etranger in France for *The Circle of Reason*, the Sahitya Akademi Award and the Ananda Puroskar for *The Shadow Lines*, the Arthur C. Clarke Award for *The Calcutta Chromosome*, the Grand Prize for fiction at the Frankfurt International e-Book Awards for *The Glass Palace* and the Hutch Crossword Book Prize for *The Hungry Tide*. The Dan David Prize that Amitav received recently is the latest recognition of his universal appeal. The $1 million award endowed by the Dan David foundation is awarded annually in three different fields – archaeology, performing arts and material science – in the three-dimensional framework of past, present and future. But this issue of awards itself is not wholly without complications. In the first place, popularity and works are so intricately related to each other that it is almost impossible now to say which precedes the other. Admittedly, in Ghosh's case, his location in New York and proximity to its academic/intellectual circuit (he had been a professor there for quite some time) has surely placed him in an advantageous position. But interestingly, at least once, Ghosh received equally large publicity in refusing to be considered for a prestigious award. Ghosh's refusal to be considered for the Commonwealth Writers' Prize in 2001 is now a well-known story. Ghosh withdrew from the competition, objecting to the classification of his novel (*The Glass Palace*) under the rubric of Commonwealth literature for, as he pointed out, the idea of categorizing the Commonwealth and its literature as such represented a certain reading of the past and the present he held as being contrary to the spirit in which the book was written.

But awards are not all. Ghosh's multiple home addresses have been an important factor for various other reasons.[20] In the first place, that Ghosh shares his time between New York and India (Goa and Kolkata) has given him an easy access between two different cultures, ambience and readership. This has, in its turn, lent strength of first-hand experience to Ghosh's narrative – he is sure of what he is writing. Secondly, one can hardly deny that his location in America (and his marriage to an American) has undoubtedly placed him ahead of many of his colleagues located (and rooted) in India exclusively, for he is never treated an outsider or an 'other' there. After being there over the years as a professor and a writer, he has of course been adopted there. Interestingly again, he also is rooted in the Bengal ethos, resorting to pure *Bangaliyana* whenever he is here, conversing in unadulterated Bangla with university students or intellectuals over cups of tea. This was my own experience when I interviewed him formally at the Tolly Club in 2009 or when I talked to him informally at Jadavpur University or in my own department at Ramakrishna Mission Residential College, Kolkata, where I had invited him to deliver the first Alumni Annual Lecture. On all those occasions or even at his home at Jodhpur Park, Kolkata, he comes across as a true-blue *Bangalee Bhadrolok*, amiable and reassuring, polished, yet never snobbish.

It is equally important to note in this connection that Ghosh maintains a close relationship with Ananda Publishers, the leading publishing house in Bengal, and with the eminent poet and former president of Sahitya Akademi, Sri Sunil Gangopadhyay. All these, of course, have given him an immense popularity, so much so that in recent years there has been a craze for him even within the readers who cannot overcome the language barrier in his novels. This explains why Ghosh has taken personal interest in the translation of *The Hungry Tide*.

Coming to the celebrated 'Ghoshean flavour', readers of Ghosh will recognize that the writer has a unique brand of language, a postcolonial variant, interpolating Bangla, Bhojpuri and Hindi words in his prose. An example from *Sea of Poppies* would not be out of place:

'Because, my dear', said Mrs Burnham with a good-natured laugh, 'he is most greatly impressed by your simple manners and your modesty. You have quite won his heart. Can you imagine, dear, what a prodigious stroke of *kismet* it will be for you to bag Mr Kendalbushe? He's a *nabob* in his own right – made a mountain of *mohurs* out of the China trade. Ever since he lost his wife every *larkin* in town's been trying to *bundo* him. I can tell you, dear, there's a *paltan* of *mems* who'd give their last *anna* to be in your *jooties*.[21]

This may be postcolonial defiance, but at the same time it is surely a next-gen language, making him more and more readable. A host of writers in India and elsewhere in South Asia have adopted this language and are using it with remarkable success – Chetan Bhagat (India) and Ali Sethi (Pakistan) are ready examples – but Ghosh has been one of the major trendsetters. Readers of this anthology need not be reminded that Rushdie, who opened up a new chapter in the history of Indian English fiction, has been severely criticized by a host of critics enquiring critically into his popularity in the West. All these critics commonly point out that Rushdie's fiction is popular in the West because it satisfies a Western commercial appetite for the exotic. Aparna Mahanta, in 'Allegories of the Indian Experience: The Novels of Salman Rushdie', rather cynically observes that his *Midnight's Children* was only the latest in a whole series of fictions catering to the Western desire to see India as a strange, sensual, fantastical land of 'others'.[22] Aijaz Ahmed similarly ascribes Rushdie's success to his privileged class position and his preference for postmodernist narrative forms authorized by the Anglo-American academe.[23] What these critics (and many others) say about Rushdie applies to a large group of post-Rushdie novelists. With all their rhetoric of India, their anxiety of being accommodated and appreciated in the West has invariably chained them up to a restrictive, predictable discourse. In a broad way, Ghosh is no exception. It would only be fair to remember in this context that transnationalism, as a project, has exposed in very recent years its flipside as well: the consequent boom in information technology, the revolution in global communication and the opening up of economic relations have, ironically, also facilitated the neocolonial tendency among the developed nations. Liberalization of the market since the '90s has encouraged the First World nations to aggressively grab these opportunities to consolidate economic power over the Third World market. With the lure of immediate commercial gain in the market ruthlessly shaping everything in the world, including even its literary activities, the concept of universal brotherhood seems at times to be acquiring only a mythical status. In such a situation as this, Ghosh, along with his colleagues in the field of Indian writing in English, can only be expected to take advantage and exploit 'local' India to capture the 'global' market. India sells, and the elite, immigrant status of Ghosh, his strong bonhomie with the American and Indian upper-class intelligentsia have been great opportunities for him, because it has readily sanctioned him the authority, as it were, to represent (or sell?) India to a global readership.

But then, what else could Ghosh (and his colleagues) have done? Transnationalism, with all its good and bad effects, is still the fate of the twenty-first-century world – in politics, economics and literature. One can hardly avoid being caught up in its vortex. And if one accepts its blessings, one must chew its evils too. Ghosh, too, can hardly ignore the demands of the market. Rather, by participating in the market actively with his project of transnational utopia, he has certainly succeeded in resisting the intended disenfranchisement of the East by the West.

Makarand Paranjape, in the introduction to *In Diaspora: Theories, Histories Texts* (2001), predicts that very shortly 'we might actually be witnessing the birth of a new global Indian identity' that will 'play an increasingly active role in world affairs'.[24] Leela Gandhi, too, in *Postcolonial Theory: A Critical introduction* (1998), focuses on the new needs of the age when she speaks of how 'the old story of clash and confrontation is (now) retold with an eye to the transactive/ transcultural aspect of colonialism'. She recommends a 'utopian manifesto for a postcolonial ethic, devoted to the task of imagining an inter-civilisational alliance against instutionalised suffering and oppression'.[25] Amitav Ghosh has so far successfully engaged himself in this task, establishing himself as a chronicler of global concerns. The worldview that he has repeatedly tried to visualize to his readers is of course utopian, but the dream of utopia can be the only succour he can offer, as a responsible chronicler of his times, to the otherwise fractured, dystopian world of the present. As Bill Ashcroft says, 'We live in an age in which hope is ever more necessary to social existence. Utopia is by definition impossible, an unachievable ideal, a fanciful dream, unrealistic and naïve. Yet utopian theory has undergone a vigorous renaissance during the post–cold war period of global empire. The concept of the utopian remains a conceptual anchor to any theory of a better world, any hope for social change and amenity. So I am determined to continue to talk about Utopia.'[26]

Meenakshi Mukherjee's 'Anxiety of Indianness' suggested that the achievement of a writer like Ghosh lies with his freedom from this anxiety about his identity. More than a decade after Mukherjee's *The Perishable Empire* (2000), her prediction about Ghosh has been conclusively proven true: the empire has perished. Who knows, the nation may also perish some day, but I guess Ghosh's project of postnational utopia will be timeless and imperishable.

Notes and References

1 Meenakshi Mukherjee, *The Perishable Empire* (New Delhi: Oxford University Press, 2000), 174.
2 Timothy Brennan, *Salman Rushdie and the Third World: Myths of the Nation* (New York: St Martin's Press, 1989), 35.
3 Bharati Mukherjee, preface to *Darkness and Other Stories* (Harmondsworth: Penguin, 1995), n.p.
4 John Hawley, *Amitav Ghosh: An Introduction* (New Delhi: Foundation Books, 2005), 4.

5 Amitav Ghosh, 'The Ghosts of Mrs. Gandhi', in *The Imam and the Indian* (New Delhi: Ravi Dayal, 2002), 62 [emphasis mine].
6 Amitav Ghosh, unpublished interview with Sajal Bhattacharya, Kolkata: Tolly Club, 12 March 2009.
7 James Clifford, 'The Transit Lounge of Culture', *Times Literary Supplement*, 3 May 1991, 7–8.
8 Paul Sharrad, 'Fabricating Community: Local, National and Global in Three Indian Novels', in *Nation in Imagination: Essays on Nationalism, Sub-Nationalism and Narration*, ed. C. Vijayashree, M. Mukherjee, H. Trivedi and T. Kumar (Hyderabad: Orient Longman, 2007), 226.
9 Amitav Ghosh, in Hawley, *Amitav Ghosh: An Introduction*, 9.
10 Mukherjee, *The Perishable Empire*, 267.
11 Murari Prasad, '*The Shadow Lines*: A Quest for "Indivisible Sanity"', in *The Novels of Amitav Ghosh*, ed. R. K. Dhawan (London: Sangam Books, 1999), 91.
12 Homi Bhabha, *The Location of Culture* (London: Routledge, 1994), 139.
13 Mukherjee, *The Perishable Empire*, 185.
14 Rakhee Moral, 'In Time of the Breaking of Nations: *The Glass Palace* as Postcolonial Narrative', in *Amitav Ghosh: Critical Perspectives*, ed. Brinda Bose (New Delhi: Pen Craft International, 2003), 151.
15 Vinita Chandra, 'Suppressed Memory and Forgetting: History and Nationalism in *The Shadow Lines*', in *Amitav Ghosh: Critical Perspectives*, ed. Brinda Bose (New Delhi: Pen Craft International, 2003), 74.
16 Amanda Anderson defines a cosmopolitan as one who operates at a 'reflective distance from [his] original and cultural affiliations, [and possesses] a broad understanding of other cultures and customs and a belief in universal humanity'. See, Amanda Anderson, *The Powers of Distance: Cosmopolitanism and the Cultivation of Detachment* (Princeton: Princeton University Press, 2001), 63. Taking a cue from this, Terri Tomsky, in his essay 'Amitav Ghosh's Anxious Witnessing and the Ethics of Action in *The Hungry Tide*', describes these characters as cosmopolitans. *Journal of Commonwealth Literature* 44, no. 1 (2009): 53–65.
17 Amitav Ghosh, *The Hungry Tide* (New Delhi: HarperCollins, 2005), 208.
18 Ibid., 353.
19 Paul Gilroy, *The Black Atlantic: Modernity and Double Consciousness* (London: Verso, 1993), 4.
20 In his infamous and provocatively titled essay 'Damme, This is the Oriental Scene for You' in the Special Fiction Issue of the *New Yorker* (23 June 1997, 50) marking 50 years of postcolonial Indian writing, Rushdie remarked that 'literature has little or nothing to do with a writers' home address'. But Ghosh definitely proves otherwise.
21 Amitav Ghosh, *Sea of Poppies* (New Delhi: Penguin, 2008), 273 [emphasis mine].
22 Aparna Mahanta, 'Allegories of the Indian Experience: The Novels of Salman Rushdie', *Economic and Political Weekly* 19, no. 6 (1984): 244.
23 Aijaz Ahmad, *In Theory: Classes, Nations, Literatures* (London: Verso 1992), 67–71.
24 Makarand Paranjape, ed, *In Diaspora: Theories, Histories, Texts* (New Delhi: Indialog Publications, 2001), vi.
25 Leela Gandhi, *Postcolonial Theory: A Critical Introduction* (New Delhi: Oxford University Press, 1998), 125.
26 Debasish Lahiri, 'Of New Centers and Old Margins: The Limits of the Postcolonial', in *Anxieties, Influences and After: Critical Responses to Postcolonialism and Neocolonialism*, ed. Kaustav Bakshi, Samrat Sengupta, Subhadeep Paul (New Delhi: Worldview Publications, 2009), 404.

Chapter Thirteen

HERE, THERE AND EVERYWHERE: VIKRAM SETH'S MULTIPLE LITERARY CONSTITUENCIES

Mala Pandurang

Vikram Seth is unique among contemporary Indian writers in English in that he has successfully defied the attempts of academicians to fix his body of work within a singular category of literary production. An Indian by birth, Seth has experienced a considerable degree of global migrancy in the course of his literary career, spanning three decades. He has lived in three continents and has written in a variety of genres. The first part of this paper offers a literary biographical overview to correlate Seth's mobility to the creative milieu of his work and reception therein. Seth, for instance, moves with ease from San Francisco 'yuppiedom' in *The Golden Gate* (1986) to medieval Chinese poetry in *Three Chinese Poets* (1992), and from the Hindi belt in immediate postindependence North India in *A Suitable Boy* (1993) to the world of classical music of Bach and Beethoven in Britain, Italy and Austria in *An Equal Music* (1999). *Two Lives* (2005) encompasses the geographical and temporal span of pre–World War II Germany and postwar Britain.

    Critics are unanimous about Seth's mastery over his craft, in both prose and verse. There are, however, varied opinions on Seth's 'belongingness' in terms of geocultural location, central to considerations of the politics of publication and reception. Seth's writing has been considered from within various theoretical brackets including the 'postcolonial', 'transnational', 'cosmopolitan' and 'diasporic'. The second part of this paper will take cognizance of debates on Seth's 'Indianness' as against his personal philosophy of an 'international universality', triggered off by the global visibility accorded to Seth with the publication of *A Suitable Boy*. Subsequently, in the postliberalization period, Seth has been applauded for his transcultural reach, and his 'capacity to enter into other lives and cultures absolutely'.[1] He has been declared 'a genuinely international man, the personification and embodiment of globalism'.[2] The paper will examine the tendency to read Seth's work from the perspective of a 'global literature', which is completely differentiated from the nationally bounded responses that have conventionally determined our understanding of 'world literature'.[3] And yet, even if we consider Seth as a participant of a larger global migrancy of the mind, a number of concerns remain unanswered. Particularly, how does one deal with the problematics of affiliation in the work of a writer who has remained steadfastly nonaligned towards political and economic concerns of the developing world, as against the impact of late-twentieth-century global capitalism.

Vikram Seth was born in Calcutta (now Kolkata) in 1952. He spent the formative years of his childhood in Patna, and then studied at the elitist Doon public school in Dehradun. By 18, he was in England for his A levels at Tonbridge School in Kent, followed by undergraduate studies at Corpus Christi College, Oxford. He moved on to the USA in 1975 for an MA in Economics, and also registered for a PhD degree at Stanford University. His fieldwork on the economic demographics of Chinese villages took him for two years to the Nanjing University in the People's Republic of China, in 1980. Seth reflects upon his Chinese experience in his only travelogue *From Heaven Lake* (1983).

Seth wrote his first work of fiction, *The Golden Gate*, while working towards his doctoral dissertation at Stanford. This unusual narrative, inspired by Pushkin's *Eugene Onegin* (1837), is entirely composed of 594 sonnets, all written in iambic tetrameter. Seth received much praise for his technical virtuosity and craftsmanship. *The Golden Gate* eventually went on to become one of the most highly praised bestsellers of 1986 and Seth was awarded the John Simon Guggenheim Memorial Fellowship. Seth sets his plot in the Bay Area of San Francisco. His five protagonists are drawn from the professional class, and Seth uses the ups and downs of their relationships to offer a thought-provoking analysis of the artificial culture of consumption of contemporary American society. Post-1990s policies of economic liberalization and the entry of multinational corporations have led to a similar culture of rampant materialism among the urban Indian middle class. In this context, Seth's critique of crisis of 'yuppiedom' moves from being culture specific to the USA alone, to a more universal comment on a rapidly spreading global phenomenon of the conspicuous consumption.

The successful reception of *The Golden Gate* allowed Seth the financial independence to return to India to work on his second novel *A Suitable Boy* (1993). It took him almost eight years to complete this extensively researched epic of 1349 pages. The novel is structured into 19 well-crafted subsections that allow Seth to move back and forth while telling the story of four extended families – the Mehras, the Chatterjis, the Kapoors and the Khans. The novel opens with a wedding ceremony that brings these four families together. Now that Mrs Rupa Mehra's eldest daughter Savita is married, she can turn her attention towards finding a bridegroom for her younger daughter Lata. Her quest for a 'suitable boy' serves as a connecting strand for Seth's multiple thematic preoccupations. It is the early winter of 1950 and India has been independent from British colonial rule for three years. In addition to the network of relationships that emerge out of these family webs, Seth also introduces a large cast of other characters drawn from across religions, languages, class and castes, to offer a fascinating survey of the operations of the postindependence Indian nation-state.

A Suitable Boy is the only book by Seth that is set in India. The novel created publishing history because of the staggering advance of £250,000 that Seth received from Orion, the largest ever paid for a 'first novel' in Britain.[4] While the ensuing media hype assured Seth of global visibility, it also drew uncharitable responses from a number of Indian critics, who accused Seth of acquiring an inflated reputation after having been co-opted into a network of mass-market publishing. C. D. Narasimhaiah, for instance, angrily suggested that the worldwide response that attended Seth's publication seemed 'very largely the handiwork of his publisher and media as they colluded in the sinister design of announcing the birth of a new star'.[5] He dismissed the novel as being 'unsuitable to the Indian mind and most unsuitable to the Indian spirit'.[6] Anita Desai accused Seth of pandering to the needs of the Western reader for the exotic: 'With the glee of an anthropologist let loose among Pacific islanders, Seth describes for us all the festivals of the Indian calendar year, from the spring festival of Holi through Rakhi, Janamashtami, Karva Chauth [...] Christmas and New Year's Eve.'[7] Ashok Jha, on the other hand, conceded that Seth had used the 'resources of his art in grappling with something which is perhaps more of a value as experience for readers of his works in India than what he has been able to do with experience of the contemporary West'.[8]

In due course, however, 'home' critics have acknowledged the complex strands of Seth's monumental novel, and have offered full-length critical anthologies that discuss Seth's presentation of feudal, caste and communal interests in Nehruvian India, along with the disintegration of secular and socialist ideals, his effective use of social realism as a narrative technique, the skilful incorporation of sociolinguistic aspects drawn from English Hindi, Urdu and Bengali, and the presentation of patriarchal structures, namely his portrayal of his female characters in public and private spaces.[9]

Seth's next novel, *An Equal Music* (1999), is set in London with Western classical music as its predominant focus. The title of the book was inspired by a sermon of Jon Donne, describing life after death. The world of Hindustani sangeet in *A Suitable Boy* makes way completely for the European classical circuit of Bach, Beethoven, Hayden and Schubert. This is a tale of an emotionally volatile musician, Michael Holden, who is second violinist in an English quartet called the 'Maggiore'. Michael was intensely in love with Julia McNicholl, a talented pianist, as a student in Vienna. They quarrel and part ways, only to meet years later in London. Julia, who is now married, is suffering from an autoimmune disease of the inner ear and is going deaf. The narrative, which explores the depths of Julia's emotional distress in her transition from the world of sounds to the world of deafness, is however constrained by the web of 'absence and vacant regret' that a highly strung Michael weaves around his lonely, near-psychotic existence. The warmth of the collective in *A Suitable Boy* gives way to the solitariness of the individual. References to Michael's childhood in the small northern England town of Rochdale are important, as they offer an insight into Michael's desire to escape from the limitations of his unprivileged background.

Extensive media coverage also accompanied the release of *An Equal Music*, and Orion reportedly earmarked £80,000 for its publicity campaign. Surprisingly, the novel received a much warmer reception from Indian reviewers than did *A Suitable Boy*. The Indian academia seemed to have bypassed its 'anxiety over Indianness' prevalent in the early 1990s, as is evident in Namita Gokhale's appreciation of Seth as a 'writer about human beings, not as a peddler of Indian exotica'.[10] Gokhale continues, 'Vikram Seth is yet a citizen of the world in the best sense. His genius should be evaluated in his control over his material, and in creating a credible world-in-itself which he can co-habit and explore.'[11]

Two Lives (2005) is a nonfictional reconstruction of the (extra)ordinary lives of Seth's maternal great uncle Shanti Behari Seth (an Indian dentist trained in Berlin who served in the British army during World War II) and his great aunt Helga Gerdo Caro or Henny (a German Jew who escaped from Berlin just a month before the war broke out). Shanti Behari stayed as a boarder with Henny's family in prewar Berlin. They reconnect in London after the war and finally marry after 18 years of friendship. The idea of *Two Lives* took seed in Seth's mind after his parents suggested that he interview his 86-year-old uncle. The novel is divided into five sections. It begins with the time that Seth spent with his great uncle and aunt, when he came to England to study at a boarding school. The childless couple adopts young 'Vicky' as the son they never had. According to Christopher Rollason, the uncle–aunt–nephew trio inhabits 'an intercultural space which may be called transcultural (Anglo-Indian-German).'[12] This bonding perhaps explains Seth's desire to commemorate the lives of his relatives in a 503-page tome. Part II consists of a series of interviews with his uncle. Part III is the most evocative section of the book, wherein Seth reconstructs Henny's story from a recovered trunk full of letters she wrote, and received, in German. There are some extremely moving moments here, as in the agonizing two-page description of the gas chambers, wherein Henny relives the terrible fate of her mother and sister Lola, killed at Auschwitz and Theresienstaddt respectively. In Part IV, Seth brings the two lives of Shanti and Henny together in an account of their courtship, until their marriage in 1951. The skeleton sketch of the love affair offers little by means of possible drama and complexity of an interracial relationship in Europe of the 1940s and '50s. Finally, in the last part, Seth delves into Shanti's decision to change his will, a cause for much bitterness among his own family members. The narrative meanders into mundane details of Seth's family. While reviewers like Frances Wilson appreciate this tale of two seemingly ordinary people as an 'exemplary memoir' that encompasses 'the major events of the twentieth century in an account of 2 unhistoric lives',[13] others are more critical of the plethora of minutiae of the day-to-day life of his great uncle and aunt. Nicholas Shakespeare remarks, 'A danger for genealogists is that they get stuck up the family tree. In his project to rescue the past of a humble but not necessarily universal couple, Seth runs the risk of everything becoming hallowed indiscriminately, so that the result does, on occasion read like Chocktaw.'[14] By and large, *Two Lives* lacks the epic scope and wide canvas of characters of *A Suitable Boy*. The narrative also falls short of the emotional drive of *An Equal Music*.

In addition to his prose writing, Seth has also published a total of five anthologies of poetry. Most of the poems in Seth's first anthology *Mappings* (1981) were written while Seth was a student, first in England and then in California. Included in this collection are translations of works by Chinese, Hindi and German poets, offering an insight into Seth's multilingual skills. *The Humble Administrator's Garden* (1985) is a slim collection of individual lyrical and satirical poems, wherein Seth describes his experience of four diverse cultural milieus – Indian, English, Chinese and Californian. *All You Who Sleep Tonight* (1990) is an anthology of miscellaneous lyric poems and brief narratives in rhymed, unrhymed and free verse, and translations and epigrams. In his introductory remarks to *Beastly Tales: From Here and There* (1991), Seth talks of how this collection of ten impish animal fables was written on a hot day in Delhi, when he could not concentrate on his work and so decided to write 'a summer story involving mangoes and a river.'[15] The collection offers us delightfully witty accounts of journeys through the fantasy world of 'Gup', as well as India, Greece, China and the Ukraine. *Three Chinese Poets* (1992) is a collection of translations by Seth of the poetry of Wang Wei, Li Bai and Du Fu, three recognized literary figures of China who lived during the reign of the Emperor Ming Huang of the Tang dynasty, in the eighth century AD. Seth has also written a libretto (i.e. an opera text), *Arion and the Dolphin* (1994), that retells the legend of a young Corinthian musician who is thrown overboard by greedy sailors and is rescued by a dolphin who becomes his protector. *From Heaven Lake* (1983) is Seth's only travelogue, and offers a detailed account of an impromptu hitchhiking trip undertaken by Vikram Seth in 1981, from Northwest China to Tibet, and then across the border into Nepal.

Seth's subjectivity can be described as 'migratory' in that it has traversed multiple geographical, national, ethnic and linguistic as well as literary constituencies. Yet, although Seth has lived for a considerable number of years both in the UK and the US, he is not an emigrant to the West in the same sense as his contemporaries Salman Rushdie, Rohinton Mistry or Bharati Mukherjee. There are certain indicators of a sense of ambivalence resulting from geocultural dislocation in his first collection of poems *Mappings* (1981). In 'Divali', Seth acknowledges that he belongs to a particular class of privileged Indians who are already alienated to some degree, even prior to migration outside the Indian subcontinent. He summarizes the 'nowhereness' of this class who will suffer some degree of deracination wherever they are: 'I know that the whole world/means exile for our breed/Who are not home at home/and are abroad, abroad.'[16] A few others in *Mappings* are located in either an airport arrival or departure lounge. In 'To a Fellow Traveller', the poet addresses himself to a copassenger who is, like himself, in perpetual transition.

The body of writing that comes from a globally dispersed community is often designated as 'diasporic', and a number of commentaries on Seth have appeared in critical anthologies on diasporic writing. Victor Ramraj, however, points out that while diasporic writing has affinities with expatriate writing, it also stands apart, although convenience often dictates that they be seen together as one corpus.[17] Ramraj explains that the sensibility that informs these conditions results in different thematic preoccupations. In a broader sense, immigrant writing could refer to any work, and is more likely to concentrate on the contemporary experience in the host society. The diasporic, on the other hand, is more likely to have a preoccupation with the lost or imaginary homeland. US-based critics like Craig Tapping (1992) and Ketu Katrak (1997) have indexed Seth's work under the category of 'North American Indian writers'[18] and 'contemporary South Asian Americans'[19] respectively, using the parameters of evaluating diasporic subjectivities. This inclusion is no doubt based on Seth's only text set in a North American milieu, *The Golden Gate*. According to Tapping, the signifying tropes of 'Indo-American ethnic literature' include the trauma of transposition into an alien context, the processes of identity reformation, the acculturation of the Asian protagonist, anxiety over the loss of the homeland and protests against racial marginalization. None of the above is applicable to *The Golden Gate*, which is depopulated of diasporic subjects and their ensuing dilemmas. Similarly, the narrative of *A Suitable Boy*, written after Seth's return to India after staying for 14 years abroad, steers clear of attempts to construct states of ambivalence or liminality that arise from cross-cultural conflicts. In this context, none of Seth's protagonists fit in with Michael Ondaatje's description of his own fictional characters as 'international bastards', born in one place but choosing to live elsewhere – 'fighting to get back to or get away from our homelands all our lives'.[20]

An Equal Music is set in London and has an all-white cast, save for the fleeting appearance of a one-dimensional Japanese student. Conspicuously missing is the multicultural fabric of a new British Society, vibrantly alive in the works of British Asian women writers like Ravinder Randhawa and Meera Sayal. This almost adds an unrealistic element to the narrative. The novel also raises questions of affiliation. Can a novel written by an Indian, with nothing 'Indian' in it, and set in England, with white British characters, be considered as the ultimate apple cart to upset conventional centre-periphery relations? The reader located outside the milieu of San Francisco may have a certain degree of familiarity with the world of *The Golden Gate* because of exposure to widespread codes and icons of American popular culture through the media. In the case of *An Equal Music*, with its central preoccupation with Western classical music, the 'experience gap' between author and his Indian recipient is likely to be much wider. The degree of the gap in communication depends on historical and geographical conditions as well as a complex multicultural grounding and a certain 'European' component in the make-up of one's identity. The question therefore arises as to which potential readership is *An Equal Music* directed at? Will only a Western/ized readership, familiar with European classical music, be able to capture the finer nuances of the text?

In an insightful analysis of *Two Lives*, which he describes as 'lying on the fault line between biography and autobiography', Christopher Rollason points out that text is 'centered on questions of expatriate diasporic identity, not easy either to place spatially and culturally within the globalizing literary economy of the early twentieth century'.[21] According to Rollason, Shanti Uncle and Aunt Henny can be seen 'as cases of subaltern lives in certain aspects, above all given their time and place(s) – Henny obviously, as a German Jew forced into exile in the 1930s, and Shanti as a British colonial subject who sacrificed himself in World War II'. He adds that the life stories of the two diasporic Indians, Shanti and Seth, 'became part of a larger world […] in which Indian history has its autonomous dynamic yet is inextricably bound with other countries histories and the whole global system'.[22]

According to Bikhu Parekh, a characteristic typical of the average Indian migrant is that she or he can coexist in several homes simultaneously, and distances need not necessarily lead to a sense of fragmentation and loss. Parekh comments, 'Far from being homeless, he (the migrant) has several homes and that is the only way he has increasingly come to feel at home in the world.'[23] This challenges the assumption that absence of geographical rootedness necessarily leads to alienation or psychological deracination. In Seth's case, it may be argued that the writer's creative consciousness thrives on the 'pleasure' of having had a multiplicity of homes. Seth experiences no angst at being a cultural traveller. His work does not fall back on predictable fictional thematic preoccupations of rootlessness and displacement, privileged in cosmopolitan discourse of the late twentieth century. Rather Seth fits in well with an emerging pocket of privileged 'international citizens' or members of an emerging 'new world order'. As Namita Gokhale puts it, 'Today's identities are no longer about passports and birth certificates. In a world without barriers, you belong to where you are.'[24] Seth's syncretic leaning and his 'multiple affiliations to multiple locations' invite the critic to explore alternative frames of analysis, while considering his oeuvre as a whole.[25] The term 'internationalized writing', for example, can be used in the context of an authorial worldview that consciously addresses audiences beyond national boundaries. Ketu Katrak used the term 'simultaneity of geography' to refer to the 'possibility of living "here" in body and "elsewhere" in mind and imagination'.[26] The experience of (mind–body) simultaneity is of a specific kind for writers in English whose sociointellectual displacement is one of choice and different in degrees from that of more economically displaced immigrants. Hence, Seth is able to present a realistic nonmythical reconstruction of home in *A Suitable Boy* in spite of the considerable number of years spent abroad. He then goes on to write a story set in London, exclusively peopled by white Britons in *An Equal Music*. Seth's narratives do not convey the feeling of being trapped in an impossible 'in-betweenness', wherein he is denied the option of identifying with either an 'Indian' or a cosmopolitan/metropolitan culture. The term 'transnational' is frequently used in contemporary discourse to theorize the complex flow of cultures and emerging fluidities that are a consequence of rapidly changing geopolitical and economic realities. It is important to understand that while this flow is undoubtedly multidirectional, it still remains dictated by the power of international capitalism. Seth's last two works (*An Equal Music* and *Two Lives*) have been written in the period of the liberalization of the Indian economy, and can be read as laudable attempts to supersede the restrictive boundaries of nationalism. Still, the fact that Seth consciously refuses to discuss the complicated terms of transnationalism within a global South–North paradigm will remain an intruding factor in any assessment of his social commitment as a writer with postcolonial roots.

Editor's notes:

1. (On Seth's reception): 'Although Seth has provided a multitude of in-person interviews and despite the existence of an unquantifiable amount of reviews and essays concerning his work, all seem to grasp the core essence of this author. The public's interest in Seth is further fuelled by its continued inability to pierce the veil that shields his reclusive and extremely private life.' See V. G. Julie Rajan, 'Vikram Seth', in *South Asian Literature in English: An Encyclopedia*, ed. Jaina C. Sanga (Connecticut: Greenwood, 2004), 282.
2. Often compared to Goethe and Tolstoy, Seth's views on the craft of writing are worth noting. He aims to be 'readable because those are the kind (of books) I like to read. [...] Basic issues of human interest – honour, ambition, love, enmity, family, money, intrigue, death – really matter, rather than the etiolated idea of writing some over-dense, over-referential literary construct.' The writer advocates simplicity of writing and believes that a novel is not a vehicle for an author's political ideas. See Seth's interview with Sheela Reddy, 'I Wish More Writers Would Fight For a Big Advance', *Outlook*, 20 July 2009, 68.

Notes and References

1. G. J. V. Prasad, *Vikram Seth: An Anthology of Recent Criticism* (New Delhi: Pencraft International, 2004), 14.
2. Jonathan Yardley, review of *Two Lives*, *Washington Post*, 20 October 2005. Online: http://www.washingtonpost.com/wp-dyn/content/article/2005/10/20/AR2005102001723.html (accessed 6 September 2010).
3. Shirley Geok-Lin Lim and Amy Ling, eds, *Reading Literature of the Asian American* (Philadelphia: Temple Press, 1992), 29.
4. Michele Field, 'Vikram Seth', *Publishers' Weekly*, 10 May 1993, 47.
5. C. D. Narasimhaiah, *Spurious Representations: Vikram Seth, Salman Rushdie and Shashi Tharoor, Essays in Commonwealth Literature* (New Delhi: Pencraft, 1995), 119.
6. Ibid., 119.
7. Anita Desai, 'Sitting Pretty', *New York Review* 41, no. 1 (1993): 25.
8. Ashok K. Jha, 'Vikram Seth: *The Golden Gate* and Other Writings', in *Recent Indian Fiction*, ed. R. S. Pathak (New Delhi: Prestige, 1994), 69.
9. See Mala Pandurang, *Vikram Seth: Multiple Locations, Multiple Affiliations* (Jaipur: Rawat Publications, 2001); G. J. V. Prasad, *Vikram Seth: An Anthology of Recent Criticism* (New Delhi: Pencraft International, 2004); Murari Prasad, *Vikram Seth's A Suitable Boy: An Anthology of Recent Criticism* (New Delhi: Pencraft International, 2005); and Rohini Mokashi Punekar, *Vikram Seth: An Introduction* (New Delhi: Cambridge University Press, 2008).
10. Namita Gokhale, 'Vikram's Vocalist Strains on the Literary Landscape', *Times of India* (Delhi), 4 May 1999, 4.
11. Ibid.

12 Christopher Rollason, 'Vikram Seth's *Two Lives*. A Literature of Global Protagonism', *The Expatriate Indian Writing in English Vol. 1*, ed. T. Vinoda and P. Shailaja. (New Delhi: Prestige, 2006), 176.
13 Frances Wilson, 'Ordinary Lives Writ Large', *Guardian*, 2 October 2005. Online: http://www.guardian.co.uk/books/2005/oct/02/biography.features1 (accessed 14 November 2010).
14 Nicholas Shakespeare, 'Marmite: You Either Love It or You Hate It', *Telegraph*, 10 October 2005. Online: http://www.telegraph.co.uk/culture/books/3647101/Marmite-you-either-love-it-or-you-hate-it.html (accessed 11 October 2010).
15 Taken from jacket of *Beastly Tales: From Here and There* (New Delhi: Penguin, 1992).
16 Vikram Seth, *Mappings* (New Dehi: Viking, 1994), 67.
17 Victor Ramraj, 'Diasporas and Multi-culturalism', in *An Introduction to Postcolonial Theory*, ed. Peter Childs and Patrick Williams (New York: Prentice Hall, 1997), 228.
18 Craig Tapping, 'South Asia Writes North America: Prose Fiction and Autobiography from the Indian Diaspora', in *Reading Literatures of the Asian American*, ed. Shirley Geok-Lin Lim and Amy Ling (Philadelphia: Temple University Press, 1992), 285.
19 Ketu Katrak, 'South Asian American Literature', in *An Interethnic Companion to Asian American Literature*, ed. King-Kok Cheung (New York: Cambridge University Press, 1997), 193.
20 See Pico Iyer, 'India Day by Day', *Times Literary Supplement*, 19 March 1993, 20.
21 Rollason, 'Vikram Seth's *Two Lives*', 172.
22 Ibid., 173.
23 Bikhu Parekh, 'Some Reflections on the Indian Diaspora', *Journal of Contemporary Thought* (1993): 106.
24 Gokhale, 'Vikram's Vocalist Strains', 4.
25 Pandurang, *Vikram Seth*, 2.
26 Katrak, 'South Asian American Literature', 201.

Chapter Fourteen

WHATEVER HAPPENED TO KAAVYA VISWANATHAN?

Shaleena Koruth

The April 2006 article in the *Harvard Crimson* that alerted the public to accusations of plagiarism in Kaavya Viswanathan's debut novel, *How Opal Mehta Got Kissed, Got Wild, and Got a Life* (2006), set off a media blitz of sorts, which catapulted the 19-year-old Harvard sophomore and author from fame and a $500,000 book contract to immediate infamy. On closer examination though, Viswanathan's mercuric rise and fall had all the symptoms that could contribute to such an anticlimax. Her life, from its involvement with IvyWise – a firm that coaches Ivy League aspirants in creating their applications – until the book deal, might have reaffirmed to the young writer that a novel can be coached and packaged, just as much as a college application. In fact, the book itself followed a path so scripted that its copyright was held by Viswanathan and the book packaging firm that worked with her. Firms such as these take targeted, even formulaic approaches toward creating media that will entertain, and Viswanathan's creative work was certainly subject to the dictates of what consumers want to read.

If originality, taken as a premise for all artistic work (especially fiction writing) can be micromanaged and 'packaged' the way *Opal* was, it might not have been unthinkable for the already overloaded Harvard sophomore to 'repackage' sections of existing novels. Add to this the hype: the writer of a novel categorized by most as 'chick lit' was awarded a $500,000 contract. Perhaps Viswanathan's fall, so feasted and commented upon by the public and the media, was our revenge on her for exacting such high expectations – even though she was never the one to have set them.

Whatever happened to Kaavya Viswanathan? The question is not about where she is in her writing career; it is understood that for some time, to say the least, the publishing world is sealed off to her. The huge plagiarism scandal that erupted tainted her enough to merit an unofficial exile from publication, a recall of her book and an immediate end to her contract with Little, Brown, the publishing firm that had signed her on. *Opal* was found to have strong similarities to two novels, *Sloppy Firsts* and *Second Helpings*, both about teenage girls from New Jersey, by Megan F. McCafferty. The question has to do instead with what made Viswanathan commit the alleged plagiarism, and while her error was egregious, to what extent it might have been associated with many different factors, which will be examined. The question also seeks an explanation for the media's reaction to her. Once the scandal broke, Viswanathan's fall from grace in the media was rapid and vengeful and completely at odds with its earlier stance of applause and admiration. The exposé spawned a deluge of articles, blogs and commentary. Whether it was hubris (she was a teenager with a six-figure book contract) or desperation (the book was written while she was enrolled in Harvard with full course load) that made her plagiarize, Viswanathan's story is one that requires examination of the subtle negotiations between the publishing world, the media and the public that transformed a first time writer of an average novel into a celebrity. It also requires addressing the changing view of authorship where novels are approached in the way that television and film are, as collaborative 'projects', and the fine line between intentional and unintentional plagiarism in genre fiction.

The Story

The book is a well-written piece of chick lit. Opal Mehta is an overachieving (a byword in articles, forums and all other discussions about Viswanathan herself), driven and talented senior in high school whose entire life has been geared towards securing admission to Harvard University. Shepherding her through this process, planned to the tees (apart from superb Scholastic Aptitude Test scores and first chair in the New Jersey regional symphony orchestra, Opal takes welding classes for six months to completely round off an already well-rounded resume) are her parents, both doctors. Opal Mehta therefore conforms to all stereotypes of the expatriate Indian community in the United States: she is the daughter of highly skilled professionals; the mother gives up her career to focus on her child's; very high standards of achievement are set for the child; the family unit is close and involved. HOWGIH (How Opal Will Get Into Harvard) is a plan, hatched and implemented by Opal's parents from the day she is born. Viswanathan conveniently lifts a stereotype of the Gujarati community in the US through a character named Kali, a cousin of Opal who works in Patel Cash-and-Carry, the ubiquitous Gujarati-owned 'Indian' store found in almost all Indian enclaves in North America. Apart from this one aspect, her awareness of the Gujarati community is superficial. The Mehta family's interactions and habits are generic and completely devoid of authentic descriptions of Gujarati culture or cuisine. Opal's family, in fact, is nonvegetarian – her mother serves *halal* meat during their family Diwali party. That said, the book has many very humorous moments; the writing is seamless and makes for a better read than many other teen blockbusters.

A disappointing early interview, where a Harvard dean points out the lack of fun element from Opal's application, propels a change in plan and HOWGIH becomes HOWGAL (How Opal Will Get A Life). The book traces Opal's transformation from achievement-obsessed nerd to popular senior, leading her to seek membership in the Haute Bitchez, a clique of the hottest girls in high school. She succeeds, but only at the cost of committing some thoughtless acts; the art of cultivating shallowness and pursuing popularity is new to Opal and in the process (hotly followed and abetted by her parents), Opal commits some gross errors, which in the end she duly corrects and more than makes amends for. The ending is a happy one; any other would not have been tenable in a book that is so intentionally entertaining. Opal enters Harvard, learning in the process that 'getting a life' is indeed challenging for it involves risks and choices that have consequences for herself and her friends.

The Behind-the-Scenes Story

No doubt, the story of Opal Mehta is in many ways the story of Kaavya Viswanathan. Both are New Jersey girls, both Indian Americans with overinvolved but well-meaning parents, and both girls subscribe to their parents dream for them: Harvard. But while Opal Mehta submitted her application to Harvard the regular way, Viswanathan's parents hired IvyWise, headed by Katharine Cohen. A college applications firm that helps prospective Ivy League applicants put together 'killer' college applications, IvyWise gave Viswanathan a leg-up in the intensely competitive process.[1] Thus the young Viswanathan was introduced, very early, to a 'collaborative' approach to essay writing and application building by 'experts' with an 'in' on the Ivy League and who, according to the IvyWise website, 'have contacts at the schools, attended the most prestigious colleges [...]', etc.[2]

It was the same Katharine Cohen, herself the author of *Rock Hard Apps: How to Write the Killer College Application* (2003), that forwarded some of Viswanathan's writing samples to her own literary agent, Suzanne Gluck, at the William Morris Agency. Another agent at the same agency, Jennifer Rudolph Walsh, looked at Viswanathan's work and was convinced of her talent. The only trouble was that Viswanathan's original idea for a novel was 'dark' and not 'commercially viable'.[3] This lead to Viswanathan being referred to Alloy Entertainment, a book-packaging firm in New York City, previously called 17th Street Productions. Asya Muchnick, the editor who worked with Viswanathan at Little, Brown, said that the book involved more 'shaping' than usual.[4] The 'Opal Mehta' pie had many fingers in it. Was it a wonder then that Viswanathan went astray in finding her own voice?

Book packaging firms such as Alloy work with authors to develop ideas and manuscripts, which are then shopped to publishers. This reduces the publisher's risk and cost involved in scouting out authors; the book's concept and some, if not all, of the manuscript is available for publishing firms to look at prior to investing in it. According to an article in the *Boston Globe*, the editors at Alloy proposed that Viswanathan scope out a lighter concept for a novel – closer to home and to her own life. They asked that she send them an email writing about herself in a light, conversational voice. The initial idea for Opal came from this email, and Viswanathan worked with editors at Alloy to come up with a concept. Jennifer Walsh loved the concept, and the offer was auctioned for, as Walsh put it, 'oodles and boodles of money'. The amount, first reported in the *New York Sun*, approached $500,000. It was, in any case, far higher than the advances first novels usually get, which are more to the tune of $20,000. The actual amount of the contract was not confirmed or denied by Viswanathan or Little, Brown.[5] Thus, in collaboration with Alloy – the firm shared the copyright for *Opal Mehta* with Viswanathan – and after it was sold to Little, Brown, the book was written during her freshman year at Harvard.[6]

The Hype-Making Machine: Book Packaging, Publishing and Marketing

Opal Mehta had the stamp of approval from Alloy Entertainment, the book-packaging firm roped in to 'fix' her initial concept and make it more saleable. Alloy Entertainment calls itself an 'integrated entertainment company' that 'originates entertainment properties and then partners with leading publishers, television networks and movie studios to deliver those properties to the world'.[7] When DreamWorks cancelled the film version of *Opal Mehta*, Alloy, as coproducer, lost out too.[8] Had the movie been made, the advertising and product plugging potential was limitless, with the littering of designer brands in the book, from Manolo Blahniks to Hermes scarves. In *Opal Mehta* lay an irresistible Hollywood vehicle for product promotion. Alloy Entertainment is in the business of creating blockbusters. The company usually retains all the intellectual property rights to a book, thus owning producer's rights to a movie or TV series, should either be a possibility.[9] *Opal Mehta* was indeed a package – irresistible to the media because of its author's very unique qualities and irresistible to its author, its publishers and cocreators as a cash cow, fattened for slaughter.

Alloy is an originator of 'tween-lit-hits' – books aimed specifically at an almost entirely female audience of preteens, teenagers and young adults. Alloy was, at the time of *Opal Mehta*'s printing, already the originator of, among others, *The Sisterhood of the Traveling Pants*, a series that produced three bestsellers for Delacorte Press and has since been made into a movie.[10] Alloy's partnership with Viswanathan explains, at least in part, the size of the advance. Once the near-$500,000 amount was reported in the press, there was no going back. Kaavya Viswanathan was big news. Interestingly though, her coauthor, Alloy Entertainment, was not. Something about the notion of authorship through the ages – the writer toiling over her manuscript, pouring into it her font of knowledge – does not lend itself to the kind of authorship that Alloy sells. Literary novelists are not driven by formulae or the market. However, when scoping out the next big novelist, editors look at many extraliterary aspects, such as 'how photogenic and articulate the author is, his age and likely productive life cycle, the fashionability and/or substance of the themes dealt with in books being pitched, the possibility of media tie-ins or product placement deals, the existing degree of celebrity of the author, rights sales, the reliability of his agent, and so on'.[11] Alloy Entertainment is, very simply, a company that taps this need for tie-ins and rights sales that concern publishing houses.

When Viswanathan fell from grace, the so far glossed-over role that Alloy Entertainment played came under scrutiny. It must be mentioned here that Alloy Entertainment was never accused with Viswanathan. She has said that the similarities were her responsibility and no other's. Oddly enough though, Claudia Gabel, an Alloy editor at the time, is thanked in the acknowledgement pages of both *Opal Mehta* and McCafferty's books. Prior to Alloy, she worked at Crown Publishing Group, an imprint of Random House that published McCafferty's books. A Random House spokesman said that Ms Gabel asserted that she never touched a word in Viswanathan's book.[12] Leslie Morgenstein, president of Alloy, has said he would not work with minors again.[13]

Alloy Entertainment is owned by Alloy Media and Marketing. It targets teens, preteens (tweens) and the 18–34 crowd: 'Ignoring the teen market? LOL. Today's teenager is a force in consumer spending, part of a highly influential $175B consumer market.'[14] Alloy recognizes that, while being a hard group to target, teens have a high spending potential since they earn 63 per cent (as per their website) of their income independently from parents and carry credit cards. As a marketing firm, Alloy's innovation lies in identifying the tween and teen market. Describing itself as a producer of 'targeted media' and 'promotional programs', Alloy is a perfect example of the marriage of product placement, merchandising and advertising to entertainment, books being only one medium; the web, television and film are others. Little wonder then that *Opal Mehta*'s brand-obsessed Haute Bitchez have so much in common with other heroines in Alloy's chick lit titles, such as *Gossip Girl*'s Serena van der Woodsen, who finds all her amazing clothes at none other than Barney's New York (according to the *Gossip Girl* blog on the CW television channel's website). Indeed, the web of product, story and media is anything but tangled; it is smooth, streamlined and sells well to publishers, whose risk is greatly reduced when buying a book with an identified market and a well-tested plotline. Add to this the continuous plugging of a certain lifestyle in many of the novels, films and TV series produced by Alloy: 'classy, professional and rich', a catchall phrase for the lifestyle that *Gossip Girl* depicts.[15] By elevating brands as a part of daily life, Alloy has perfected what the *Boston Globe* called a 'kind of total immersion'.[16]

The Alloy method, typically, is to hash out concepts in editorial meetings and then either use in-house talent or hire a writer to write the first ten chapters or so of the book. This method is not set in stone though, and writers sometimes enter the picture very early; in Viswanathan's case, her agent referred her to the firm. Once the first ten chapters – called the 'first act' within the firm – looks good, it is pitched to publishers. Some writers look upon this collaborative approach as a useful start to a career in an industry that offers few, if any, breaks for wannabe writers. One of the creators and author of the *Gossip Girl* series, Cecily von Ziegesar, published her novel *Cum Laude* in 2010, written independently of Alloy. Ann Brashares, the creator of *The Sisterhood of the Traveling Pants*, told the *New Yorker* that it was unlikely for the many voices of collaboration to find its way into the sentence-level writing. Alloy – which generally owns a fifty per cent stake in the authors work – took a huge share of the money, but was willing to leave her alone in the actual writing of her novels.[17]

Alloy's invisibility is its most beguiling quality. The company's name is not on the spines of most of its books and the fact that it often uses company-owned pseudonyms instead of the writers' real names gives the illusion of a single, dedicated author, though this is not the case. No doubt, the interest value of *Opal Mehta* would have gone down had it been made known that a group worked on it. Company bylines don't sell books; individuals do.

Publicity: The Making and Unmaking of Viswanathan

It is evident that the near $500,000 two-book advance and the DreamWorks movie deal propelled Viswanathan immediately into the public eye. As for the book itself, the quality of her prose, though good, is not interesting, and while there were some very amusing points, her fiction is by no means a work of staggering genius; it is formulaic, it promises to please and is simply not memorable in any real sense. It is, however, a quick and entertaining read. But its achievement lies as much in this as in its being the creation of a very young author who managed to take a full course load as a freshman at Harvard while writing it. Which raises the question: why did Viswanathan receive such a huge advance for a piece of chick lit, when literary novelists like Jonathan Safran Foer – who would turn up their noses and beam themselves out of any room containing *Opal Mehta* – receive similar amounts?[18] The answer lies in hype and the publishing industry's continuous search for 'the next big thing', according to Dr David Emblidge, an industry expert and faculty member at Emerson College. He spoke to me at length about American publishing's hype machine, vis-à-vis Viswanathan. In his case study of the Viswanathan case, he discusses it thus: 'Viswanathan is manna from heaven for Little, Brown. Sex sells, and she's gorgeous. Youthfulness sells, and she's a college student. Exotic ethnicity sells, and she looks Indian although, really, as a second generation American from the Jersey suburbs, she's as American as apple pie. […] As a stock to bet on, Viswanathan looks like a really good tip.'[19] A teenage writer, a Harvard affiliation and an attractive face – especially a minority (Indian) attractive face – adds up to a lot. Think Zadie Smith, author of *White Teeth* (2000), touted by the *Guardian* in an early interview as 'young, black and British'.[20] Viswanathan was hotter than her book.

The other aspect of the advance was its reflection on the book itself. Though advances are determined based on the returns expected from book sales, the amount of the advance implicitly carries a connotation of 'quality'. For it to be worth so much, the book must be unique in some sense. But *Opal Mehta* is not a *White Teeth* or *Everything is Illuminated* (2002), both novels by writers in their twenties, both of which were critically acclaimed and both of which received very large, six-figure advances.[21] Morris Holbrook makes the point that the connection between literary excellence and popularity, or sales, is next to nil. The role of the capitalist hallmarks – standardization and mass production – in creating formulaic and banal popular entertainment has long been the subject of cultural commentators.[22] Alloy Entertainment's focus on creating blockbusters and its role in shaping Viswanathan's book concept to the point where it was seen as 'commercially viable', is ample demonstration of this phenomenon. Add to this Viswanathan's representation by the reputed William Morris Agency and one can see another trend: the appropriation of high culture by mass consumption.[23]

Journalistic reviews and profiles, book publicists, editors, buyers and prize committees – in other words, book publishing, journalism and, in recent decades, the mass market with its possibilities for film, TV and internet distribution – have created an 'invisible screening' process for literature that is closely linked with what the market wants.[24] For publishers and agents, nurturing talent is less important than marketing. *Opal Mehta* in particular makes the case for the observation that book publishing has become part of the entertainment business, leading therefore to the 'deification of the bestseller' by publishing firms.[25] Projected as a bestseller, *Opal Mehta* was never meant to be associated with literary merit. However, the big names and big money associated with the book – Harvard, William Morris – conflated high art with middlebrow work and connoisseurs with chick lit fans, resulting in that other marketing phenomenon, hype. And because literary publishing is associated with art, *Opal Mehta* was, too.[26] As the American publishing industry locks hands with the television, film and video game industry (a nonexhaustive list) through firms like Alloy, a new 'mediocracy' is created, with 'dumbed down' rather than 'wised up' products occupying the same exalted status as high art traditionally did.[27]

While advances are often determined using formulae based on sales projections for a book, big publishing houses like Little, Brown often make huge bets on manuscripts based on factors that include the saleability of a genre, how 'hot' the author is, how good a fit she is for the firm itself and the potential for movie/TV rights. This sort of 'gambling' is over the top, but big trade houses do it all the time because, sometimes, they are right: 'If you could find the next Toni Morrison or the next Stephen King, or somebody whose sales and reputation would happen at that level, you'd pay anything for it, right?' Emblidge goes so far as to call the size of Viswanathan's advance 'off the charts'.[28] Many authors are not even expected to earn back the amount of their advances since these amounts, once reported in the press, become free publicity for the publishing house.[29]

Viswanathan's agent at William Morris, Jennifer Walsh, speaking to the *Boston Globe*, seamlessly spun her appearance and manner with her talent and potential. 'Kaavya had the craftsmanship, she's beautiful and charming, she just needed to find the right novel that would speak to her generation and to people beyond her years as well. We worked on it some more and sold it for oodles and boodles of money'.[30] Attractive and articulate, Viswanathan was an excellent candidate to build a publicity campaign around; publishing firms have been known to hire coaches who will 'polish' the personalities of less urbane and presentable authors. People tend to view profiles and interviews of stars – publicity – as less likely to be manipulated and paid for by studios than paid advertising or promotion. The high end of the American publishing industry recognizes this and, consequently, devotes money and staff towards the effort. Marketing meetings in the publishing firm determine which selected titles among the many publications slated for the season get the 'full treatment – the six-figure print run, the lavish book jacket,[31] the pressure on the news media, the 10 city tour, the television interviews, the advertisements, the four-color posters and bookstore displays'.[32] Given the size of her advance, Viswanathan's campaign would have certainly included some, if not all of these. And the many profiles of Viswanathan in the *New York Times* and the *Harvard Crimson*, to name a few publications, is evidence of the publishing industry and the news media working to add to the hype around her. In a culture that dedicates itself to the pursuit of youth and brands, Viswanathan was an irresistible package herself, associated with the greatest brand in education, Harvard.

Yet today's authors are complicit in creating the hype around them. After all, authors must promote themselves; the private writer becomes the public author.[33] Almost all published authors now have a website where they blog, revealing mundane details about their life and work, stepping down to the level of the reader and fan from the otherwise elevated position they hold as celebrities. Staring at us on the website of Aimee Nezhukumatathil, a successful and respected Indian American poet in New York State, is a photograph of her reclining, a bare arm and shoulder in the foreground, the rest of her draped in something very soft and possibly silky.[34] Jhumpa Lahiri, known to guard her privacy fiercely, has a stunning photo on her official Facebook page, with fan photos that include wedding pictures! Even the literary end of the celebrity spectrum buys into a middle ground of spectacle and personal packaging. In book jacket photos and photo ops we see authors presenting themselves to the camera and in turn to their admiring readers. For writers needing to earn their keep, reclusiveness is not an option. A story-hungry media fixates on what makes the author special, by focusing on her very ordinariness. The negotiation between writer and interviewer, between celebrity and journalism is a tough one to untangle, for both feed off each other, all the time. Though Viswanathan was denied the possibility of some of these venues for self-promotion because of the scandal, she did present herself as an 'everyman' Harvard student (an irony in itself) who, along with a full course load, was a member of a sorority and partied on weekends. She waved away the pressure on her to produce, academically and contractually, by disarmingly saying that writing the book was nothing extraordinary: 'It's just, you go to meals, you sleep, you write.'[35]

The Rise and Fall of Celebrity: Kaavyagate

Viswanathan was the perfect example of what Daniel Boorstin, in his analysis of celebrity, called 'the Human Pseudo-Event'. Centuries ago, greatness was a prerequisite to fame. In this age though, wrote Boorstin in 1961, people manufacture greatness, with the help of the media. So quickly and effectively do the papers, television, radio and now the Internet make the unknown well known, that the users of these media willingly conflate the quality of being well known, or fame, with greatness.[36] Viswanathan was an instant celebrity. It was a glimpse into our preoccupation with the romantic view of authorship – that the author is the sole, divinely inspired creator of her work.[37] As the teenage daughter of Indian immigrants, Viswanathan made it seem that it was indeed possible to transcend social categories and do it all.[38]

The exposing of Viswanathan as a plagiarist led to a media blitz. Her notoriety far exceeded her celebrity. Articles and discussions about the plagiarism were followed by articles about the manner in which her downfall was feasted upon by the media; the debacle was called 'Kaavyagate' by some bloggers, reminiscent of the Watergate scandal that led to the resignation of President Nixon in the '70s, and the media frenzy compared to a 'lynch mob'.[39] No doubt this feeding fest was a case of *Schadenfreude*, the enjoyment obtained from the troubles of others, especially a cosseted, overachieving, rich girl.

The scandal itself was good for the publishing industry since it sparked interest in *Opal Mehta*; the book rose from number 64 on Amazon's sales list to number 10 the day after Little, Brown announced that it was pulling it off the shelves. McCafferty's first book also saw a spike in sales.[40] The fall of a celebrity is always a great news story. It is, after all, an acknowledgement of the public's power – to crown and to dethrone.[41] That the allegations against Viswanathan provoked so much interest is a reflection on the nature of celebrity today – while being out of reach, it is simultaneously within reach and available for analysis. 'In a peculiarly contemporary way', celebrity journalism has become a way for the public to explore the personal through the celebrity's actions; the allegations of Viswanathan's plagiarism handed the public the moral higher ground.[42]

The Allegations of Plagiarism

Plagiarism was recognized as a problem as far back as 1751, when Dr Johnson wrote about it.[43] A more recent definition of plagiarism in creative work, provided by a copyright lawyer, identifies it as: 'intentionally taking the literary property of another without attribution and passing it off as one's own, having failed to add anything of value to the copied material and having reaped from its use an unearned benefit'.[44]

In the final analyses of Viswanathan's work, she was accused of almost forty instances of plagiarism, across five writers.[45] Without doubt and to say the least, Viswanathan's youth and ambition definitely got the better of her; the number of similarities to existing literature are simply too many to dismiss. The question is not whether she committed plagiarism – she did – but whether the plagiarism was intentional or unintentional. By the time the scandal began to make its exit from the news – the general judgement was that the number of similarities across the books was large enough to demonstrate intent. Though she insisted that all copying was 'unintentional and unconscious', she herself admitted that it was confusing to her because it seemed to have happened so many times.[46]

Parse through the indignation and outcry though, and one can find dissenters, who either believe that the plagiarism was not intentional or that given the formulaic nature of the genre itself and the fact that she was writing about consumerist adolescent angst of the anti-Holden Caulfield sort, the odds of being completely original were not in her favour.[47] Discussing the multiple similarities to other works found in Viswanathan's work, a vice president at Simon Pulse told the *Boston Globe* that within the genre of young adult chick lit, there are similarities across the board: 'The teenage experience is fairly universal.'[48] In a blog entry about the case, Malcolm Gladwell asked, citing one incriminating example of Viswanathan's appropriation of McCafferty's *Sloppy Firsts*, whether it was even possible to write a teen novel without using sentences such as these.

McCAFFERTY: Bridget is my age and lives across the street. For the first twelve years of my life, these qualifications were all I needed in a best friend. But that was before Bridget's braces came off and her boyfriend Burke got on, before Hope and I met in our seventh-grade honors classes.

VISWANATHAN: Priscilla was my age and lived two blocks away. For the first fifteen years of my life, those were the only qualifications I needed in a best friend. We had first bonded over our mutual fascination with the abacus in a playgroup for gifted kids. But that was before freshman year, when Priscilla's glasses came off, and the first in a long string of boyfriends got on.[49]

Viswanathan's mentoring by Alloy laid the expectations: to produce something that would sell, on the lines of existing tales. It must be noted here that Alloy Entertainment only worked with Viswanathan on the first four chapters of the novel. After that, she worked almost entirely with Asya Muchnick. Viswanathan has said that Alloy provided only 'minor suggestions' during this process.[50] Viswanathan is alleged to have copied from McCafferty, Meg Cabot, Sophie Kinsella and Salman Rushdie. Another Indian American writer, Tanuja Desai Hidier, has also claimed that Viswanathan copied from her novel about an Indian American girl titled *Born Confused*. Hidier was approached by Alloy Entertainment but refused to work with them,[51] which raises the question: was it not too early to throw in one's lot with a book packager if one was serious about a literary career?[52]

All art exists as a response to its precedents, with reproduction and imitation being one possible response. In Virginia Woolf's words: 'Reading Yeats turns my sentences one way: reading Sterne turns them another.' Discussing the phenomenon of plagiarism, Thomas Mallon describes the writer's pen as one that is pushed by whatever literary ghost he's just entertained.[53] One can imagine Viswanathan drowning herself in chick lit before and while writing out her own manuscript. Was it, therefore, so surprising that *Opal Mehta* contained so many 'samplings' from other novels in the genre? Was it even entirely avoidable?

Dr Richard Shiffrin, director of the memory and perception lab at Indiana University says that verbatim reproduction of texts is unlikely; ideas, though, are learnt and absorbed and reproduced, but given the absence of tools that detect intentionality on the part of the author, it is hard to label an act as intentional plagiarism. People usually see intent if the amount of plagiarism crosses the line, but in the end it's a judgment call. Dr Shiffrin looked through some examples of Viswanathan's versions of McCafferty's passages and said that, in his view, they were not so far out of the normal unconscious borrowing that you might see that you could establish a strong case – however, there's no way to tell.

There is a case for unconscious copying, the sort that George Harrison was found guilty of with his song 'My Sweet Lord', where information from another source is misattributed to oneself, partly because its easier to remember information than its source and partly because of 'implicit memory', which allows us to remember information without knowing that we're remembering it.[54] However, an alert intellect can guard against such oversights; evidently Viswanathan let too many of her own barriers down.

The question that does not have an answer is: if there were intent, why would she not be cleverer about plagiarizing so blatantly in popular fiction? In the end, intentionality did not matter; the plagiarism did. Little, Brown could not risk its reputation.[55] And so, Viswanathan was banished, at least for a time – there is hope, even for plagiarists. Two giants accused of plagiarism include the American historians, Doris Kearns Goodwin and Stephen Ambrose, whose success was barely tainted by the scandals. More recently, Ian McEwan was accused of borrowing in his novel *Atonement*, but has been defended by his literary standing and the fact that the novel he built upon the borrowed text is outstanding and original. Viswanathan's building upon existing texts was original too; no one accused her of borrowing narrative and plot, but she lacked the benefit of a mature, proven career and 'friends in high places'.[56] In my analysis of Viswanathan's case, I think she is guilty of intellectual sloth, by permitting herself to appropriate, though even she was probably not aware of the extent to which she was doing so. As Rushdie put it, she was a victim of her own ambition.[57]

While writing this essay, my efforts at attributing sources have bordered on paranoia; yet in this prediction I cite my intuition. I think Viswanathan will be forgiven (eighteen is a shaky age) and will return – the question is, without a six-figure advance and the delicious publicity, will the writer publish and will the readers read? Cue an analysis of the postdated advantages of negative literary publicity.

Notes and References

1. Ann Hulbert, 'How Kaavya Got Packaged and Got Into Trouble', *Slate*, 27 April 2006. Online: http://www.slate.com/id/2140683 (accessed 18 March 2010).
2. Online: http://www.ivywise.com (accessed 15 March 2010).
3. David Mehegan, 'The Six-Figure Sophomore', *Boston Globe*, 22 February 2006. Online: http://www.boston.com/ae/books/articles/2006/02/22/the_six_figure_sophomore (accessed 19 March 2010).
4. Hulbert, 'How Kaavya got Packaged'.
5. Mehegan, 'The Six-Figure Sophomore'.
6. Motoko Rich and Dinitia Smith, 'First Idea, Plot and Characters: Then a Book Needs an Author', *New York Times*, 27 April 2006. Online: http://www.nytimes.com/2006/04/27/books/27pack.html (accessed 20 March 2010).
7. Alloy Entertainment, press release for Samurai Girl. Online: http://editorial.sidereel.com/Text/Samurai_Girl_Press_Release.html (accessed 21 January 2013).
8. Robin Abcarian, 'Now "Opal" won't get a movie', *Los Angeles Times*, 29 April 2006. Online: http://articles.latimes.com/2006/apr/29/entertainment/et-ruttenside29 (accessed 23 March 2010).
9. Rebecca Mead, 'The Gossip Mill: Alloy, the Teen Entertainment Factory', *New Yorker*, 19 September 2009. Online: http://www.newyorker.com/reporting/2009/10/19/091019fa_fact_mead (accessed 15 March 2010).
10. Rich and Smith, 'First Idea, Plot and Characters'.
11. Daragh O'Reilly, 'Martin Amis on Marketing', in *Consuming Books: The Marketing and Consumption of Literature*, ed. Stephen Brown (New York: Routledge, 2006), 74.
12. Rich and Smith, 'First Idea, Plot and Characters'.
13. Mead, 'The Gossip Mill'.
14. Centre for Digital Democracy, 'CDD and USPIRG File Comments with FTC on Privacy and Behavioral Targeting', 4 November 2009. Online: http://www.democraticmedia.org/cdd-uspirg (accessed 21 January 2013).
15. Online: http://www.fanpop.com/clubs/blair-and-chuck/links/10384364/title/cw-couples-know-fashion (accessed 10 January 2013).
16. David Mehegan, 'Opal Aided by Marketing Firm that Targets Teens', *Boston Globe*, 8 May 2006. Online: http://www.boston.com/ae/books/articles/2006/05/08/opal_aided_by_marketing_firm_that_targets_teens (accessed 22 March 2010).
17. Mead, 'The Gossip Mill'.
18. Sarah Bernard, 'A Fan's Notes', *New York*, 15 April 2002. Online: http://nymag.com/nymetro/arts/features/5879 (accessed 10 March 2010).

19 David Emblidge, 'The Viswanathan Dilemma at Little, Brown, Publishers', *International Journal of the Humanities* 5, no. 3 (2007): 7–13.
20 Stephanie Merritt, 'She's Young, Black, British – and the First Publishing Sensation of the Millennium', *Observer*, 16 January 2000. Online: http://www.guardian.co.uk/books/2000/jan/16/fiction.zadiesmith (accessed 12 March 2010).
21 Stephen Moss, 'White Teeth by Zadie Smith', *Guardian*, 26 January 2000. Online: http://www.guardian.co.uk/books/2000/jan/26/fiction.zadiesmith (accessed 12 March 2010).
22 Morris B. Holbrook, 'On the Commercial Exaltation of Artistic Mediocrity', in *Consuming Books: The Marketing and Consumption of Literature*, ed. Stephen Brown (New York: Routledge 2006), 100–110.
23 Joe Moran, *Star Authors* (London: Pluto Press, 2000), 48.
24 Ibid., 48.
25 Holbrook, 'Commercial Exaltation', 106.
26 O'Reilly, 'Martin Amis on Marketing', 74.
27 Moran, *Star Authors*, 46–8.
28 David Emblidge, interview by author, Bloomington, Indiana, 9 April 2010.
29 Moran, *Star Authors*, 39.
30 Mehegan, 'The Six-Figure Sophomore'.
31 Moran, *Star Authors*, 40.
32 Ibid., 38.
33 Ibid., 70.
34 Online: http://aimeenez.net/category/multimedia/ (accessed 20 March 2010).
35 Mehegan, 'The Six-Figure Sophomore'.
36 Daniel J. Boorstin, 'From Hero to Celebrity', in *The Human Pseudo-Event: The Celebrity Culture Reader*, ed. P. David Marshall (New York, London: Routledge, 2006), 73.
37 Rebecca Moore Howard, *Standing in the Shadow of Giants: Plagiarists, Authors, Collaborators* (Stamford: Ablex, 1999), 83.
38 P. David Marshall, 'Intimately Intertwined in the Most Public Way: Celebrity and Journalism', in *The Celebrity Culture Reader*, ed. P. David Marshall (New York, London: Routledge 2006), 317.
39 See Bill Poser, 'Kaavyagate Update', *Language Log* (blog), 8 April 2008. Online: http://itre.cis.upenn.edu/~myl/languagelog/archives/003089.html (accessed 20 March 2010); and Manish Vij, 'KaavyaGate Reloaded', *Sepia Mutiny* (blog). Online: http://www.sepiamutiny.com/sepia/archives/003324.html (accessed 10 March 2010).
40 Motoko Rich and Glen Rifkin, 'For a Harvard Student and Aggrieved Novelist, Plagiarism Generates Interest', *New York Times*, 29 April 2006. Online: http://www.nytimes.com/2006/04/29/books/29book.html (accessed 12 March 2010).
41 Marshall, 'Intimately Intertwined', 316–21.
42 Ibid., 322.
43 Thomas Mallon, *Stolen Words: Forays Into the Origins and Ravages of Plagiarism* (New York: Ticknor & Fields, 1989), 10.
44 Laurie Stearns, 'Copy Wrong: Plagiarism, Process, Property, and the Law', in *Perspectives on Plagiarism and Intellectual Property in a Postmodern World*, ed. Lisa Buranen and Alice M. Roy (Albany: State University of New York Press, 1999), 7.
45 See Motoko Rich and Dinitia Smith, 'Publisher to Recall Harvard Student's Novel', *New York Times*, 28 April 2006. Online: http://www.nytimes.com/2006/04/28/books/28author.html (accessed 13 March 2010); David Zhou and Paras D. Bhayani,

'"Opal" Similar to More Books', *Harvard Crimson*, 2 May 2006. Online: http://www.thecrimson.com/article/2006/5/2/opal-similar-to-more-books-kaavya/ (accessed 15 March 2010); and Tanuja Desai Hidier, 'Tanuja Desai Hidier on Born Confused and Opal Mehta', Desi Club, 2006. Online: http://www.desiclub.com/community/culture/culture_article.cfm?id=265 (accessed 15 March 2010).

46 Dinitia Smith, 'Harvard Novelist Says Copying Was Unintentional', *New York Times*, 25 April 2006. Online: http://www.nytimes.com/2006/04/25/books/25book.html (accessed 13 March 2010).
47 See Bill Poser, 'In Defense of Kaavya Viswanathan', *Language Log* (blog), 25 April 2006. Online: http://itre.cis.upenn.edu/~myl/languagelog/archives/003068.html (accessed 20 March 2010); and Malcolm Gladwell, 'Viswanathan-Gate', Gladwell.com (blog), 30 April 2006. Online: http://gladwell.typepad.com/gladwellcom/2006/04/viswanathangate.html (accessed 5 April 2010).
48 Rich and Smith, 'First Idea, Plot and Characters'.
49 Gladwell, 'Viswanathan-Gate'.
50 Rich and Smith, 'First Idea, Plot and Characters'.
51 Hidier, 'Born Confused & Opal Mehta'.
52 Whitney Otto, 'Unoriginal Sins', *New York Times*, 12 May 2006. Online: http://www.nytimes.com/2006/05/12/opinion/12otto.html (accessed 18 March 2010).
53 Thomas Mallon, *Stolen Words*, 3.
54 Russ Juskalian, 'You Didn't Plagiarize, Your Unconscious Did', *Newsweek*, 6 July 2009. Online: http://www.newsweek.com/2009/07/06/you-didn-t-plagiarize-your-unconscious-did.html (accessed 18 March 2010).
55 Emblidge, 'The Viswanathan Dilemma'.
56 Charles McGrath, 'Plagiarism, Everybody Into the Pool', *New York Times*, 7 January 2007. Online: http://www.nytimes.com/2007/01/07/education/edlife/07books.html (accessed 20 March 2010).
57 Anirudh Bhattacharyya, 'Salman Rushdie Writes off Kaavya', IBN Live, 2 May 2006. Online: http://ibnlive.in.com/news/salman-has-no...for-kaavya/9223-2.html (accessed 10 March 2010).

Chapter Fifteen

OF WIN AND LOSS: KIRAN DESAI'S GLOBAL STORYTELLING

Sara-Duana Meyer

'Born in India, educated in India, England and the United States.' These sparse bits of information, found on the dust jackets of Kiran Desai's novels, already tell a story of their own. It is a global story – that of a talented daughter of an internationally acclaimed novelist, that of an upper-class nonresident citizen of a postcolonial country on the way to become one of the economic players of the 'new' empire, and that of a cosmopolitan writer and permanent resident of the US moving casually within the transnational league of what used to be termed 'diaspora writing'.

This essay will trace some of these storylines and investigate their conjunctions against the background of global processes. Kiran Desai, I suggest, tells global stories to a, more or less, global audience. And yet, I would like to add, Kiran Desai tells emphatically Indian stories. Inherently, these assertions entail manifold and well-worn questions of the localization of culture, agency and the self-positioning of a writer within and with literature. Also, in the scope of this anthology and its explicit focus, the question of audience and the mechanisms of the market cannot be omitted.

By a close reading of Desai's work this essay will follow up the various journeys that she embarked on through and in her writing, thus trying to trace the particular topics, concerns and major themes of her work, and accentuate the radical process her writing underwent from the first to the second novel. It will be, true to Desai's various stories, a journey that goes back and forth between the local and the global, the individual and the universal.

Born in 1971, Kiran Desai spent her childhood in India, mostly Delhi, surrounded by her mother Anita Desai's writing and literature from all over the world. A German maternal grandmother, a grandfather from Bangladesh and another grandfather educated in England imply various inherited cultural influences and might be read as a foreboding of a life lived in and between several worlds of East and West. In the mid-80s, aged 14, Desai continued her ancestors' journeys and moved with her then-separated mother to England. A year later they relocated to the US where Kiran Desai has studied, lived and worked ever since, with regular short- and long-term visits both to England and India.

So far Kiran Desai has written two enormously successful novels. The first, *Hullabaloo in the Guava Orchard*, was published in 1998, one year after the 50th anniversary of India's independence, when the world had already pricked up its ears due to the huge media rumpus and numerous Indian writers were published in the US. The novel was highly praised by Salman Rushdie, who listed Desai among 'the best writing since independence' in his controversial anthology *50 Years of Indian Writing* – which, without wanting to undermine the value of Desai's work, since a novel always both anticipates and participates in the global process of its own commercial promotion, surely smoothened the way ever so slightly.

Desai won the Betty Trask Award[1] for her first novel and after that it became quiet around the young author while she worked on her second novel, travelling back and forth between the US and India since she had realized that she 'had to return to India for the other half of the story'.[2] Some eight years later, her second novel *The Inheritance of Loss* (2006) came out with a bang, receiving the Man Booker Prize in 2006 along with several other awards.[3] True to her ancestry, Desai spent a great part of the next year on reading tours all over the world and since then innumerable interviews and reviews as well as an anthology of essays on her work have followed.[4] She was the featured author of the Asia House Festival of Asian Literature in 2007, has been included into the academic canon of postcolonial writing and is, judging by the recent updates on her Wikipedia site that disclose juicy bits of her personal life, still a person of public interest despite the prolonged time lags between her books.[5]

The media, always in need of a tag, have called her an expatriate writer or Indian-American author, with and without the hyphen that has, despite its ostensive insignificance, split bearings. Along with the coeval blurring of the boundaries of time/space and the rise of global networks, the definitions and terms of belonging have equally shifted, thus leading attempts of classification onto a sticky wicket. The uncertainty of how to nationalize a writer like Kiran Desai points to a common feature of writers of Indian origin living and working mostly, but not exclusively, abroad, and moving between several cultural and geographical 'homes', both physically and in their writing. North America especially takes pride in providing fertile grounds for the most successful literary representatives of the so-called *desi*-diaspora, a term that (nowadays) focuses on transnational processes and implies the recognition of a necessary heterogeneity and diversity. In fact, the national claim on a famous author like Desai leads to herself being located as a matter of course on the contemporary literary map of both the US and India and to her writing being conceived as a cultural commodity with a certain flavour not wanted to be missed anymore in a global consumer society. While literature by writers like Desai can hardly be listed among the export goods of postliberalization India, the ethnic label or brand, depending on the viewpoint, sticks. 'India' is a commercial cultural marker and Graham Huggan, who discusses the condition and consumption of postcolonial writings in a global, late-capitalist system, states, 'Part of the reason, surely, that Indian literature in English has become so fashionable is that it has been made to stand in metonymically for India itself as an object of conspicuous consumption.'[6] To Desai's double pressure of second-generation fame and first-rate talent, then, a third aspect is added, namely that of the politics of representation – yet another inheritance that comes along with the cultural capital of postcolonial writing and leads inevitably to the pesky question of which audience a cosmopolitan Indian American writer might be aiming at, and to its twin sister, the loathed inquiry whether s/he is exoticizing India for a Western audience.[7] Amit Chaudhuri's fuming essay on that very subject points out that by 'bringing the audience into the picture, the emphasis and the debate shift from writerly practice to cultural, social, and economic transactions [...], from meaning to the production of meaning'.[8] Since reading as much as writing is always culturally presupposed, the audience constitutes a crucial point, though, especially in the context of this anthology. And while Chaudhuri falls short in acknowledging that meaning is never simply 'there' and is mostly a reciprocal product of writerly and readerly practice, it seems pretty obvious that cosmopolitan writers like Desai might not aim at or write for a particular readership, but certainly are aware of their global reception. After all, the 'exotic' aspect that, let's face it, adds considerably to the market value of a work if carefully balanced, depends substantially on where and how an international readership positions that particular work: 'The exotic is not, as is often supposed, an inherent *quality* to be found "in" certain people, distinctive objects, or specific places; exoticism describes, rather, a particular mode of aesthetic *perception* – one which renders people, objects and places strange even as it domesticates them, and which effectively manufactures otherness even as it claims to surrender to its immanent mystery.'[9]

Arguably a diasporic writer can radically avoid the prestressed tag of postcolonial writing along with this discussion by choosing a literary topic that doesn't address any pivotal issues. However, for Desai, who admitted in various interviews that she saw 'everything through the lens of being Indian'[10] and that 'the perspective was too important to give up', this 'choice' clearly was not an option. Quite the opposite: 'Being part of the Indian diaspora gives one a precise emotional location to work from, if not a precise geographical one.'[11]

India, then, is the setting that Desai chose for both her debut novel and the greater parts of the global tale of her second novel. It is an India that she left as a teenager, before the economic liberalization process started, and has ever since only returned to as a visitor – an India, 'truly a land of miracles', as she states in her first novel only half tongue-in-cheek.[12] Her first novel, *Hullabaloo in the Guava Orchard* (*HGO*), stages ironically and cunningly the story of Sampath Chawla, a young man unfit for mundane life or – in short – a loser, who climbs a guava tree in search of a moment of peace and solitude and unintentionally becomes a worshipped holy man. It is an account of the author's coming to terms with what she 'was in the inevitable process of losing'.[13] Although this evokes Salman Rushdie's well-known warning to fellow expatriate writers to be aware of their creating 'imaginary homelands' when writing about the *desh* from outside India, Desai's first novel does not resonate any overly sentimental emotions.[14] Quite the contrary: migration is not an issue, the story is simple, the scene is Shahkot – an average Indian town that provides along with its inhabitants and the nearby orchard the narrative setting, leaving the world beyond peculiarly vague. Thus Desai's emotional statement strikes one as slightly odd, given the evident criticism of big topics like spirituality as the most lucrative business in India, the denunciation of administrative corruption and the obvious disapproval of a strict patriarchal family system that Desai expresses in this book.

The narrative approach chosen by the author underlines this rather critical perception. Throughout this well-crafted novel, the narrator's voice maintains an amused distance from the events and characters, keeping the reader at bay by never allowing complete identification with the characters. Rather, the reader witnesses an 'India' that is without doubt depicted with vivid and pointed strokes, but bears unmistakable traits of a rather satirical social study of 'Indian' habits and customs, seen from the perspective of an outsider-insider. This portrayal involves corruption and abuse of power in the government service along with domestic acts of illegality like tapping water or electricity from the hospital supplies as a matter of course, includes sly acts of insubordination like the dismantling of the barbed wire fence around the post office since people 'discovered a sudden need for wire' (*HGO*, 27), and goes on to parody the malfunctioning phone system in a scene that reminds one of a classical Shakespearean comedy of errors. The inevitable breakdown of electricity when it rains is amended by the street lights that 'wouldn't work, everyone knew, until the next local election' (*HGO*, 16) and the microcosm of Shahkot is described at length as a bustling market scene with all the necessary 'typically Indian' ingredients of 'cows and pigs and water buffalos' right next to 'clerks from the asthma institute' and an 'orange-robed sadhu' (*HGO*, 28).

Overall an exhaustive portrayal of Indian society in a small town, one might assume, which, in addition to the formerly discussed, brings to mind an essay by Lisa Lau on the differing representations of South Asia by female writers within and outside of India. She argues that since 'American Indians [...] are the most prolific of the contemporary South Asian women writers [...], it is predominantly the diasporic women writers who are the creators and keepers of the global literary image of South Asian culture, and this trend looks set to continue.'[15]

This 'task' can surely be traced in Desai's vivid account of Shahkot, which, apparently, stands *pars pro toto* for the Indian society at large, on display for an international readership, thus opening the local again towards the global. Despite its restricted setting, the psychological features discussed in the novel are universal. It is a story about family matters, generation conflicts and the petty strive of average people for something bigger while balancing on the edge of normality. The question of the norm and its limits runs strong in the novel, closely tied to its counterpart of the collective in stark contrast to the individual. Not able to conform to social regulations by working regular jobs and behaving 'normal', the main character Sampath eventually falls out of the machinery of society by his explicitly 'queer'[16] behaviour at a classically enacted Hindu wedding, where he sneaks into a 'room piled high with wedding finery' (*HGO*, 37) and dresses up. This gives the author an occasion to elaborate on well-known imagery: 'fabrics and saris of every colour imaginable [...] with embroidered parrots and lotus flowers [...], rich plum and luminous amber shades. There were dark velvets and pale milk-like pastels' (*HGO*, 37). This almost tangible visual abundance is continued at an olfactory level and Desai conjures up the fragrances of the Orient: 'rose-water and [...] the scent of musk, [...] sandalwood oil' (*HGO*, 37).

Characteristically, Desai applies throughout the novel a remarkably light tone that sometimes deceives the dark undercurrents of futility and desperation that are part of her characters. While Sampath (and with him the reader and presumably also the author) indulges in this feast of the senses, his physical and social trespassing can, on a heavier note, be read as a mute but radical sign and the only way of making his desperate situation finally understood – thus evoking ever so faintly Spivak's subalterns. His dress-up culminates in a grotesque drag show with a grand striptease in the fountain in front of the whole wedding party. Normality shatters to pieces and Sampath, who literally 'found a crack' (*HGO*, 48), escapes at last from social duties and family obligations.

The peace and bliss Sampath has found, of being 'in the right place at last' (*HGO*, 51) in his guava tree (after a flight that is enacted by Desai as a frenzy bordering on hysteria), is not meant to last for long. He is quickly made into a holy man after he displays traits of clairvoyance, an unrightfully acquired knowledge of people's secrets that turns into an unintended Foucauldian kind of power. Desai artfully points out the sly identity of the involuntary Baba, while she also shows his innocent ambivalence. She doesn't follow a blatant narratological solution to explain the whole thing as a fraud. Rather, she carves out the human longing for a spiritual leader and the joyous – presumably not exclusively Indian – belief in wonders.

Though delivered with a knowing wink, Desai's disapproval of spiritual and material consumerism, at times impossible to distinguish, is tangible in the obvious critique of the successful marketing machinery carried out by Sampath's father-turned-manager, which includes billboards, devotional objects and shares taken by rikshawalas. The same applies to her critique of a society prone to superstition and the supernatural that could not bear the slightly odd behaviour of a misfit, while his allegedly supernatural and utmost abnormal traits are willingly accepted and reinforced into a religious travesty.

As distinct as she makes her point, Desai still avoids a clear-cut drawing of generic boundaries between reality and truth, which might resonate with her own experiences of oscillating between several worlds and blurred borders. A touch of magic remains in the novel that goes beyond the showing off of superstition. By using well-proven tools of magic realism, Desai suggests that there might be more to Sampath than just a little madness, ironically hinted at in his final escape (or 'transformation') into a guava at the undoubtedly open end of the novel.

The dichotomy of nature in crass contrast to the humdrum of the town life is another trail that can be traced throughout the novel. Lush, wild and untamed nature as an almost metaphysical experience is repeatedly enacted and staged in the first and also the second novel, suggesting that this for Desai is a typical trait of India. The poetical description of distinct climatic markers like the monsoon displays the human exposure and commitment to nature's arbitrary abundance: 'The world would grow silent and fragrant […]. Soon the winged ants would be flying and lizards would grow fat on dozens of multiplying insects. […] Doors would swell […]. Fungus and mould would sprout green and voluptuous […] under the sink' (*HGO*, 12). This portrayal of animated nature literally encroaching upon the materialistic world can be found again in *The Inheritance of Loss* and strikes the reader as essentially prolific and sensual, even more so as it is the view of Sampath's young mother Kulfi, who has just given birth. Kulfi is probably the darkest character, in whom Desai blends a variety of the novel's central themes. The relationship between magic and nature is enacted in her grotesque pregnancy. In Kulfi's insatiable hunger and her obsession with food, the thin line of sanity seems to be particularly fragile, which can be read as yet another hint at the fissures in the society Desai depicts. Again we find the question of normality as a dark undercurrent of the novel, although light-heartedly and wittily narrated, while the focalization zooms in and out of Kulfi's rambling desires. What keeps her sane during her pregnancy is a metafictional twist, namely the creation of an entirely fictional world of food: 'With a feeling bordering on hysteria, she began to draw on the dirty, stained walls of the house' (*HGO*, 7). Thus Kulfi conjures up in a creative act what she misses most, which resonates with Desai's statement about recreating a world that she herself was going to lose.

Food as a cultural marker plays a major role in Desai's novels: the refusal of Shahkot's new (Indian) district collector to eat any more English food, which results in the resignation of his offended (Indian) cook, is echoed and taken further in the English-food-only politics of the Anglophile judge in *The Inheritance of Loss*. Desai clearly evokes stereotypes when she marks the bluntness of English food in stark contrast to the varieties of Indian dishes. It is literally Kulfi's cooking pot where several major themes are blended into a delicious and exotic dish, which yet again gives the author the opportunity to relish in Indian cuisine and parade 'food abundant in all its many incarnations' (*HGO*, 4). However, along with typical ingredients, other condiments are mentioned that strike even the reader familiar with the Indian cuisine as exotic: 'Cumin, quail, mustard seeds, pomelo rind, [...] spider leaf, lotus root [...]' (*HGO*, 101), 'a porcupine, a mongoose' (*HGO*, 154). These ingredients find Kulfi, sketched with fond strokes, as an increasingly happy and wild woman in the 'deepest parts of the woods, losing herself amidst the bamboo groves, the sal forests, the towering moss-laden trees' (*HGO*, 100), by which – subtly but unmistakably – a link is established between Kulfi's cooking, exuberant nature and magic or, more specifically, witchcraft. Similarly, Desai's descriptions of the dishes Kulfi creates read like those of psychedelic drugs: '[...] full of strange hints and dark undercurrents, leaving you on firm ground one moment, dragging you under the next' (*HGO*, 102). This foretells the fate of the spy, who, certain that Sampath's secret lies in Kulfi's magic potions and desperate to uncover a fraud, falls into (and possibly drowns in) Kulfi's biggest cauldron.

This disturbing end – suggesting cannibalism and raising yet again the question of the border between human and animal, reason and madness – shows clearly that Desai's debut novel is certainly more than her fond memories of her country of origin. Rather, it is a furious account and social study of common stereotypes, spiced with local flavour and topped with the bitter-crisp device of satire.

There are, however (and despite severe criticism), obviously some 'typical' characteristics of a surprisingly homogenous India that include even the at-times stereotypical display of fissures and flaws in the Indian society. And while Rushdie famously states in the introduction to *Mirrorwork* (1997) that 'literature has little or nothing to do with a writer's home address'[17] and Huggan confirms this view by downplaying the 'national distinctiveness' of Indian writing in English, since the latter, he argues, is 'to a large extent a transnational, diasporic phenomenon and [...] literary works are rarely if ever direct expressions of national identity, with characteristics that might go some way toward "explaining" aspects of national culture'.[18] However, several (Indian) critics come to a rather devastating verdict on Desai's first novel. For Shubha Tiwari, 'basically it is a Western way of looking and analyzing India. Although no one can deny the grotesque details of our country, nevertheless the novel appears to be a slice of India served to the egoistic West.'[19] Likewise, Haris Qadeer criticizes the 'hegemonic view of India' that Desai conveys and accuses her of reinforcing the 'Oriental' image of India by presenting 'a kaleidoscopic picture of Indian culture, tradition and ethos which down the ages have attracted the attention of the West'.[20]

While I wouldn't agree that Desai's geocultural living circumstances don't matter at all, nor that there isn't any Indian 'distinctiveness' marked as such, I would like to borrow once more Lau's approach. According to her, it is particularly common for diasporic women writers to put more emphasis on a comprehensive portrayal of the country they have left – surely not only due to nostalgic reasons but also due to an 'outsider view' that comes along with an implied responsibility of writing as a representative, as she goes on to explain. The novel clearly harks back at Desai's nostalgia and her attempts at '"explaining" aspects of national culture' are unmistakable, however subtle. Still, I would suggest to perceive Desai as her own audience applying a peculiar and possibly unavoidable outsider-insider view in a process of remembering and rediscovering, which eventually conjures up the peculiarities of an India she is about to forget.

In my reading, both of Desai's novels are a 'return journey to the fact of being Indian'[21] and a global tale at the same time. *The Inheritance of Loss*, focusing on India in relation to the rest of the world and awarded with the Booker Prize in 2006, presumably marks a turning point in Desai's – although so far certainly not unsuccessful – career. Considering the ambivalent status of one of the top prestigious prizes of the world, due to its colonial heritage and inherently authorizing power, the query as to whether Desai seriously contemplated turning down the award seems justified. Then again, the same could be said about her explicit answer: 'I'm not crazy! [...] Nooo! NO! Because you can drag that ethical dilemma into every single aspect of your life.'[22]

Even though the prize has contributed to raising awareness of the global dimensions of literature in English, Huggan's critique of its hidden politics (namely the commodification of difference and an Anglocentric patronizing discourse) is certainly justified, 'as English-language literature splinters into a variety of commercially viable "othered" forms'.[23] The lure, however, is virtually irresistible. Sales triple or quadruple and as 'the stakes get ever higher the Prize exerts a major influence over the cultural perceptions, as well as the reading habits, of its consumer public.'[24]

The heightened interest in Indian authors in the US at the end of the '90s coincided with a reciprocally growing publishing industry in India, which eventually led, as Desai remarks, to a global recognition of Indian literature produced in India: 'It used to be the case that really you had to be published abroad in order to make a living as a writer and to have access to this whole machine, this publishing machine of the west.' The global impact of the Booker, however, was incommensurably greater, both in India – which, as Desai explains, 'always followed the Booker' – and in the rest of the world.[25] It might be no accident that the novel addresses an equally big topic, namely that of the postcolonial condition of not only India but an ever-shrinking globalized world.

Globalization, of course, is not an entirely new phenomenon. The process might have started in the watershed year of 1492 or much earlier; the colonial endeavour, in any case, is a thoroughly global project. Over the past few decades, the firm dichotomy between the global and the local has dwindled more and more, giving way to an intensified global awareness on a local level and in turn a valorization of local structures through global perspectives – a process that the sociologist Roland Robertson termed 'glocalization' and which relates also to the mechanisms of the Booker.

Surely there is a lot of Desai's own experience of moving and living in and between several worlds and histories in her second novel that addresses themes like the colonial past of India, the legacy of class and the more recent history of separatism, but also migration, economic inequality, hybridization and the question of the nation-state. Again the drawing and crossing of borders (and with it the notation of the 'norm') is the leitmotif of the novel, this time on a global scale. While in Desai's first novel the world remains 'large and mysterious beyond Shahkot' (*HGO*, 12), in *The Inheritance of Loss* (*IL*) the whole world makes up the scene, aptly showcased in the prefacing poem by Jorge Luis Borges that anticipates key themes and adds yet another global flavour. The plot stretches far, geographically and historically: the narrative takes the reader in several parallel storylines into several realities that go back and forth from the extreme landscape of the Northeast Himalayas via academic Cambridge to the 'underbelly of the nation' in New York, and from the mid-1980s (the time when

Desai left India) to the last decade of the British Empire. The narrative anchor of the novel is India – more precisely a specific borderland of the country that inherently defies 'Indianness' and the British heritage of national concepts. In Kalimpong, a hill station in the Northeast Himalayas, lives a retired judge, his old pitiable cook and his orphaned granddaughter, Sai, none of them native to the place, amidst wild and beautiful nature in a huge crumbling house, where time seems either preserved or abandoned: 'a space so big it reached both backwards and forward' (*IL*, 47). Desai accentuates aptly the intense solitude of the setting, and with it the immense weight of history. The Anglophile judge, more an archetype than a character, is the well-known mimicry man – albeit without the subversive potential that Homi Bhabha suggested. His education in England during the 40s makes up one of the parallel storylines, told in flashbacks and memories. It is a story of shame, loneliness and social failure. Despite the humiliation suffered and without having aligned the 'real' England with his ideals, he returns to India as a 'brown sahib' and accomplishes the task of becoming more English than the English, recuperating his bashed self-esteem by mortifying his wife: 'He loathed Indians. He worked at being English with the passion of hatred and for what he would become, he would be despised by absolutely everyone, English and Indians, both' (*IL*, 161). With this character, Desai sketches the colonial past, or rather the harms it has done to India's cultural assertiveness, and one cannot but be reminded of Macaulay's notorious 'Minute on Education'.[26] The author raises the question of identity constructed along the coordinates of ethnicity, nationality, class and culture, and balances the tricky issue of willing surrender with the involuntary inheritance of the colonial past that the judge's granddaughter, Sai, experiences. The 17-year-old anglophone and convent-educated orphan could be called a mimicry girl by upbringing, who, despite having never been outside India, doesn't really belong to India either. The young girl is the stereotypical teenager – pondering questions of identity, experiencing her first love and adopting universal teenager styles: 'khaki pants and a T-shirt that said "Free Tibet". Her feet were bare and she wore her short hair in two untidy braids ending just before her shoulders' (*IL*, 90). However, Sai on no account corresponds to the image of an average Indian woman, as her secret lover and tutor, young Indian-Nepalese Gyan, on his quest for national identity points out: '[Sai] who could not eat with her hands; could not squat down on the ground on her haunches to wait for a bus; who had never been to a temple but for architectural interests; never chewed a *paan* and […] thought it vulgar to put oil in your hair and used paper to clean her bottom' (*IL*, 234).

Not only does Sai's lack of 'Indianness' become obvious in this picture of a (stereo)typical Indian woman, but also the class divide and with it the exploitation of the working class. Desai's prose turns acrid when she illustrates the construction of the mansion: 'As always, the price for such romance had been high and paid for by others' (*IL*, 16). Walled up in his castle and refusing to speak the local language, the judge embodies an anglicized ruling class whose legacy is, as Desai claims, reinvented and reinforced by the class represented by the cook who in an act of self-abasement begs for punishment or, literally, to be put in his place: 'It's your duty to discipline me. It's as it should be' (*IL*, 428). Sarcastically, Desai points out the century-old mechanisms of this class divide: 'Poor people needed certain lines; the script was always the same, and they had no option but to beg for mercy: The cook knew instinctively how to cry' (*IL*, 8). And, Desai makes clear, the class divide does certainly not cease to exist by leaving India.

Migration, one of the key features of globalization, is probably the biggest topic in *The Inheritance of Loss*. While Desai juxtaposes the judge's traumatic but successful education in England with the horrid working and living conditions of the cook's son, Biju, in New York, several issues are being illustrated. The question of the localization of culture is apparently inseparably connected to the postcolonial condition; however, the impact of global economy has led to a shifting focus in the choice of country as well. Biju (and with him the reader) learns that the Indian 'ethnoscape'[27] might be found everywhere: 'Everywhere you look, practically, Indians' (*IL*, 28). Still, Desai chose the USA as the setting for Biju's story, which is certainly but not solely influenced by her personal experiences. In fact, the US as the number one immigration country has outrun the values that used to be assigned to England, and with this shift the facets of desperation, deprivation and degradation have also changed, as Desai suggests. The author illustrates vividly the high hopes that the poor of 'the global south' pin on the 'promised land' and dismantles these aspirations by sketching the messy map of globalization in the restaurant kitchens of New York, 'perfectly first-world on top, perfectly third-world twenty-two steps below' (*IL*, 30). In this context, both Biju and the reader receive a lesson in cultural stereotyping when Desai confronts them with Biju's own, arguably typically Indian, prejudices, and presents then a list of 14 seemingly random countries from all over the world that either 'would throw them out', 'hate them' or 'don't like them'. Not even Guadeloupe: 'They love us there? No' (*IL*, 104–5). Noticeable is the narrative shift from 'them' to 'us', which might be a tiny but significant sign for the narrator positioning herself alongside Biju, notwithstanding class, hence making the list presumably all the more startling for many of her (Indian) readers. However, it is not a unique Indian experience that Desai depicts in this American nightmare. The story is universal in an age of global fluidity of every kind and Biju stands for a whole class and generation of immigrants, yet another feature of the global state of postcoloniality that, according to Huggan, 'capitalises both on the widespread circulation of ideas about cultural otherness and on the worldwide trafficking of culturally "othered" artifacts and goods'.[28] To the flows of global capitalism is added the export of cheap labour, albeit clandestine. The only choice left to the economically disadvantaged from 'unwanted' countries is to go illegal – and be all the same exploited and deprived, suggesting that social inequality can certainly not be made up by the American dream turned nightmare.

While on a bigger scale the universal problems of the nation-state and global inequality are being discussed, Desai balances this rather broad perspective with the focus on the local political situation, thus anchoring the narrative both temporally and spatially and drawing an analogy between Indian immigrants in the US and Nepali immigrants in India. The border zone and 'messy map' (*IL*, 13) of the Northeast Himalayas, 'where India blurred into Bhutan and Sikkim' (*IL*, 12) and different ethnic groups overlap and interweave, provides an ample playground for a separatist movement.

Noticeably, the author operates on several levels. While the bleary and entirely fictional notion of borders and their transgression runs as the perpetual undercurrent through the novel, the fights taken out on 'homeground' affect directly the lives of the main characters and thus become all the more substantial. Informed by Desai's own familiarity with the actual place,[29] the narrative switches back and forth between the personal approach, lengthy lessons on the politically and historically complex background, and a more general viewpoint: 'There was a report of new dissatisfaction in the hills, gathering insurgency, men and guns. It was the Indian-Nepalese this time, fed up with being treated like the minority in a place where they were the majority' (*IL*, 12). Evidence yet again for Desai's self-asserted task to represent an India true to the facts, one might conclude. However, flashes of irony, like the description of the 'universal guerrilla fashion' (*IL*, 5) worn by 'the boys', turn out to be much more cynical than expected by unmasking the local strive as yet another global phenomenon – without the consolation of a possible worldwide brotherhood in the struggle against inequality or the power of the 'multitude' that Michael Hardt and Antonio Negri, in their seminal work on the new world order – or 'Empire' – so aptly adjure.[30] Obviously, her wider geographical range has trained Desai to look more broadly, but eventually even India in general, or rather North India, is depicted as mutually fractured and fissured by listing turmoils and insurgencies. 'The country, Sai noted, was coming apart at the seams' (*IL*, 145) – a bleak and certainly more ambivalent account than the India depicted in her debut novel.

Similarly, the recurring theme of food is used as a cultural marker in the second novel. However, while in her debut novel food served the main purpose of conjuring up memory and adding to a bright, sensual and arguably exotic picture of India, the second displays the many aspects of food closely related to the overall questions of (national) identity and cultural commodification. Cultural differences are chiefly acted out in the tea ceremony, the core ritual of Englishness – which seems all the more fitting considering the nearby tea plantations and thus the emblem of colonial exploitation. However, the dwindling British influence and with it the hubris of the whole colonial enterprise is articulated in the judge's complaint: 'This was a travesty that undid the very concept of tea time' (*IL*, 4). Sai, on the other hand, is yet again shown in her constraint that deprives her of cultural knowledge without offering her an adequate alternative: 'She had no idea how to properly make tea this way, the Indian way. She only knew the English way' (*IL*, 9). The blandness of English dishes, like 'water-logged green beans, and a head of cauliflower under cheese sauce that looked like a shrouded brain' (*IL*, 44), is put in stark contrast to the local cuisine, and Desai makes a point of emphasizing both an insider view (hers and that of a certain readership) and the strange (and therefore exotic) aspect for those of her readers who are, like Sai, unfamiliar with '*loki*, *tinda*, *kathal*, *kaddu*, *patrel*, and the local *saag* in the market' (*IL*, 234).

On the other hand, the transfer from the local to the global, or rather glocal, orbit and back also happens via the culturally charged *topos* of food. Sai's elderly lady friends teach their Sherpa-servant to cook 'Indonesian *saté*' (*IL*, 91) along with Chinese and Hungarian dishes, the fact that 'chicken tikka masala has replaced fish and chips as the number one take out dinner in Britain' (*IL*, 63) and the menus at Biju's different places of work in New York are ample examples of food as just one more cultural commodity.

While many of the themes addressed in her first novel are hence deconstructed during the narrative process of the second, nature and the specific climate remain cultural markers that firmly locate the respective plots in India. The fierce beauty of the Northeast Himalayas evokes a poetic vocabulary of grandness and striking images that seem in fact the only elements in the novel depicted without the otherwise finely nuanced but prevailingly stylistic device of irony and, at times, sarcasm. The insignificance of petty human striving and aspiration are put in stark contrast with the natural sublime – climatic inevitabilities like the monsoon mock the judge's need of propriety and control, and the sheer size of the mountains and their exuberant intimidating beauty 'proved a man to be so small that it made sense to give it all up, empty it all out' (*IL*, 39).

Although the questions of 'home', of identity and belonging, remain unanswered, the end of the novel eventually turns the experience of nature into the metaphysical artist's formula that beauty is truth and truth is beauty: 'The five peaks of Kanchenjunga turned golden with the kind of luminous light that made you feel, if briefly, that the truth was apparent. All you needed to do was to reach out and pluck it' (*IL*, 433).

Although Sai's decision to leave Kalimpong opens up the global perspective anew and evokes yet again the undercurrent of border crossing, this seemingly positive ending cannot overcome the overall themes of alienation, loss and failure that run through Desai's second novel along with the legacies of impotence that are somehow 'inherited' and the widening chasm of global poverty and humiliation. Despite her own success as a cosmopolitan writer living in several worlds, Desai expresses a rather pessimistic view of hybridization. In particular, the experience of migration seems mostly a traumatic one in her novel, which performs the visual and literal 'vocabulary of immigration, of exile, of translation, [which] inevitably overlaps with a realization of the multiple options for reinvention, of myriad perspectives, shifting truths, telling of lies', as Desai states.[31]

Consequently, Desai's second novel is much less received as a portrayal of 'India' than as an aesthetic account of a global condition, albeit seen from Desai's personal and expressly Indian viewpoint – which adds a local flavour and has led to overall praise, in which the accusation of exoticizing India (the major criticism of her first book) remains almost completely absent. In fact, reviewers and critics alike seem to agree with the (thanks to first-grade media coverage) evenly and globally conveyed statement by the head judge of the Booker Foundation, Hermione Lee, that *The Inheritance of Loss* is 'a magnificent novel of humane breadth and wisdom, comic tenderness and powerful political acuteness'.[32]

Interesting, however, is the massive critique from a rather unexpected side. Desai's portrayal of Kalimpong and its inhabitants did not go down well with people of Nepalese descent, who had mostly been alerted to it by the ensuing global media coverage and felt utterly misrepresented – yet another example of global reception and the detours that global flows at times take.[33]

Both of Desai's novels tell global, or rather glocal, stories. In an age of global deterritorialization, Desai suggests, the coordinates of time and space that constitute the even more elusive dimensions of place and identity are both entirely dispensable and yet vitally crucial.

The related notion of shifting geographies, by which former centres and margins often acquire a radically new quality, invokes in reference to a country like India the vocabulary of First and Second World – but, as Desai suggests, since both the First and Second or even Third World can be found in the same place right next to each other, these notions have to be adapted.[34] The global commodification of cultural difference remains, not only in the context of this anthology, a major topic, and the attempt to narrate 'India' proves to be a tricky task. Obviously there are flaws in Desai's accounts, both in the peculiarities and the abundance of India in the microcosm of a town – which conveys a peculiarly manageable, somehow homogeneous, image – as much as in the assumption of a whole country 'coming apart at the seams', despite the geographically and culturally restricted focus on North India covered by the narrative frame.

The writer as cultural interpreter who sets out on a conversation with the world bears the load of his/her audience's own imaginations and experiences. The question of whether this image has to be accurate, then, has necessarily to be answered by another question, namely the crucial query of whether there ever is such an image at all. No one has been accused so far of showcasing globalization – presumably due to the fact that literally everyone is affected by these processes, or, as Arif Dirlik put it: 'In the age of flexible production, we all live in the borderlands.'[35]

Desai's quest of retrieving her personal India and thus 'Indianness' is unmistakably subjective, although rather common for a cosmopolitan diasporic writer. Her thematic concerns, and with them her approach, are informed by these circumstances, as argued by Lau, who states that place and cultural identity even in a deterritorialized world still matter a great deal: 'Geographical locations of the authors influence, to no small degree, […] the audience for whom they write, and the concerns which they choose to draw attention towards.'[36]

Desai's global profile, however, is twofold. On the one hand, it carries an undeniable advantage in terms of visibility and marketability. On the other, her perception as representative of 'India' and a possible conveyer of cultural 'otherness' leads to a peculiar vulnerability of her work to both being seen and used as a means of reconfirming an exoticist image. In order to avoid this, Huggan suggests the subversive and self-protective act of 'rehearsing a continuing history of imperialist perceptions of an "othered" India', which ironically might increase its commercial value.[37]

To date there is no trace in Desai's work of what Huggan calls 'strategic' exoticism or 'metaexoticism'. Even so, Kiran Desai's story so far was a story of success. It runs in the family, one could say, or else simply this: it is surely not the last time we have heard from Kiran Desai.

Notes and References

1 This prize is given to the best new novels by Commonwealth writers under the age of 35.
2 Kiran Desai, interview by Sophie Rochester, Man Booker Prize, 2007. Online: http://www.themanbookerprize.com/perspective/qanda/40 (accessed 22 December 2010).
3 *The Inheritance of Loss* was selected as one of *Publishers Weekly* Best Books of the Year 2006, as one of the *New York Times Book Review* 100 Notable Books of the Year, as an ALA Notable Book of the Year 2006, subsequently awarded the National Book Critics Circle Fiction Award in 2007 and shortlisted for several other prizes.

4 See http://wiki.angl-am.uni-oldenburg.de/index.php/Kiran_Desai,_The_Inheritance_of_Loss_(2006) for a selection of reviews (accessed 24 December 2010). Unfortunately, the anthology of critical essays on Desai's work edited by P. D. Nimsarkar and published in 2008 might not exactly be a prime example. It assembles a variety of, it has to be said, at times rather peculiar viewpoints, and brims with an utterly astonishing quantity of obvious typing, spelling and other mistakes.
5 http://en.wikipedia.org/wiki/Kiran_Desai (accessed 21 January 2013).
6 Graham Huggan, *The Postcolonial Exotic: Marketing the Margins* (London: Routledge, 2001), 81.
7 The equally tedious controversial discussion on the choice of language shall not be expatiated here. Instead I will simply outline what others before me have stated, namely that English indeed has become a first language in India, and that undoubtedly English is the language of choice for maximum chances on the global market.
8 Amit Chaudhuri, 'The East as a Career: On "Strangeness" in Indian Writing', in *Clearing a Space: Reflections on India, Literature and Culture* (Oxford: Peter Lang, 2008), 87.
9 Huggan, *The Postcolonial Exotic*, 13.
10 Kiran Desai, interview by Laura Barton, 'A passage from India', *Guardian*, 12 Oct 2006. Online: http://www.guardian.co.uk/books/2006/oct/12/bookerprize2006.thebookerprize (accessed 22 December 2010).
11 Kiran Desai, interview by Sophie Rochester.
12 'And so the post office stood in the middle of the hustle and bustle of Shahkot. Schoolchildren, beggars, potters and signboard painters. Cows and pigs and water buffaloes ... A fish woman. Flies ... An orange-robed sadhu smiling and bowing despite the heat. (Truly India is a land of miracles)' (*HGO*, 28).
13 Kiran Desai, interview by Laura Barton.
14 See Salman Rushdie's essay of the same name in his collection of essays and criticism, *Imaginary Homelands: Essays and Criticism 1981–1991* (London: Granta, 1992), 9–21.
15 Lisa Lau, 'Making the Difference: The Differing Presentations and Representations of South Asia in the Contemporary Fiction of Home and Diasporic South Asian Women Writers', *Modern Asian Studies* 39, 1 (2005): 239.
16 In a double sense, considering Desai's play with gender attributions.
17 Salman Rushdie and Elizabeth West, eds, *Mirrorwork: 50 Years of Indian Writing, 1947–1997* (New York: Picador 1997), xiii.
18 Huggan, *The Postcolonial Exotic*, 66.
19 Shubha Tiwari, 'Kiran Desai's Hullabaloo in the Guava Orchard as a Satirical Novel', *Indian English Literature: A Post-Colonial Response*, ed. Gajendra Kumar and Uday Shankar Ojha (New Delhi: Sarup & Sons, 2005), 137.
20 Haris Qadeer, 'Essentially Oriental: The Image of India in Kiran Desai's Hullabaloo in Guava Orchard' [sic], in *Kiran Desai: The Novelist, An Anthology of the Critical Essays*, ed. P. D. Nimsarkar (New Delhi: Creative Books 2008), 85.
21 Kiran Desai, interview by Sophie Rochester.
22 Kiran Desai, interview by Laura Barton.
23 Huggan, *The Postcolonial Exotic*, 111.
24 Ibid., 108.
25 Kiran Desai, interview with *Bold Type* for Random House, May 1999. Online: http://www.randomhouse.com/boldtype/0599/desai/interview.html (accessed 23 December 2010).

26 The politician and historian Thomas Babington Macaulay infamously opted, in his 'Minute of 2 February 1835 on Indian Education', for a class of 'interpreters between us and the millions whom we govern [...], Indian in blood and colour, but English in taste, in opinions, in morals, and in intellect' and presumed to claim that 'a single shelf of a good European library was worth the whole native literature of India and Arabia.' (Online: http://dart.columbia.edu/library/indian-education/indian-education.html (accessed 21 January 2013).)

27 In reference to Manuel Castells' 'spaces of flows', Arjun Appadurai lists five dimensions of global cultural flows, namely that of people, media, technologies, money and ideologies: ethnoscapes, mediascapes, technoscapes, financescapes and ideoscapes. ('Disjuncture and Difference in the Global Cultural Economy', in *Global Culture: Nationalism, Globalization and Modernity*, ed. Mike Featherstone (London: Sage, 1990), 295–310.)

28 Graham Huggan, *The Postcolonial Exotic*, 28.

29 See Kiran Desai, interview by Laura Barton.

30 Hardt and Negri assert not so much the territory to this term but the notion of a ubiquitous, global power.

31 Kiran Desai, interview by Sophie Rochester.

32 Hermione Lee, quoted in 'Kiran Desai gets Booker Prize', *Overseas Indian*, October 2006. Online: http://www.overseasindian.in/2006/oct/news/23dia3.shtml (accessed 24 December 2010).

33 Randeep Ramesh, 'Book-burning Threat Over Town's Portrayal in Booker-Winning Novel', *Guardian*, 2 November 2006. Online: http://www.guardian.co.uk/world/2006/nov/02/books.india (accessed 23 December 2010).

34 The sociologist Saskia Sassen, who coined the term 'global city', states that the new geographies of global networks nowadays include cities such as Mexico City or Mumbai alongside the 'old' centres of power. (See: 'The Global City: Strategic Site/New Frontier', in *Democracy, Citizenship, and the Global City*, ed. Engin F. Isin (London: Routledge, 2000), 51). Interestingly, and despite her own urban experience of Indian as well as US megacities, so far Desai has chosen rather rural Indian settings for her novels.

35 Arif Dirlik, *After the Revolution: Waking to Global Capitalism* (Hanover: Wesleyan University Press, 1994), 87.

36 Lisa Lau, 'Making the Difference', 237–8.

37 Graham Huggan, *The Postcolonial Exotic*, 81.

Chapter Sixteen

IMMIGRANT DESIRES: NARRATIVES OF THE INDIAN DIASPORA BY CHITRA BANERJEE DIVAKARUNI

Tutun Mukherjee

> Travel is usually thought of as displacement in space. This is an inadequate conception. A journey occurs simultaneously in space, in time and in the social hierarchy.
>
> Claude Lévi-Strauss (*Tristes Tropiques*)[1]

It is often stated that demography changes through three processes: fertility, mortality and migration. In demographic terms, then, the last criterion of migration makes the twentieth century a remarkable period. Large-scale movements of people across the globe have impacted the socioeconomic dynamics of many countries in unprecedented ways, which in turn have led to the birth of new experiences, perspectives and attitudes to life and their examination with regard to the politics of identity and location. The 'migrant' as a term is a floating signifier, as there exists no universally accepted definition for it. The term migrant is usually understood to cover all cases where the decision to migrate is taken freely by the individual/s for reasons of 'personal convenience' and without intervention of any external compelling factor. It can therefore describe persons or groups moving to another country or region to better their material or social conditions and improve the prospects for themselves and/or their family. A large section of Indian migrants have flocked – and continue to flock – to America for economic betterment and career prospects, and constitute a large section of the Indian diaspora. According to Amitav Ghosh, 'the Indian Diaspora is one of the most important demographic dislocations of Modern Times [and is] representative of a significant force in global culture.'[2]

Diaspora is a complex term that brings to mind various contested ideas and images. Diasporic discourses focus invariably on issues of 'identity' either in a positive way of sociocultural assimilation or reflect anxiogenic irresolution of losing that identity. Diaspora is also a popular term in current research as it captures various phenomena that are prevalent in the numerous discourses devoted to transnational globalization, as for instance the issues concerning borders, migration, 'illegal' immigration, repatriation, exile, refugees, assimilation, multiculturalism and hybridity. It is not necessary here to judge whether the term can encapsulate all the sociopolitical dimensions of these issues. For the purposes of this paper, it serves adequately as a useful and constructive tool and metaphor in an explicitly literary context. Diaspora becomes the site on which to engage with a matrix of diverse cultures, languages, histories, people, places and times. As Sandra Ponzanesi writes, 'Within the category of literary diaspora, the two senses – elation and distress – seem to merge. Playing out between centre and periphery, literatures of the diaspora highlight many of the conflicts and paradoxes that characterize our "global village" proclaiming affiliation with the global while asserting their representation of the local.'[3] There are certain affiliations of themes and tropes that all diasporic writers seem to share regardless of the countries of their origin. These are, for example, the sense of duality – of straddling spaces, cultures, languages and ethnicities; the sense of displacement, uprootedness, alienation and the multiplicity of margins; and the feeling of 'the "unhomely" or a kind of haunting otherness'.[4] These themes operate as the causal connections for the sense of hybridity, nostalgia and search for identity for the diasporic individual/writer who negotiates her/his 'location' through the expressive medium.

To recall Amitav Ghosh's comment (cited above), it is an incontestable fact that writing by the Indian diaspora constitutes a significant and critically acclaimed body of literature today. Increasingly, the works of the Indian diaspora top the sales charts globally and are gaining prominence in the teaching syllabuses around the world. Much has been and is being discussed and written about them. This certainly marks a change from the time when, as Kamala Visweswaran and Sucheta Mazumdar point out in their separate discussions, Asian immigrants were seen as huddled masses seeking 'change and choice',[5] and then sweepingly described as living happily ever after as the newcomers. The nation was 'transformed by assimilation' and the mythical dream of 'having arrived'[6] economically and socially was realized, because the initial motivation for their lateral movement across space had been the quest for economic stability and vertical mobility in the social hierarchy. It is noteworthy that to a large extent, the diasporic writers have succeeded in defining new paradigms to contextualize the socioeconomic realities of Asian American migrations within the history of transnational migrations in the twentieth century, with special reference to global capital and labour movements, and have thus complicated the facile understanding of the processes of assimilation in a new land.

Perhaps the most important contribution to this body of writing is that of women writers who have provided the 'interiority of female/gendered subjectivity' of the immigrant experience and have thereby created, and in the process acquired for themselves, an increased visibility of those migrants from the Indian subcontinent now being referred to as the 'newest Americans'.[7] What their writings make evident are the processes of adaptation and construction – adaptation to changes, dislocations and transformations, and the construction of new forms of knowledge and ways of seeing the world from other perspectives.

The focus of this discussion is the selected fiction by an eminent woman writer of Indian origin, Chitra Banerjee Divakaruni, who has an impressive list of poetry and fiction to her credit. Divakaruni is often bracketed with Indian diasporic writers like Bharati Mukherjee, Jhumpa Lahiri and Sunetra Gupta, obviously because of their roots in Bengali culture and the Kolkata connection that is often an overt and invariably a covert presence in their writing, and also because of some shared preoccupations made manifest in their fictive worlds, whether based in the US or in England. Commenting on female Indian diasporic writers, Ponzanesi says, 'Each of these writers employs and deploys strategies of home and homelessness to sketch her own literary odyssey which can be entangled or disentangled from the notion of Indianness.'[8] This paper focuses on two novels by Divakaruni, an early one titled *The Mistress of Spices* (1997), which topped international bestseller lists on publication, and a later, critically acclaimed one titled *Queen of Dreams* (2004). The novels are selected to highlight some persisting thematic interests of the writer as well as the creative journey undertaken by her from the 1990s into the twenty-first century, motivated by her motto: 'The art of dissolving boundaries is what living is all about.'[9]

All writers are storytellers, and the gifted ones hold the readers captive forever. According to Walter Benjamin, what distinguishes the storyteller of yore (of the oral epic or romance tradition) is the post-Gutenberg dependence on the book, the idea of the 'author' as the solitary individual writing in seclusion and the scientific inclination for analyses and rationalization. Benjamin argues that, post-Enlightenment, the mystery of 'far away places' that traveller-storytellers (like the Ancient Mariner) could bring near and make 'believable' is lost, replaced by explanations that tear away opacity the of myth and magic and hammer the inexplicable to fit into the explicated, straitjacketed mundane. For Benjamin, 'a story is different. It does not expend itself. It preserves and concentrates its strength and is capable of releasing it even after a long time'. He explains that in the earlier mode of story telling, 'the most extraordinary things, marvelous things, are related with the greatest accuracy, but the psychological connection of the events is not forced on the reader. It is left up to him to interpret things the way he understands them, and thus the narrative achieves the amplitude that information lacks.'[10] It is my contention that Divakaruni reveals herself as a Benjaminian storyteller with her penchant for delving into the inexplicable realms of the human mind to search for the magical aspects of life, which she explores in sensuous, evocative and lyrical prose. In his review of one of her novels for Amazon.com, Mike Birman comments, 'Through Divakaruni's creative alchemy we are drawn to the power of stories to reveal who we were, what we are and what we hope to become. The author shows us with stunning simplicity and skill that after we die all that may remain are our stories. And for the solace they offer and the instruction they bring, these stories need to be told as much as they need to be heard.'[11] Divakaruni herself says, 'I don't want to explain things in my books. I want the culture to be presented without dilution.' Her efforts are to weave observations of social realities with 'the element of myth, magic and ancient culture alongside contemporary culture. I try to bring those things together – a sense of ancient culture and the daily realities of immigrant life.'[12] It does seem that the dreams of the diasporic narrator are translated as the dreams of her immigrant heroines, who have ostensibly chosen to move away from the stultifying rituals of the old home/country only to remain suspended in a dream world of hopes and desires.

Spices are integral to Indian cuisine and brought the Western traders to the subcontinent. Their use is like alchemy that creates the magic of cooking, augmenting the aroma and taste, to suit every Indian palate, household, region, climate or culture. Spices can govern health and hence control the spirit of life. A grandmother's kitchen is also her pharmacy/*pharmakon*. The queen/king of the spices is revered and honoured and is expected to pass on the secret legacy down the generations. The cover blurb describes the novel thus:

> Magical, tantalizing, and sensual, *The Mistress of Spices* is the story of Tilo, a young woman born in another time, in a faraway place, who is trained in the ancient art of spices and ordained as a mistress charged with special powers. Once fully initiated in a rite of fire, the now immortal Tilo – in the gnarled and arthritic body of an old woman – travels through time to Oakland, California, where she opens a shop from which she administers spices as curatives to her customers. An unexpected romance with a handsome stranger eventually forces her to choose between the supernatural life of an immortal and the vicissitudes of modern life. Spellbinding and hypnotizing, *The Mistress of Spices* is a tale of joy and sorrow and one special woman's magical powers.[13]

The story is that of a baby girl abducted by bandits, who is later adopted by a group mother and taught the secret power of the spices. She is named Tilo, the mistress of sesame seeds, and like the others must follow the three dictums to retain her control over spices that empower her to find lost things as well as forecast calamities. She is instructed to secure the desires of those who seek her help, never leave her spice store and never touch anyone else's skin. Tilo is comfortable within the confines of the store and is able to help several people with her extraordinary abilities until she meets an American and his girlfriend. She is sexually attracted to the man and must make a life-transforming decision and choose either her forbidden desire or her magical powers.

Divakaruni's 2004 novel *Queen of Dreams* is written in the aftermath of the September 11 attacks. The story begins with the death of Rakhi's mother, who had the extraordinary ability to interpret dreams and guide those who sought her help through their fates. Rakhi is a young artist and a divorced mother living in Berkeley, California. She struggles to balance her relationship with her ex-husband, her family, career and a small business in an environment shaken and changed by the horrors of the tragedy. Perhaps when she needs her mother most, she loses her in a freak car accident. In an attempt to assuage her father's loneliness, she begins to read her mother's journals with him as they are written in Bengali, the language she has lost touch with. Thus begins Rakhi's journey of understanding her mother and her cultural roots, her mother's reflections on the illusory power of the world and the truths about relationships – all leading to her introspection and self-discovery. 'A dream is a telegram from the hidden world', Rakhi's mother writes in her journals.[14] With her mother's words working as catalyst, Rakhi begins to wonder if dreams carry messages from the past or hints for the future? Why does an individual dream? What purposes do dreams serve in one's life? In the post-Freudian scenario, such questions are not new nor regarded as pointless, as the acquaintance with the inchoate world of the unconscious was made possible through the psychoanalytical explorations of Western philosophers, right from Aeschylus and Plato through Sigmund Freud, Carl Jung, Kurt Gödel, Thomas Kuhn, Jorge Luis Borges, Pablo Picasso, Ernst Gombrich and many others. Moreover, scholars like Mircea Eliade and Wendy Doniger O'Flaherty have done extensive research on non-Western studies on dreams, especially O'Flaherty, whose 1984 book *Dreams, Illusions and Other Realities*, focusing on ancient Indian texts like the *Yogavasistha*, projects dreams as vivid and meaningful, offering the way to connect with numinous energies.

The two novels by Divakaruni revolve around a 'spice whisperer' and a 'dream teller' who control primal instinctive forces and are empowered by supernormal and magical domains of knowledge, which enable them to probe into human desires, motivations and wants that in ordinary circumstances one cannot easily articulate. These specially gifted women understand that most human wants are driven by the subconscious/unconscious, and that individuals may not even be aware of being compelled into action by these impulses. Divakaruni's lyrical prose creates elusive mystical worlds where the magical seems plausible and where the mysterious and the mundane collide. The competent structuring of the narratives introduce different points of view with careful character development, move back and forth in time, span spaces, splice enchantment into the prosaic, weave hope into disillusion – all features reminiscent of the spellbinding art of storytelling of Scheherazade.

The matter that is of equal interest here is to examine what role these two characters play in Divakaruni's diasporic reconnaissance. I argue that Tilo, the mistress of spices, and Mrs Gupta, the interpreter of dreams, who inhabit secret, sensuous worlds of feminine understanding and power, work in Divakaruni's oeuvre as metaphors of immigrant desires: one, the desire to bridge dualities – of the inexplicable pulls of old cultural roots against that of the new, of the past and the present; two, the desire to confidently handle anxieties, which in the case of a diasporan is the capacity to deal with the complexities of assimilation, acculturation and adaptation and overcome feelings of uncertainty and ambivalence towards the host society, especially in the face of growing xenophobia; three, the desire to retain ethnic identity yet not appear alienated; and finally, the desire to contribute to the host society in a meaningful and humanitarian way by bringing forth the precious healing knowledge of other ancient traditions and cultures. Divakaruni's narrative world is that of the Asian diaspora (particularly Indian), where journey and transformation are two persuasive motivations for travel and relocation to new lands. Journeying is related to the way the past, present and future is defined and is subject to redefinition. For diasporic lives, the journey is more than a philosophical way of viewing entire lives or segments within them. It becomes an important mode for interpreting past and future in the context of the present. It symbolizes the aspiration for happiness while adjusting to harsh existential realities. Haunted by subliminal fears, the diasporan does not forsake the hope of new love and understanding in an unfamiliar milieu. In the same manner, transformation too can be a physical, social or mental manifestation, and is in some cases all three. Whether planned or unplanned, undertaken forcibly or by choice, journey and transformation involve substantive or circumstantial change of a significant nature intrinsic to diasporic experience. Another inescapable awareness of the diasporic existence is the sensitivity to boundaries – of inclusion and exclusion, of being the 'other'. The boundary or the border operates as a powerful metaphor as it implies values about social class and status, and combines inevitably with memories, feelings, bodies and sociocultural surroundings (the classic study by Gloria Anzaldúa is a case in point).¹⁵ It is my contention that in Divakaruni's narratives Tilo and Mrs Gupta are deployed as percipient metaphors for journey, transformation and boundaries to make manifest the complexities of diasporic experience and yearning, of having to make difficult choices between what one should do and what one can do. Admittedly, the metaphors operate sometimes as a thin cover for political statements, but can one ever escape the politics of 'location'? Divakaruni's views, however, are not given as 'agendas' but as facts: the 'host' country can indeed be unfair, people of other ethnicities and race do face bias and prejudice, hopes are often dashed in the face of discrimination. Yet, migrations continue to take place; people are still eager to undertake the transitions that immigration into new societies and cultures will make imperative. The presence of life-transforming characters like Tilo and Mrs Gupta are indicative of the universal and individual qualities of the search for meaning in life, as well as the timelessness of this search.

No discussion on the writers of the diaspora can disregard the critique aimed at them. For instance, women writers like Bharati Mukherjee, Jhumpa Lahiri and Chitra Banerjee Divakaruni have been accused of fetishizing and exoticizing the notion of immigration. For example, in her essay 'Of Foreigners and Fetishes', Sheetal Majithia writes, 'While these narratives appear to celebrate the fluidity and mobility of immigrant identity, they reduce the historical contexts to tensions in the text that are too easily resolved through the tropes of romance. In effect, they serve to *fetishize* the experience of immigration, so as to perpetuate easy translation and dubious interpretation, processes that uncannily resemble Orientalist and imperial projects of literary and critical representation.' These authors 'ignore the social contradictions that constitute the conditions of immigration and citizenship, the very conditions that also produce this literature in the first place. Their narratives displace the experiences of immigration out of the time and space of the present into a temporality of nostalgia. The present issues of immigration: access to rights, political participation, representation, and economic disparity, are met and resolved formally within the cozy embrace of the domestic romance. It is here that nostalgia repeats and reproduces tropes of romance, which continually defer the act of resolving these contradictions in any substantive way.'¹⁶ Majithia argues that Divakaruni falls into a similar trap of 'romanticizing India' and offering romance as resolution by allowing the tensions of immigrant experiences to be worked out within sexual and romantic dynamics. Majithia very astutely argues that the identification with the characters of the novels numbs the cutting edge contradictions of the immigrant experience. She highlights the limitations of romance as an appropriate strategy for contending with the violence that often accompanies the issues of citizenship that get problematized for the diaspora.

Thus there are contending views regarding the 'success' of diaspora literature. Does being visible and reader-friendly minimize the need for this body of literature to address the economic and sociopolitical issues that immigrants face in their new environments? And in this particular context, how would one assess the contribution of narratives like those discussed above to this need? Whether Divakaruni's novels 'fetishize' the immigrant experience in strange lands cannot be summarily resolved. It cannot, however, be denied that Divakaruni's narratives present the complex play of pain, pleasure and desire interwoven with the politics of the diaspora. Told by a gifted storyteller, they entice and captivate. They do not remain rooted in the particular but transcend the dictates of the 'here and now' to focus on everlasting issues of human relationships, disappointments and hopes, as well as pride associated with one's heritage and how confidence in it can shape individual identity in times of transition. They anticipate and satisfy novelistic pleasures and therein lies Chitra Banerjee Divakaruni's achievement as a writer.

Notes and References

1 Claude Lévi-Strauss, *Tristes Tropiques*, trans. John and Doreen Weightman (London: Pan, 1989), 104.
2 Amitav Ghosh, quoted in Shaleen Singh, 'Diaspora Literature: A Testimony to Realism', Ezine Articles, 13 June 2004. Online: http://EzineArticles.com/1362004 (accessed 20 July 2012).
3 Sandra Ponzanesi, *Paradoxes of Postcolonial Culture: Contemporary Women Writers of the Indian and Afro-Italian Diaspora* (New York: State University of New York Press, 2004), 10.
4 Ibid., 11.
5 Kamala Visweswaran, 'Diaspora by Design: Flexible Citizenship and South Asians in US Racial Formations', *Diaspora* 6, no. 1 (Spring 1997): 5–29 (14, 22).
6 Sucheta Mazumdar, 'Asian American Studies and Asian Studies: Rethinking Roots', *Asian Americans: Comparative and Global Perspectives*, ed. Shirley Hune et al. (Pullman: Washington State University, 1991): 29–44 (29–30).
7 Leonard, Karen Isaaksen, 'Indian (Asian Indian) Immigrants' in *Multicultural America: An Encyclopedia of the Newest Americans*, vol. 1, ed. Ronald H. Baylor (New York: ABC Clio, 2011), 969–1026.
8 Ponzanesi, *Paradoxes of Postcolonial Culture*, 23.
9 http://en.wikipedia.org/wiki/Chitra_Banerjee_Divakaruni (accessed July 18 2012).
10 Walter Benjamin, 'The Storyteller: Reflections on the Works of Nikolai Leskov', 4–5. Online: http://www.slought.org/files/downloads/events/SF_1331-Benjamin.pdf (accessed 18 July 2012).
11 Mike Birman. Online: http://www.amazon.com/Amazing-Thing...Divakaruni/.../1401340997 (accessed 18 July 2012).
12 Ismat Sarah Mangla, 'Writing from Two Worlds', *Nirali*, 1 October 2004. Online: http://niralimagazine.com/2004/10/writing-from-two-worlds (accessed 18 July 2012).
13 Cover blurb, Chitra Banerjee Divakaruni, *The Mistress of Spices* (New York: Doubleday, 1997).

14 Chitra Banerjee Divakaruni, *Queen of Dreams* (New York: Doubleday, 2004), 34.
15 Gloria Anzaldúa, *Borderlands / La Frontera: The New Mestiza* (San Francisco: Aunt Lute Books, 1999).
16 Sheetal Majithia, 'Of Foreigners and Fetishes', *Samar* 14. Online: http://samarmagazine.org/archive/articles/59 (accessed 12 July 2012).

GLOSSARY OF INDIAN WORDS

Word	Approximate English Meaning
adivasi	tribal
andolan	agitation, movement
arbit	(abbreviated) arbitrary
ashram	a place for hermits
Bangalee Bhadrolok	elitist Bengalis
bhaji	vegetable
Brahmin	an Indian caste
chawls	slums
dabbawalas	people who carry lunch for office workers in metro cities
desi	Indian
dhamaka	blast
dharna	a mode of demonstrating protest
gullels	slingshots
haveli	mansion
idli-sambhar	a South Indian meal
kanchas	marbles
loki	gourd
maidan	ground
malikini	mistress/landlady
mem	an Englishwoman/a woman from upper-class society
muggu	a rote learner
putli	a small bundle of clothes

(Continued)

Word	Approximate English Meaning
rasgullas	a kind of Indian sweet
rikshawalas	a kind of human-powered transport
saag	vegetables
sadhu	an ascetic
samosa	a deep fried and spicy Indian delicacy
tapori	someone off the streets
tharavaad	ancestral home
utra hua tel	used / stale oil
vada	a fried, South Indian dish

LIST OF CONTRIBUTORS

A. N. Dwivedi, an award-winning poet, worked as a professor in the Department of English, University of Allahabad. He has published about 100 research articles in local and international journals and a dozen books of literary criticism, three books of translation and five books of poetry. His collections of poetry are: *Random Reflections* (New Delhi: BRPC, 1994), *Fine Frenzy* (Allahabad: Kitab Mahal, 1998), *Protest Poems* (Calcutta: Writers Workshop, 2002), *Beyond Borders* (New Delhi: Adhyayan Publishers, 2008), and *Wayward Wanderings* (New Delhi: Authorspress, 2012). He is on the advisory board of *Transnational Literature* (University of Flinders, Australia) and *Journal of Postcolonial Cultures and Societies* (USA).

Angshuman Kar is reader at the Department of English, University of Burdwan. He did his PhD on Raja Rao's fiction and his present areas of interest are Indian English literature, contemporary theories and new literatures in English. He was awarded the Australia-India Council Fellowship in 2006. He is the secretary of the Centre for Australian Studies, University of Burdwan and also a member of the Advisory Board (Bengali) of Sahitya Akademi (the National Academy of Letters in India). He has presented papers and chaired sessions in different national and international seminars and conferences in India and abroad. He has five books and twenty articles to his credit. His most recent book is *The Politics of Social Exclusion in India: Democracy at the Crossroads* (published by Routledge and coedited with Harihar Bhattacharya and Partha Sarkar).

Aysha Iqbal Viswamohan did her PhD in American drama. She is associate professor in the Department of Humanities and Social Sciences, Indian Institute of Technology, Madras, India. She teaches, guides and writes on drama, film studies, contemporary fiction and English language teaching. She has published over thirty papers in the areas of language and literature.

Chinmoy Banerjee was educated in Scindia School, Gwalior, St Stephen's College, Delhi and the University of Delhi, where he took his MA. He did his PhD at Kent State University, Ohio on the works of Laurence Sterne. He taught at the Department of English, Simon Fraser University in BC, Canada until retirement. He is the founding president of the South Asian Film Education Society in Vancouver, BC.

Chinnadevi Singadi is assistant professor in the Department of Commonwealth Literary Studies at the English and Foreign Languages University, Hyderabad, India, where she teaches and guides research on literature from South Asia. She studied at Fatima Convent and received her BA from Chowgule College, Goa. Her doctoral thesis, 'Art Hunts for Avenues to Life: A Study of Select Novels of John Gardner', asserts the life-saving value of art, and she recently published *Ishq ka Asar: Songs of Love*, her first collection of *ghazals* and songs in Hindi. She co-convened *Postcoloniality in Transition: Cosmopolitanism, Transnationalism and Globalization*, an international conference held at EFL University in January 2013 that featured illuminating sessions by Bill Ashcroft and Tabish Khair. She will be Visiting Fellow at Technische Universität Dresden, Germany in the 2013 summer semester.

John Masterson is a senior lecturer in the Department of English at the University of the Witwatersrand, Johannesburg. He has published work on a range of writers, including Chinua Achebe, Chimamanda Ngozi Adichie, Kiran Desai, Dave Eggers and Abdulrazak Gurnah, and topics, including the Rwandan genocide and 'postcolonial conflict.' His book, *The Disorder of Things: A Foucauldian Approach to the Work of Nuruddin Farah*, will be published by Wits University Press in 2013.

Laura Moss is associate professor at the University of British Columbia, the associate editor of *Canadian Literature: A Quarterly of Criticism and Review* and the former director of the UBC International Canadian Studies Centre. With Cynthia Sugars, she coedited the two-volume *Canadian Literature in English: Texts and Contexts* (2008, 2009). She is also the editor of *Leaving the Shade of the Middle Ground: The Poetry of F. R. Scott* (2011), *Is Canada Postcolonial: Unsettling Canadian Literature* (2003) and a scholarly edition of Frances Brooke's *The History of Emily Montague* (2001). She has published articles on multiculturalism and public arts policy, fractals and short stories, Margaret Atwood's international iconicity, self-parody in Salman Rushdie, postcolonial reading strategies and J. M. Coetzee, and mainstream hybridity in the work of Zadie Smith, among others.

Letizia Alterno is the editor-in-chief of the Raja Rao Publication Project and the director of Rao's official website (http://www.therajaraoendowment.org). She authored Rao's obituary article published by the *Guardian* as well as a recent article on the legacy of Rao's work in the *Times of India*. Her published and current work focuses on a postcolonial reading of Raja Rao's production. She has translated two of Rao's works into Italian and is currently editing a critical volume, which investigates the significance of his writings in the transnational era. She is also working, together with Rao's wife Susan, on a biography of the author.

Maria Ridda is an associate lecturer at the University of Kent. She is currently working on a monograph exploring literary representations of Bombay, London and New York in texts written by South Asian diasporic authors from the 1990s to the present day. She has published articles and essays on South Asian American writing, Bollywood cinema and postliberalization Indian writing. Maria is on the editorial board of the *Journal of Postcolonial Cultures and Societies*.

Om Prakash Dwivedi is assistant professor in English at MITS (Deemed University, Rajasthan, India). He has published scholarly articles in many international journals. He is particularly interested in postcolonial literature and cultural studies. His forthcoming book is called *Literature of Indian Diaspora* (New Delhi: Pencraft International).

Patricia Gruben is associate professor of film, director of the Praxis Centre for Screenwriters and director of the India Field School in the School for the Contemporary Arts at Simon Fraser University, Vancouver, Canada. She has written and directed two dramatic feature films as well as several prize-winning shorts and documentaries. She has also written a number of academic articles and book chapters on narrative structure in international cinema. She is currently developing three screenplays set in South Asia and is working with Martin Gotfrit on *The Secret Doctrine*, a multimedia theatre piece funded by a major SSHRC research-creation grant.

Sajalkumar Bhattacharya is associate professor in the Department of English, Ramakrishna Mission Residential College, Kolkata. He has worked on the theme of 'Family-Nation Interface in Indian English Fiction with Special Reference to Select Novels of Salman Rushdie and Amitav Ghosh' for his doctoral thesis. His areas of interest include postindependence Indian fiction in English and Bhasa literature. He has authored a book, *In Search of Some Blessed Hope – A Critical Inquiry into Hardy's Meliorism*, and presented and published papers both at national and international levels.

Mala Pandurang is head of the Department of English, Dr BMN College, Mumbai, India. She is also a postdoctoral fellow of the Alexander von

Humboldt Foundation, Bonn. She has taught at the University of Texas at Austin as senior Fulbright visiting professor. Her publications include *Postcolonial African Fiction: A Crisis of Consciousness* (1997), *Articulating Gender* (ed.) (2000), *Vikram Seth: Multiple Locations, Multiple Affiliations* (2003), *Mediating Indian Writing in English: German Responses* (coed.) (2005, 2006), *Chinua Achebe: An Anthology of Recent Criticism* (ed.) (2006), *Ngugi Wa Thiong'o: An Anthology of Recent Criticism* (ed.) (2007) and *African Women Writers: Re-imaging Gender* (coed.) (2010).

Shaleena Koruth is a US-based interactive designer and freelance journalist. She received a master's in new media design at Indiana University, Bloomington and studied mass communications at Sophia Polytechnic, Mumbai, India. She holds a BA in economics from Stella Maris College, USA. She has written for the *Hindu*, the *Indian-American*, the *Atlantic* and other publications.

Sara-Duana Meyer is a curator, writer, literary scholar and cultural producer currently based in both Munich, Germany and Cairo, Egypt. She has taught literature, cultural theory and visual studies at the University of Osnabrück, the SNDT Women's University in Mumbai, India, and the department for Comparative Literature at the LMU Munich, and has been working with several cultural institutions and festivals in Europe and the MENA region. Her main work and research interests include art of resistance and art in public space, urbanism and urban culture, globalisation, city literature, postcolonialism, gender studies and visual culture. She is a member of the Arts Rights Justice network and is the artistic director of Spring Lessons Initiative, a platform for sociocultural projects and artistic research, which she cofounded in 2011.

Tutun Mukherjee is professor of comparative literature at University of Hyderabad, India. She has specialized in literary criticism and theory and has research interest in translation, women's writing, theatre and film studies. Her publications cover her diverse interests.

BIBLIOGRAPHY

Abcarian, Robin. 'Now "Opal" Won't Get a Movie'. *Los Angeles Times*, 29 April 2006. Online: http://articles.latimes.com/2006/apr/29/entertainment/et-ruttenside29 (accessed 23 March 2010).

About.com. 'An Interview with Vikram Chandra'. About.com, Fiction Writing. Online: http://fictionwriting.about.com/od/interviews/a/chandra.htm (accessed 20 March 2010).

Adam, Ian and Helen Tiffin, ed. *Past the Last Post: Theorizing Post-Colonialism and Post-Modernism*. New York: Harvester Wheatsheaf, 1991.

Adiga, Aravind. *The White Tiger*. London: Atlantic Books, 2008.

_____. *Between the Assassinations*. London: Atlantic Books, 2009.

Adil, Alev. 'The Bus Stopped by Tabish Khair'. *Independent*, 24 May 2004. Online: http://www.uni-saarland.de/fileadmin/user_upload/Professoren/fr43_ProfGhoshSchellhorn/Tas_Datenbank/South_Asia___Diasporas/Khair_The_Independent.pdf (accessed 21 January 2013).

Afzal-Khan, Fawzia and Kalpana Seshadri-Crooks, eds. *The Pre-Occupation of Postcolonial Studies*. Durham, NC: Duke University Press, 2000.

Agamben, Giorgio. *Homo Sacer: Sovereign Power and Bare Life*, translated by Daniel Heller-Roazen. California: Stanford University Press, 1998.

Agamben, Giorgio. *Means Without End: Notes on Politics*. Minneapolis: Minnesota University Press, 2000.

Ahmad, Aijaz. *In Theory: Classes, Nations, Literatures*. London: Verso, 1992.

Alcoff, Linda Martin and Eduardo Mendieta, edited by *Identities: Race, Class, Gender and Nationality*. Oxford: Blackwell, 2003.

Amin, Samir. *Empire of Chaos*. New York: Monthly Review Press, 1992.

Anderson, Amanda. *The Powers of Distance: Cosmopolitanism and the Cultivation of Detachment*. Princeton: Princeton University Press, 2001.

Anderson, Benedict. *Imagined Communities: Reflections on the Origins and Spread of Nationalism*. London: Verso, 1983.

Aneesh, A. *Virtual Migration: The Programming of Globalization*. Durham, NC: Duke University Press, 2006.

Anzaldúa, Gloria. *Borderlands / La Frontera: The New Mestiza*. San Francisco: Aunt Lute Books, 1999.

Appadurai, Arjun, ed. *The Social Life of Things*. New York: Cambridge University Press, 1988.

_____. *Modernity at Large*. Minneapolis: University of Minnesota Press, 1996.

_____. 'Disjuncture and Difference in The Global Cultural Economy'. April 2003. Online: http://www.intcul.tohoku.ac.jp/~holden/MediatedSociety/Readings/2003_04/Appadurai.html (accessed 17 December 2010).

Appelbaum, Richard and William Robinson. *Critical Globalization Studies* (New York: Routledge, 2005.
Appiah, Kwame Anthony. 'Is the Post- in Postmodernism the Post- in Postcolonial?' *Critical Inquiry* 17 (1991): 336–57.
Ashcroft, Bill. *Post-Colonial Transformation*. London and New York: Routledge 2001.
Ashcroft, Bill, Gareth Griffiths and Helen Tiffin, eds. *The Empire Writes Back: Theory and Practice in Post-Colonial Literatures*. London: Routledge, 1989.
_____, eds. *Key Concepts in Post-Colonial Studies*. London: Routledge, 1998.
Babu, B. Ramesh, ed. *Globalization and the South Asian State*. New Delhi: South Asian Publishers, 1998.
Bahri, Deepika and Mary Vasudeva, eds. *Between the Lines: South Asians and Postcoloniality*. Philadelphia: Temple University Press, 1996.
Bakshi, Kaustav, Samrat Sengupta and Subhadeep Paul, eds. *Anxieties, Influences and After: Critical Responses to Postcolonialism and Neocolonialism*. New Delhi: Worldview Publications, 2009.
Balakrishnan, Gopal, ed. *Debating Empire*. London: Verso, 2003.
Barton, Laura. 'A Passage from India'. *Guardian*, 12 October 2006. Online: http://www.guardian.co.uk/books/2006/oct/12/bookerprize2006.thebookerprize (accessed 22 December 2010).
Basu, Kaushik. *The Retreat of Democracy and Other Itinerant Essays on Globalization, Economics and India*. Ranikhet: Permanent Black, 2007.
Bauman, Zygmunt. *Globalization: The Human Consequences*. New York: Columbia University Press, 1998.
Bayor, Ronald H., ed. *Multicultural America: An Encyclopedia of the Newest Americans*. New York: ABC Clio, 2011.
Begamudre, Ven. 'Greetings from Bangalore, Saskatchewan'. *Canadian Literature* 132 (Spring 1992): 8–14.
Benjamin, Walter. *Illuminations*, edited by Hannah Arendt and translated by Harry Zohn. Glasgow: Fontana, 1977.
_____. 'The Storyteller: Reflections on the Works of Nikolai Leskov'. Online: http://www.slought.org/files/downloads/events/SF_1331-Benjamin.pdf (accessed 18 July 2012).
Benson, Eugene and L. W. Conolly, eds. *Encyclopedia of Postcolonial Literatures in English*. London: Routledge, 1994.
Bernard, Sarah. 'A Fan's Notes'. *New York Magazine*, 15 April 2002. Online: http://nymag.com/nymetro/arts/features/5879 (accessed 10 March 2010).
Bhabha, Homi. *Nation and Narration*. London: Routledge, 1994.
_____. *The Location of Culture*. London: Routledge, 1994.
_____. 'On the Irremovable Strangeness of Being Different'. In 'Four Views on Ethnicity'. *PMLA* 113, no. 1 (January 1998): 34–9.
Bhagat, Chetan. *Five Point Someone: What Not to Do at IIT*. New Delhi: Rupa, 2004.
Bharucha, Nilufer E. *Rohinton Mistry: Ethnic Enclosures and Transcultural Spaces*. Jaipur: Rawat Publications, 2003.
Bhattacharyya, Anirudh. 'Salman Rushdie Writes off Kaavya'. IBN Live, 2 May 2006. Online: http://ibnlive.in.com/news/salman-has-no...for-kaavya/9223-2.html (accessed 10 March 2010).
Boehmer, Elleke. *Colonial and Postcolonial Literature: Migrant Metaphors*. Oxford: Oxford University Press, 1995.
Bold Type. Interview with Kiran Desai. Random House, May 1999. Online: http://www.randomhouse.com/boldtype/0599/desai/interview.html (accessed 23 Dec 2010).

Boorstin, Daniel J. 'From Hero to Celebrity', in *The Human Pseudo-Event: The Celebrity Culture Reader*, edited by P. David Marshall. New York and London: Routledge, 2006.
Bose, Brinda, ed. *Amitav Ghosh: Critical Perspectives*. New Delhi: Pen Craft International, 2003.
Breckenridge, Carol A., ed. *Consuming Modernity: Public Culture in South Asia*. Minneapolis: University of Minnesota Press, 1995.
Brennan, Timothy. *Salman Rushdie and the Third World: Myths of the Nation*. New York: St Martin's Press, 1989.
———. *At Home in the World: Cosmopolitanism Now*. Cambridge, MA: Harvard University Press, 1997.
Brians, Paul. *Modern South Asian Literature in English*. Westport, CT: Greenwood Press, 2003.
Brouillette, Sarah. *Postcolonial Writers in the Global Literary Marketplace*. Hampshire: Palgrave Macmillan, 2007.
Brown, Mark. 'Booker Longlist Pits Fiction's Finest Against First Kiss-and-Tell Chimp'. *Guardian*, 28 July 2009. Online: http://www.guardian.co.uk/books/2009/jul/28/booker-prize-longlist-me-cheeta (accessed 24 September 2010).
Brown, Stephen, ed. *Consuming Books: The Marketing and Consumption of Literature*. New York: Routledge, 2006.
Bruce-Novoa, Juan. 'Offshoring the American Dream'. *CR: The New Centennial Review* 3, no. 1 (2003): 109–145.
Bummiler, Elisabeth. 'A Novelist Beginning With a Bang'. *New York Times*, 29 July 1997. Online: http://nytimes.com/1997/07/29/books/a-novelist-beginning-with-a-bang.html (accessed 18 October 2010).
Butcher, Maggie, ed. *The Eye of the Beholder: Indian Writing in English*. London: Commonwealth Institute, 1983.
Chandra, Vikram. *Love and Longing in Bombay*. London: Penguin, 1997.
———. *Sacred Games*. London: Faber & Faber, 2006.
Chatterjee, Partha. *The Nation and Its Fragments: Colonial and Postcolonial Histories*. Princeton: Princeton University Press, 1993.
Chaudhuri, Amit, ed. *The Picador Book of Modern Indian Literature*. London: Picador, 2001.
———. 'The East as a Career: On "Strangeness" in Indian Writing', in *Clearing a Space: Reflections on India, Literature and Culture*, 85–99. Oxford: Peter Lang, 2008.
Cheung, King-Kok. *An Interethnic Companion to Asian American Literature*. New York: Cambridge University Press, 1997.
Childs, Peter and Patrick Williams, ed. *An Introduction to Postcolonial Theory*. New York: Prentice Hall, 1997.
Choudhury, Chandrahas. 'English Spoken Here: How Globalization is Changing the Indian Novel'. *Foreign Policy* (November/December 2009).
Clifford, James. 'The Transit Lounge of Culture'. *Times Literary Supplement*, 3 May 1991.
———. *Routes: Travel and Translation in the Late Twentieth Century*. Cambridge, MA: Harvard University Press 1997.
Cohen, Robin. *Global Diasporas: An Introduction*. Seattle: University of Washington Press, 1997.
Crane, Ralph J. *Inventing India: A History of India in English Language Fiction*. New York: Macmillan, 1992.
Cronin, Richard. *Imagining India*. London: Macmillan, 1989.
Culler, Jonathan. *On Deconstruction: Theory and Criticism After Structuralism*. New York: Routledge and Kegan Paul, 1983.

Dash, Michael J. 'In Search of the Lost Body: Redefining the Subject in Caribbean Literature'. *Kunapipi* 11, no. 1 (1989): 14–26.
Deb, Siddhartha. 'Memory on Wheels'. *Outlook*, 3 May 2004. Online: http://www.outlookindia.com/article.aspx?223760 (accessed 25 June 2011).
Desai, Anita. 'Sitting Pretty'. *New York Review* 41, no. 1 (1993): 22–6.
Desai, Jigna. *Beyond Bollywood: The Cultural Politics of South Asian Diasporic Film*. New York and London: Routledge, 2004.
Desai, Kiran. *The Inheritance of Loss*. London: Penguin, 2006.
Dhar, Subir, ed. *Romancing the Strange: The Fiction of Kunal Basu*. Kolkata: Avantgarde Press, 2004.
Dhawan, R. K., ed. *The Novels of Amitav Ghosh*. London: Sangam Books, 1999.
———, ed. *Writers of the Indian Diaspora*. New Delhi: Prestige Books, 2001.
Didur, Jill. '"An Unremembered Time": Secular Criticism in Pankaj Mishra's *The Romantics*'. *Journal of Commonwealth Literature* 44, no. 2 (2009): 65–85.
Dilwale Dulhania Le Jayenge (Lovers win brides). DVD. Directed by Adtiya Chopra, 1995.
Dirlik, Arif. *After the Revolution: Waking to Global Capitalism*. Hanover: Wesleyan University Press, 1994.
Divakaruni, Chitra Banerjee. *The Mistress of Spices*. New York: Doubleday, 1997.
———. *Queen of Dreams*. New York: Doubleday, 2004.
Dodiya, Jaydipsingh, ed. *Perspectives on Indian English Fiction*. New Delhi: Dominant, 2002.
Driscoll, Mark. 'Reverse Postcoloniality'. *Social Text* 22, no. 1 (2004): 59–84.
Dudrah, Rajinder K. *Sociology Goes to the Movies*. New Delhi and London: Sage, 2006.
Dugger, Celia. 'An Indian Novelist Turns Her Wrath on the US'. *New York Times*, 3 November 2001.
During, Simon. 'Postcolonialism and Globalisation: A Dialectical Relation After All?' *Postcolonial Studies* 1, no. 1 (1998): 31–47.
Durrix, Jean-Pierre. *Mimesis, Genres and Postcolonial Discourses: Deconstructing Magic Realism*. London: Macmillan, 1998.
Edwards, Justin D. *Postcolonial Literature: A Reader's Guide to Essential Criticism*. Basingstoke: Palgrave Macmillan, 2008.
Economist (US Edition). 'Not Losing Hope', 7 April 2005.
Emblidge, David. 'The Viswanathan Dilemma at Little, Brown, Publishers'. *International Journal of the Humanities* 5, no. 3 (2007): 7–13.
Emerson, Caryl and Holoquist Michael, eds. *Speech Genres and Other Late Essays*. Texas: University of Texas Press 1994.
Ezekiel, Nissim and Meenakshi Mukherjee, eds. *Another India: An Anthology of Contemporary Indian fiction and Poetry*. New Delhi: Penguin, 1990.
Featherstone, Mike, ed. *Global Culture: Nationalism, Globalization and Modernity*. London: Sage Publications, 1990.
Field, Michele. 'Vikram Seth'. *Publishers Weekly*, 10 May 1993.
Fisher, Susan. 'Teaching Rohinton Mistry's *A Fine Balance*: Two Cheers for Universalism?' *Canadian Literature* 190 (Autumn 2006): 180–87.
Foster, John Bellamy. 'The Rediscovery of Imperialism'. *Monthly Review* 54, no. 6 (November 2002): 1–16.
Fukuyama, Francis. *The End of History and the Last Man*. New York: Free Press, 1992.
Killam, G. D. *The Literature of Africa*. Santa Barbara: Greenwood Publishing Group, 2004.
Gandhi, Leela. *Postcolonial Theory: A Critical Introduction*. Edinburgh: Edinburgh University Press, 1998.

Genetsch, Martin. *The Texture of Identity: The Fiction of M. G. Vassanji, Neil Bissoondath, and Rohinton Mistry*. Toronto: TSAR, 2007.
George, Rosemary Marangoly. *The Politics of Home: Postcolonial Relocations and Twentieth-Century Fiction*. Berkeley: University of California Press, 1996.
Ghosh, Amitav. *The Imam and the Indian*. New Delhi: Ravi Dayal, 2002.
_____. *The Hungry Tide*. New Delhi: HarperCollins, 2005.
_____. *Sea of Poppies*. New Delhi: Penguin, 2008.
Ghosh, B. N. and Halil M. Guven, eds. *Globalization and the Third World: A Study of Negative Consequences*. Hampshire: Palgrave Macmillan, 2006.
Gikandi, Simon. 'Globalization and the Claims of Postcoloniality'. *South Atlantic Quarterly* 100, no. 3 (2001): 627–58.
Gikandi, Simon and Evan Mwangi. *The Columbia Guide to East African Literature in English Since 1945*. New York: Columbia University Press, 2007.
Gilroy, Paul. *The Black Atlantic: Modernity and Double Consciousness*. London: Verso, 1993.
_____. *After Empire: Melancholia or Convivial Culture?* London: Routledge, 2004.
Gladwell, Malcolm. 'Viswanathan-Gate'. Gladwell.com (blog), 30 April 2006. Online: http://gladwell.typepad.com/gladwellcom/2006/04/viswanathangate.html (accessed 5 April 2010).
Gokhale, Namita. 'Vikram's Vocalist Strains on the Literary Landscape'. *Times of India*, 4 May 1999.
Gopal, S. and Sujata Moorti, eds. *Global Bollywood: Travels of Hindi Song and Dance*. Minneapolis: University of Minnesota Press 2008.
Gopalkrishnan, Lakshmi. 'Booker Snooker'. *Slate*, 26 October 1997. Online: http://www.slate.com/id/1837 (accessed 10 November 2010).
Gorra, Michael. *After Empire: Scott, Naipaul, Rushdie*. Chicago: University of Chicago Press, 1997.
Green, Martin. *Dreams of Adventure, Deeds of Empire*. London: Routledge and Kegan Paul, 1980.
Green, William, Madhur Singh and Jyoti Thottam. 'Prodigal Pen'. *Time International* (Atlantic Edition), 27 October 2008.
Gregg, Allen. Interview with M. G. Vassanji. TV Ontario, 29 March 2009. Online: http://www.youtube.com/watch?v=a0sCN8jz2Rk (accessed June 2010).
Gupta, Dipankar. *Mistaken Modernity: India Between Worlds*. New Delhi: HarperCollins, 2000.
Hall, Stuart. 'When was the Post-Colonial? Thinking at the Limit'. In the *Post-Colonial Question: Common skies, Divided Horizons*, edited by Iain Chambers and Lidia Curtis, 242–60. London: Routledge, 1996.
_____. 'Conclusion: The Multi-Cultural Question'. In *Un/settled Mutliculturalisms: Diasporas, Entanglements, Transruptions*, edited by Barnor Hesse, 209–41. London: Zed, 2000.
Hawley, John. *Amitav Ghosh: An Introduction*. New Delhi: Foundation Books, 2005.
Heble, Ajay. 'A Foreign Presence in the Stall: Towards a Poetics of Cultural Hybridity in Rohinton Mistry's Migration Stories'. *Canadian Literature* 137 (Summer 1993): 51–61.
Held, David and Anthony McGrew, eds. *The Global Transformations Reader*. Cambridge: Polity Press, 2000.
Herbert, Caroline. '"Dishonorably Postnational?" The Politics of Migrancy and Cosmopolitanism in Rohinton Mistry's A Fine Balance'. *Journal of Commonwealth Literature* 43, no. 11 (2008): 11–28. Online: http://jcl.sagepub.com/content/43/2/11.full.pdf+html (accessed 16 December 2012).

Hidier, Tanuja Desai. 'Tanuja Desai Hidier on Born Confused and Opal Mehta'. Desi Club, 2006. Online: http://www.desiclub.com/community/culture/culture_article.cfm?id=265 (accessed 15 March 2010).

Hindu. 'Penguin India Bags Rights for Kiran Desai's New Novel, *Pamuk*'. 6 October 2010. Online: http://www.thehindu.com/arts/books/article816256.ece (accessed 2 November 2010).

Hogan, Patrick Colm and Lalita Pandit, eds. *Literary India: Comparative Studies in Aesthetics, Colonialism, and Culture.* Albany: State University of New York Press, 1995.

Holbrook, Morris B. 'On the Commercial Exaltation of Artistic Mediocrity'. In *Consuming Books: The Marketing and Consumption of Literature*, edited by Stephen Brown, 100–110. New York: Routledge, 2006.

Holgate, Andrew. 'Lost in the City'. *New Statesman*, 4 September 2006.

Holoquist, Michael, ed. *Dialogic Imagination: Four Essays by M. M. Bakhtin.* Austin: University of Texas Press, 1992.

Hoogvelt, Ankie. *Globalization and Postcolonialism.* London: Macmillan, 1997.

Howard, Rebecca Moore. *Standing in the Shadow of Giants: Plagiarists, Authors, Collaborators.* Stamford: Ablex, 1999.

Huggan, Graham. *The Postcolonial Exotic: Marketing the Margins.* London: Routledge, 2001.

Hulbert, Ann. 'How Kaavya Got Packaged and Got Into Trouble'. *Slate*, 27 April 2006. Online: http://www.slate.com/id/2140683 (accessed 18 March 2010).

Hutcheon, Linda. *Irony's Edge: Theory and Politics of Irony.* New York: Routledge, 1995.

Inda, Jonathan Xavier and Renato Rosaldo, eds. *The Anthropology of Globalization: A Reader.* Oxford: Blackwell Publishers, 2008.

Iyer, Pico. 'India Day by Day'. *Times Literary Supplement*, 19 March 1993.

Jana, Reena. 'The Salon Interview: Arundhati Roy'. *Salon*, 30 September 1997. Online: http://www.salon.com/1997/09/30/00roy/ (accessed 10 October 2010).

Joshi, Priya. *In Another Country: Colonialism, Culture, and the English Novel in India* (New York: Columbia University Press, 2002).

Juskalian, Russ. 'You Didn't Plagiarize, Your Unconscious Did'. *Newsweek*, 6 July 2009. Online: http://www.newsweek.com/2009/07/06/you-didn-t-plagiarize-your-unconscious-did.html (accessed 18 March 2010).

Kaarsholm, P., ed. *City Flicks: Indian Cinema and The Urban Experience.* London, New York and Kolkata: Seagull Books, 2007.

Kachru, Upendra. *Extreme Turbulence: India at the Crossroads.* Delhi: HarperCollins, 2007.

Kakutani, Michiko. 'Melodrama as Structure for Subtlety'. *New York Times*, 3 June 1997. Online: http://www.nytimes.com/1997/06/03/books/melodrama-as-structure-for-subtlety.html (accessed 16 August 2012).

Kal Ho Naa Ho (Tomorrow may never come). DVD. Directed by Nikhil Advani, 2004.

Kamboureli, Smaro and Roy Miki, eds. *Trans.Can.Lit: Resituating the Study of Canadian Literature.* Waterloo, ON: Wilfrid Laurier University Press, 2007.

Kapur, Akash. 'Sentimental Education: Review of *The Romantics*'. *New York Times Book Review*, 27 February 2000.

Kapur, Manju. *The Immigrant.* London: Faber & Faber, 2009.

Kaur, R. and A. J. Sinha, eds. *Bollyworld. Popular Indian Cinema Through a Transnational Lens.* New Delhi: Sage, 2005.

Khair, Tabish. *An Angel in Pyjamas.* Delhi: HarperCollins, 1995.

———. *The Bus Stopped.* London: Picador, 2004.

———. 'Whose Identity is it Anyway?' *Guardian*, 12 November 2005. Online: http://www.guardian.co.uk/books/2005/nov/12/featuresreviews.guardianreview1 (accessed 8 March 2012).

———. *Filming: A Love Story*. London: Picador, 2007.

Khilnani, Sunil. *The Idea of India*. London: Penguin, 1998.

Krishnaswamy, Revathi and John C. Hawley, eds. *The Postcolonial and the Global*. Minneapolis: University of Minnesota Press, 2008.

Kuch Kuch Hota Hai (Sometimes things do happen). DVD. Directed by Karan Johar, 1998.

Kumar, Amitava. 'Bad News: Authenticity and the South Asian Political Novel'. *Boston Review* (November/December 2008).

———. *Bombay-London-New York: A Literary Journal*. New York: Routledge, 2002.

Gajendra Kumar, Gajendra. *Indian English Literature: A New Perspective*. New Delhi: Sarup, 2001.

Kumar, Shiv S. 'When Lives Intersect'. *Hindu*, 2 May 2004. Online: http://www.hindu.com/lr/2004/05/02/stories/2004050200180300.htm (accessed 25 June 2011).

Lakoff, George and Mark Johnson. *The Metaphors We Live By*. Chicago: University of Chicago Press, 1980.

Lau, Lisa. 'Making the Difference: The Differing Presentations and Representations of South Asia in the Contemporary Fiction of Home and Diasporic South Asian Women Writers'. *Modern Asian Studies* 39, 1 (2005): 237–56.

Lazarus, Neil, ed. *The Cambridge Companion to Postcolonial Literary Studies*. Cambridge: Cambridge University Press, 2006.

Lévi-Strauss, Claude. *Tristes Tropiques*, translated by John and Doreen Weightman. London: Pan, 1989.

Lim, Shirley Geok-Lin and Amy Ling, eds. *Reading Literature of the Asian American*. Philadelphia: Temple Press, 1992.

Shirley Geok-Lin Lim, Shirley Geok-Lin and Amy Ling, eds. *Reading Literature of the Asian American*. Philadelphia: Temple Press, 1992.

Mahanta, Aparna. 'Allegories of the Indian Experience: The Novels of Salman Rushdie'. *Economic and Political Weekly* 19, no. 6 (1984), 244–7.

Majithia, Sheetal. 'Of Foreigners and Fetishes'. *Samar* 14. Online: http://samarmagazine.org/archive/articles/59 (accessed 12 July 2012).

Mallon, Thomas. *Stolen Words: Forays Into the Origins and Ravages of Plagiarism*. New York: Ticknor & Fields, 1989.

Man Booker Prize. Online: http://www.themanbookerprize.com (accessed 10 November 2010).

Man Group PLC. Online: http://www.mangroupplc.com (accessed 10 November 2010).

Mangla, Ismat Sarah. 'Writing from Two Worlds'. *Nirali*, 1 October 2004. Online: http://niralimagazine.com/2004/10/writing-from-two-worlds (accessed 18 July 2012).

Marquand, Robert. 'Not New Export: Prose Passages from India'. *Christian Science Monitor*, 1 February 2000. Online: http://www.csmonitor.com/2000/0201/p1s4.html (accessed 17 January 2013).

Marshall, P. David, ed. *The Celebrity Culture Reader*. New York and London: Routledge, 2006.

Mazumdar, Sucheta. 'Asian American Studies and Asian Studies: Rethinking Roots'. In *Asian Americans: Comparative and Global Perspectives*, edited by Shirley Hune et al., 29–44. Pullman: Washington State University, 1991.

McGrath, Charles. 'Plagiarism, Everybody Into the Pool'. *New York Times*, 7 January 2007. Online: http://www.nytimes.com/2007/01/07/education/edlife/07books.html (accessed 20 March 2010).

McHale, Brian. *Postmodernist Fiction* (New York: Methuen, 1987).

Mead, Rebecca. 'The Gossip Mill: Alloy, the Teen Entertainment Factory'. *New Yorker*, 19 September 2009. Online: http://www.newyorker.com/reporting/2009/10/19/091019 fa_fact_mead (accessed 15 March 2010).

Mee, John. 'After Midnight: The Novel in 1980s and 1990s'. In *An Illustrated History of Indian Literature in English*, edited by Arvind Krishna Mehrotra, 318–36. Delhi: Permanent Black, 2003.

Mehegan, David. 'Opal Aided by Marketing Firm that Targets Teens'. *Boston Globe*, 8 May 2006. Online: http://www.boston.com/ae/books/articles/2006/05/08/opal_aided_by_marketing_firm_that_targets_teens (accessed 22 March 2010).

Mehegan, David. 'The Six-Figure Sophomore'. *Boston Globe*, 22 February 2006. Online: http://www.boston.com/ae/books/articles/2006/02/22/the_six_figure_sophomore (accessed 19 March 2010).

Mehta, Suketu. *Maximum City*. London: Headline Review, 2005.

_____. 'Bollywood Confidential'. *New York Times Sunday Magazine*, 14 November 2004. Online: http://www.suketumehta.com/nytm.html (accessed 20 March 2010).

Menon, Ritu. 'The Age of Innocence'. *Women's Review of Books* 14, no. 12 (September 1997): 1–4. Online: http://www.jstor.org/stable/4022771 (accessed 30 September 2010).

Menon, Sudha. 'After "Slumdog", Danny Boyle set to film "Maximum City"'. LiveMint. com, 30 May 2009. Online: http://www.livemint.com/2009/05/30014715/After-8216Slumdog8217-D.html (accessed 20 April 2010).

Merritt, Stephanie. 'She's Young, Black, British – and the First Publishing Sensation of the Millennium'. *Observer*, 16 January 2000. Online: http://www.guardian.co.uk/books/2000/jan/16/fiction.zadiesmith (accessed 12 March 2010).

Mishra, Pankaj. 'Edmund Wilson in Benares'. *New York Review of Books*, 9 April 1998, 25–32.

_____. 'A New, Nuclear India'. *New York Review of Books*, 25 June 1998. Online: http://www.nybooks.com/articles/archives/1998/jun/25/a-new-nuclear-india/ (accessed 25 June 2011).

_____. *The Romantics*. London: Picador, 1999.

_____. 'Behold the Good European'. *New Statesman*, 7 February 2000. Online: http://www.newstatesman.com/node/136832 (accessed 25 June 2011).

_____. 'Death in Kashmir'. *New York Review of Books*, 21 September 2000. Online: http://www.nybooks.com/articles/archives/2000/sep/21/death-in-kashmir/ (accessed 25 June 2011).

_____. *An End to Suffering: The Buddha in the World*. New York: Farrar, Straus & Giroux, 2004.

_____. 'A Sepulchral Chill in the Soul'. *New Statesman*, 16 February 2004. Online: http://www.newstatesman.com/node/147304 (accessed 24 March 2011).

_____. *Temptations of the West: How to Be Modern in India, Pakistan and Beyond*. London: Picador, 2006.

Mishra, Vijay. *Bollywood Cinema: Temples of Desire*. New York and London: Routledge, 2002.

_____. *The Literature of the Indian Diaspora: Theorizing the Diasporic Imaginary*. London and New York: Routledge, 2007.

Mistry, Rohinton. *'Swimming Lessons' and Other Stories from Firozsha Baag*. Toronto: McClelland & Stewart, 1987.
———. *A Fine Balance*. Toronto: McLelland & Stewart, 1995.
Montgomery, Isobel and David Jays. 'Whales, Tales and the Funny Side of a Hijacking'. *Guardian*, 16 April 2005. Online: http://www.guardian.co.uk/books/2005/apr/16/featuresreviews.guardianreview22 (accessed 21 December 2010).
Moore, Geoffrey, ed. *The Penguin Book of American Verse*. London: Penguin, 1989.
Moran, Joe. *Star Authors*. London: Pluto Press, 2000.
Morey, Peter. *Fictions of India: Narrative and Power*. Edinburgh: Edinburgh University Press, 2000.
Morey, Peter. *Rohinton Mistry*. Manchester: Manchester University Press, 2004.
Moseley, Merritt. 'Recent British Novels'. *Sewanee Review* 106, no. 4 (Fall 1998): 675–82. Online: http://www.jstor.org/stable/27548605 (accessed 14 December 2011).
———. 'The Booker Prize for 2000'. *Sewanee Review* 109, no. 3 (Summer 2001): 438–46. Online: http://www.jstor.org/stable/27549063 (accessed 14 December 2011).
Moss, Laura. 'Can Rohinton Mistry's Realism Rescue the Novel?' In *Postcolonizing the Commonwealth: Studies in Literature and Culture*, edited by Rowland Smith, 157–65. Waterloo: Wilfrid Laurier Press, 2000.
Moss, Stephen. 'White Teeth by Zadie Smith'. *Guardian*, 26 January 2000. Online: http://www.guardian.co.uk/books/2000/jan/26/fiction.zadiesmith (accessed 12 March 2010).
Mukherjee, Arun. *Postcolonialism: My Living*. Toronto: TSAR, 1998.
Mukherjee, Bharati. Preface to *Darkness and Other Stories*. Harmondsworth: Penguin, 1995.
Mukherjee, Meenakshi. *The Twice Born Fiction: Themes and Techniques of the Indian Novel in English*. New Delhi: Heinemann, 1971.
———. *The Perishable Empire*. New Delhi: Oxford University Press, 2000.
Mullaney, Julie. *Arundhati Roy's The God of Small Things: A Reader's Guide*. London and New York: Continuum, 2002.
Muppidi, Himadeep. *The Politics of the Global*. Minneapolis: University of Minnesota Press, 2004.
Museum of Learning, 'Nava Rasas'. Online: http://www.museumstuff.com/learn/topics/Nava_rasas (accessed 20 May 2010).
Naik, M. K. and Shyamala A. Narayan. *Indian English Literature 1980–2000: A Critical Survey*. Delhi: Pencraft, 2001.
Nandy, Ashis. *The Intimate Enemy: Loss and Recovery of Self Under Colonialism*. New Delhi: Oxford University Press, 1983.
Narasimhaiah, C. D. *Spurious Representations: Vikram Seth, Salman Rushdie and Shashi Tharoor, Essays in Commonwealth Literature*. New Delhi: Pencraft, 1995.
Natarajan, Nalini. *Handbook of Twentieth-Century Literatures of India*. Westport, CT: Greenwood Press, 1996.
Nayar, Pramod K. *Postcolonial Literature: An Introduction*. Delhi: Pearson Longman, 2008.
Negus, Keith. 'The Work of Cultural Intermediaries and the Enduring Distance Between Production and Consumption'. *Cultural Studies* 16, no. 4 (2002): 501–15.
Nelson, Cary and Lawrence Grossberg, eds. *Marxism and The Interpretation of Culture*. Urbana: University of Illinois Press, 1988.
Nelson, Emmanuel, ed. *Writers of the Indian Diaspora: A Bio-Bibliographical Critical Sourcebook*. Westport, CT: Greenwood Press, 1993.

Otto, Whitney. 'Unoriginal Sins'. *New York Times*, 12 May 2006. Online: http://www.nytimes.com/2006/05/12/opinion/12otto.html (accessed 18 March 2010).

Overseas Indian. 'Kiran Desai gets Booker Prize'. October 2006. Online: http://www.overseasindian.in/2006/oct/news/23dia3.shtml (accessed 24 December 2010).

Paranjape, Makarand, ed. *In Diaspora: Theories, Histories, Texts*. New Delhi: Indialog Publications, 2001.

Parekh, Bikhu. 'Some Reflections on the Indian Diaspora'. *Journal of Contemporary Thought* (1993): 105–52.

Parker, Peter. 'Bioscope-wallah'. *Times Literary Supplement*, 3 August 2007.

Pathak, R. S., ed. *Recent Indian Fiction*. New Delhi: Prestige, 1994.

Patt, L., ed. *Benjamin's Blind Spot: Walter Benjamin and the Premature Death of Aura*. California: The Institute of Cultural Inquiry, 2001.

Penguin India. Online: http://www.penguinbooksindia.com (accessed 14 June 2010).

Pinto, Jerry. 'The Write Moment'. *Outlook*, 2006.

Pollock, Sheldon, ed. *Literary Cultures in History: Reconstructions from South Asia*. Berkeley: University of California Press, 2003.

Ponzanesi, Sandra. *Paradoxes of Postcolonial Culture: Contemporary Women Writers of the Indian and Afro-Italian Diaspora*. New York: State University of New York Press, 2004.

Poser, Bill. 'In Defense of Kaavya Viswanathan'. *Language Log* (blog), 25 April 2006. Online: http://itre.cis.upenn.edu/~myl/languagelog/archives/003068.html (accessed 20 March 2010).

———. 'Kaavyagate Update'. *Language Log* (blog), 8 April 2008. Online: http://itre.cis.upenn.edu/~myl/languagelog/archives/003089.html (accessed 20 March 2010).

Prasad, G. J. V. *Vikram Seth: An Anthology of Recent Criticism*. New Delhi: Pencraft International, 2004.

Qadeer, Haris. 'Essentially Oriental: The Image of India in Kiran Desai's Hullabaloo in Guava Orchard'. In *Kiran Desai: The Novelist, An Anthology of the Critical Essays*, edited by P. D. Nimsarkar, 81–85. New Delhi: Creative Books, 2008.

Radhakrishnan, R. 'Globalization, Desire and the Politics of Representation'. *Comparative Literature* 53, no. 4 (2001): 315–32.

Ramesh, Randeep. 'Book-burning Threat Over Town's Portrayal in Booker-Winning Novel'. *Guardian*, 2 November 2006. Online: http://www.guardian.co.uk/world/2006/nov/02/books.india (accessed 23 Dec 2010).

Ray, David and Amritjit Singh, eds. *India: An Anthology of Contemporary Writing*. Columbus: Ohio State University Press, 1983.

Ray, Manas. 'Chalo Jahoji: Bollywood in the Tracks of Indenture to Globalization'. In *City Flicks*, edited by P. Kaarsholm, 140–82. London, New York and Kolkata: Seagull Books, 2007.

Reddy, Sheela. 'The Blurb Bubble'. *Outlook*, 4 December 2006. Online: http://www.outlookindia.com/article.aspx?233278 (accessed 24 July 2011).

Rich, Motoko and Dinitia Smith. 'First Idea, Plot and Characters: Then a Book Needs an Author'. *New York Times*, 27 April 2006. Online: http://www.nytimes.com/2006/04/27/books/27pack.html (accessed 20 March 2010).

———. 'Publisher to Recall Harvard Student's Novel'. *New York Times*, 28 April 2006. Online: http://www.nytimes.com/2006/04/28/books/28author.html (accessed 13 March 2010).

Rich, Motoko and Glen Rifkin. 'For a Harvard Student and Aggrieved Novelist, Plagiarism Generates Interest'. *New York Times*, 29 April 2006. Online: http://www.nytimes.com/2006/04/29/books/29book.html (accessed 12 March 2010).

Robertson, Roland. 1992. *Globalization: Social Theory and Global Culture*. London: Sage, 1992.
Rochester, Sophie. Interview with Kiran Desai. Man Booker Prize, 2007. Online: http://www.themanbookerprize.com/perspective/qanda/40 (accessed 22 Dec 2010).
Rollason, Christopher. 'Vikram Seth's *Two Lives*. A Literature of Global Protagonism'. In *The Expatriate Indian Writing in English*, vol. 1, edited by T. Vinoda and P. Shailaja, 171–82. New Delhi: Prestige, 2006.
Ross, Robert. 'Seeking and Maintaining Balance: Rohinton Mistry's Fiction'. *World Literature Today* 73 (1999): 239–44.
Roy, Arundhati. *The Algebra of Infinite Justice*. London: Flamingo, 2002.
———. *The God of Small Things*. New Delhi: Penguin, 2002.
———. *The Shape of the Beast*. New Delhi: Penguin, 2009.
Rushdie, Salman. 'The Empire Writes Back with a Vengeance'. *Times*, 3 July 1982.
———. *Imaginary Homelands: Essays and Criticism 1981–1991*. London: Granta, 1992.
Rushdie, Salman and Elizabeth West, eds. *Mirrorwork: 50 Years of Indian Writing, 1947–1997*. New York: Picador, 1997.
———, eds. *The Vintage Book of Indian Writing, 1947–1997*, New York: Vintage, 1997.
Sam, David L. and John W. Berry. *The Cambridge Handbook of Acculturation Psychology*. Cambridge: Cambridge University Press, 2006.
San Juan, E. *Beyond Postcolonial Theory*. New York: St Martin's Press, 1998.
Sanga, Jaina C., ed. *South Asian Novelists in English: An A-to-Z Guide*. Westport, CT: Greenwood Press, 2003.
———, ed. *South Asian Literature in English: An Encyclopedia*. Westport, CT: Greenwood Press, 2004.
Sassen, Saskia. *Losing Control? Sovereignty in an Age of Globalization*. New York: Columbia University Press, 1996.
Sawka, Karma. Review of *Family Matters*. *Mostly Fiction Book Reviews*, 12 December 2002. Online: http://www.mostlyfiction.com/world/mistry.htm
Scannell, Paddy. *Radio, Television and Modern Time*. London: Wiley-Blackwell, 1996.
Schirato, Tony and Jen Webb. *Understanding Globalization*. London: Sage, 2003.
Segalen, Victor. *Essay on Exoticism: An Aesthetics of Diversity*, translated and edited by Yael Rachel Schlick. Durham, NC: Duke University Press, 2002.
Sengupta, Chandak. '*Filming: A Love Story* by Tabish Khair'. *Independent*, 29 June 2007. Online: http://www.independent.co.uk/arts-entertainment/books/reviews/filming-a-love-story-by-tabish-khair-455065.html (accessed 25 June 2011).
Shakespeare, Nicholas. 'Marmite: You Either Love It or You Hate It'. *Telegraph*, 10 October 2005. Online: http://www.telegraph.co.uk/culture/books/3647101/Marmite-you-either-love-it-or-you-hate-it.html (accessed 11 October 2010).
Sharrad, Paul. 'Fabricating Community: Local, National and Global in Three Indian Novels'. In *Nation in Imagination: Essays on Nationalism, Sub-Nationalism and Narration*, edited by C. Vijayashree, M. Mukherjee, H. Trivedi and T. Kumar, 212–28. Hyderabad: Orient Longman, 2007.
Shea, Rachel. 'New in Paperback'. *Washington Post*, 6 November 2005.
Shukla, Sandhya. *India Abroad: Diasporic Cultures of Postwar America and England*. India: Orient Longman, 2005.
Smith, Dinitia. 'Harvard Novelist Says Copying Was Unintentional'. *New York Times*, 25 April 2006. Online: http://www.nytimes.com/2006/04/25/books/25book.html (accessed 13 March 2010).

Smith, Stan, ed. *Globalisation and Its Discontents: Writing the Global Culture*. Cambridge: D. S. Brewer, 2006.

Smith, Stephen. 'Rohinton Mistry: Back in Bombay'. *Quill & Quire*, May 2002. Online: http://www.quillandquire.com/authors/profile.cfm?article_id=2369 (accessed 20 October 2010).

Spivak, Gayatri Chakravorty. *A Critique of Postcolonial Reason: Toward a History of the Vanishing Present*. Cambridge, MA: Harvard University Press, 1999.

Sreedharan, Chindu. 'Booker or Not, Arundhati's Still in the Dock'. *Rediff On The NeT*, 15 October 1997. Online: http://www.rediff.com/news/oct/15case.htm (accessed 19 September 2010).

Srinivas, Smriti. *Landscapes of Urban Memory: The Sacred and the Civic in India's High-Tech City*. Minneapolis: University of Minnesota Press, 2001.

Statistics Canada. 'Ethnic Diversity and Immigration'. Online: http://www41.statcan.gc.ca/2007/30000/ceb30000_000-eng.htm (accessed 14 May 2010).

Stearns, Laurie. 'Copy Wrong: Plagiarism, Process, Property, and the Law'. In *Perspectives on Plagiarism and Intellectual Property in a Postmodern World*, edited by Lisa Buranen and Alice M. Roy. Albany: State University of New York Press, 1999.

Sutherland, John. 'The American Scene'. *New Statesman*, 14 November 2005.

Swarup, Vikas. *Six Suspects*. London: Doubleday, 2008.

———. *Slumdog Millionaire*. Toronto: Harper Perennial, 2008.

Tait, Theo. 'In His Own Words'. *Guardian*, 12 April 2008. Online: www.guardian.co.uk/books/2008/apr/12/featuresreviews.guardianreview22 (accessed June 2010).

Tickell, Alex, ed. *Arundhati Roy's The God of Small Things*. New York: Routledge, 2007.

Times of India. 'Mistry cancels US tour over racial profiling', 3 November 2002. Online: http://articles.timesofindia.indiatimes.com/2002-11-03/news-interviews/27294154_1_canadians-airports-publisher (accessed 5 January 2013).

Tivnan, Tom. 'Rising Tide'. *Bookseller*, 12 March 2009. Online: https://www.futurebook.net/profile/rising-tide.html (accessed March 2010).

Tiwari, Shubha. 'Kiran Desai's Hullabaloo in the Guava Orchard as a Satirical Novel'. In *Indian English Literature: A Post-Colonial Response*, edited by Gajendra Kumar and Uday Shankar Ojha, 133–7. New Delhi: Sarup & Sons 2005.

Tomlinson, John. *Globalization and Culture*. Chicago: University of Chicago Press, 1999.

Tomsky, Terri. 'Amitav Ghosh's Anxious Witnessing and the Ethics of Action in *The Hungry Tide*'. *Journal of Commonwealth Literature* 44, no. 1 (2009): 53–65.

TSAR Books. Online: http://www.tsarbooks.com (accessed 12 June 2010).

Tucker, Vincent. 'The Myth of Development: A Critique of Eurocentric Discourse'. In *Critical Development Theory: Contributions to a New Paradigm*, edited by Ronaldo Munck and Denis O'Hearn, 1–26. London: Zed, 1999.

Various authors, *From There to Here: Sixteen True Tales of Immigration to Britain*. London: Penguin, 2007.

Vassanji, M. G. *A Meeting of Streams: South Asian-Canadian Literature*. Toronto: TSAR, 1998.

———. 'Am I a Canadian Writer?' *Canadian Literature* 190 (Autumn 2006): 7–13.

———. 'Some Personal Notes on the Books'. December 2009. Online: http://www.mgvassanji.com/PersonalNotes1.htm (accessed 15 June 2010).

Verma, K. D. *The Indian Imagination: Critical Essays on Indian Writing in English*. New York: Palgrave, 2000.

Vij, Manish. 'KaavyaGate Reloaded'. *Sepia Mutiny* (blog). Online: http://www.sepiamutiny.com/sepia/archives/003324.html (accessed 10 March 2010).

Visweswaran, Kamala. 'Diaspora by Design: Flexible Citizenship and South Asians in US Racial Formations'. *Diaspora* 6.1 (Spring 1997): 5–29.
Walder, Dennis. *Post-Colonial Literatures in English: History, Language, Theory*. Oxford: Blackwell, 1998.
Waters, Malcolm. *Globalization*. London: Routledge, 1995.
Weiss, John. *Industrialisation and Globalisation: Theory and Evidence from Developing Countries*. London: Routledge, 2002.
Wilson, Frances. 'Ordinary Lives Writ Large'. *Guardian*, 2 October 2005. Online: http://www.guardian.co.uk/books/2005/oct/02/biography.features1 (accessed 14 November 2010).
Yardley, Jonathan. Review of *Two Lives*. *Washington Post*, 20 October 2005. Online: http://www.washingtonpost.com/wp-dyn/content/article/2005/10/20/AR2005102001723.html (accessed 6 September 2010).
Zhou, David and Paras D. Bhayani. '"Opal" Similar to More Books'. *Harvard Crimson*, 2 May 2006. Online: http://www.thecrimson.com/article/2006/5/2/opal-similar-to-more-books-kaavya/ (accessed 15 March 2010).

INDEX

2 States (Bhagat, Chetan) 26–7
3 Idiots (Chopra, Vidhu Vinod) 26
3 Mistakes of My Life, The (Bhagat, Chetan) 27

A

About a Boy (Hornby, Nick) 19
Achebe, Chinua 32, 73, 198, 200
Adiga, Aravind 44, 51–66; see also *Between the Assassinations*; *White Tiger, The*
Adivasis 37–8
Advani, Nikhil: see *Kal Ho Naa Ho*
Aeschylus 189
Afghanistan 2, 4
Africa xii–xiii, xviii, 31–3, 36, 54, 64, 67–8, 70–75, 104, 135
Agamben, Giorgio 60, 66, 78, 85
Ahmed, Aijaz 44, 49, 138, 140
ALA Notable Book of the Year 181
Allahabad, University of 1–2, 6, 39
'Allegories of the Indian Experience: The Novels of Salman Rushdie' (Mahanta, Aparna) 138
Alloy Entertainment 154–8, 161, 163
Alloy Media and Marketing 155
All You Who Sleep Tonight (Seth, Vikram) 145
Almost Single (Kala, Advaita) 20
Amazon 7, 160, 188, 192
Amar Akbar Anthony 38
Ambani, Anil 31
Ambrose, Stephen 162
'America' (Ginsberg, Allen) 59, 66
Amis, Martin 53, 163–4
Amriika (Vassanji, M. G.) 68, 71
Andolan 42

Anglo-American 57, 64, 138
Anglo-American Academy 138
Anand, Mulk Raj 11
Ananda Publishers 137
Angel in Pyjamas, An (Khair, Tabish) 104–6, 110–11; Asadullah Khan Ghalib 105; Delhi 105, 111; Phansa 105
Anglocentric 175
Anthropology of Globalization: A Reader, The 64, 66
anti-American 24–5
'Anxiety of Indianness, The' (Mukherjee, Meenakshi) 127, 133
Anzaldúa, Gloria 190–91
Appadurai 56, 64, 66, 183; see also 'Disjuncture and Difference in the Global Cultural Economy'
Arendt, Hannah 96, 101
Arion and the Dolphin (Seth, Vikram) 146
Arthur C. Clarke Award xv, 136
Arundhati Roy's The God of Small Things (Tickell, Alex) 48
Arundhati Roy's The God of Small Things: A Reader's Guide (Mullaney, Julie) 48
Ashcroft, Bill 10, 139
Asia House Festival of Asian Literature 168
Aslam, Nadeem 104
Assassin's Song, The (Vassanji, M. G.) 68, 71
At Home in the World (Brennan, Timothy) 51, 64
Atonement (McEwan, Ian) 162
Atwood, Margaret 53, 123, 198
Austen, Jane 123
Australia xii–xiii, 36, 53, 103, 116, 136

B

Babri Masjid 5
Babu Fictions: Alienation in Contemporary Indian English Novels (Khair, Tabish) 103
Babu Fictions: Alienation in Indian English Novels (Khair, Tabish) 104
Bachchan, Amitabh 37
Badami, Anita Rau xx–xxi, 71, 75
Baldwin, Shauna Singh 75
Balzac, Honoré de 113, 116
Bangalee Bhadrolok 137
Bangaliyana 137
Bangalore 55, 59–62, 65, 125
Bangla xi, 137
Bannerji, Himani 75
Banville, John 53
Barnes, Malcolm 17
Bartholomew's atlas 132
Barucha, Nilufer E. 120
Basu, Kunal xvii, 9, 13–15, 17–18
BBC 25, 31, 54, 65, 116
Beastly Tales From Here and There (Seth, Vikram) 145, 156; 'Gup' 145
Beauvoir, Simone de 83
Begamudre, Ven 122–3, 125
'Behold the Good European' (Mishra, Pankaj) 4–5
Benares 1–2, 4–5
Benares Hindu University (BHU) 1–2
Benjamin, Walter 96, 101, 187–8, 192
Bennett, Arnold 116
Berry, John 81, 84–5
Bertelsmann Group 73
Betty Trask Award 168
Between the Assassinations (Adiga, Aravind) xvi, 52–5, 59–60, 66; Indira Gandhi 54, 59; Kittur 54–5; Rajiv 54
Bhabha, Homi 120, 176
Bhagat, Chetan xv, xvii, 19–27, 128
Bhagavad-Gita 79
Bissoondath, Neil 71, 75
BJP 42, 95
Black Atlantic: Modernity and Double Consciousness, The (Gilroy) 135
Bleak House (Dickens, Charles) 120
Boeke Prize 31
Bollywood xviii, 5, 12, 25, 57, 87–91, 93–9
Bombay 34, 37–9, 74, 87–95, 97, 99, 113–14, 117–18, 120
Booker of Bookers xv, 10, 53
Booker Prize 3, 10, 41–2, 44–5, 55, 63, 114, 168, 174
Booker Prize for literature in English 44
Book of Secrets, The (Vassanji, M. G.) 68, 70, 72
Boorstin, Daniel 159
Borges, Jorge Luis 175, 189
Born Confused (Hidier, Tanuja Desai) 161
Boston Globe 154, 156, 158, 161
bourgeois 35, 134
Boyle, Danny 31, 39, 87; see also *Shallow Grave*; *Slumdog Millionaire*; *Trainspotting*
Brand, Dionne 71
Brashares, Ann 156
Brennan, Timothy 51–2, 54, 63, 128; see also *At Home in the World*; *Cosmopolitanism Now*; *Salman Rushdie and the Third World*; 'Third World Cosmopolitans'
Bridge on the River Kwai (Mistry, Rohinton) 120
Bridget Jones's Diary 19
British East India Company xii
Brouillette, Sarah 52, 63
Buddha, Guatama 2
Buddhism 104
Bummiler, Elisabeth 46
Bus Stopped, The (Khair, Tabish) 104–6, 110–11; Chottu 107; Gaya 106–7, 111; Irfan 106; Mangal Singh 106; Patna 107; Phansa 106–7; Shankar 106; Sunita 106; Zeenat 106
Butter Chicken in Ludhiana: Travels in Small Town India (Mishra, Pankaj) 1–5; Kottayam 3; Mary Roy 3; Murshidabad 3; Muzaffarnagar 3
By the Sea (Gurnah, Abdulrazak) 81; Mr Shaaban 81

C

Cabot, Meg 161
Caine, Sir Michael 44

INDEX 217

Calcutta Chromosome, The (Ghosh, Amitav) xv, 136
Cambridge Handbook of Acculturation Psychology, The (Berry, John; Sam, David) 81
Canada xii–xix, 53, 67–74, 77–8, 80–81, 84, 103, 113–14, 118, 121–3
Canadian Governor General's Award for fiction 114
Canadian Literature (Vassanji, M. G.) 70
Canadian Multiculturalism Act 78
CanLit (Canadian literature) 68–71, 113, 121–3
Canongate 73
Can You Hear the Nightbird Call (Badami, Anita Rau) 71
Carey, Peter 53
caste xviii, 4, 46, 115, 117, 121, 134–5, 143
Castell, Manuel 183
Catcher in the Rye, The (Salinger, J. D.) 23, 27
Caulfield, Holden 27, 161; see also *Catcher in the Rye, The*
Certainty (Thien, Madeleine) 71
Chadha, Gurinder 39
Challakere, Padmaja 1, 7
Chandra, Vikram xv, xviii, 32, 87–9, 95, 99, 113; Commonwealth Writers Prize for Best First Book xv; see also *Cult of Authenticity, The*; *Love and Longing in Bombay*; *Red Earth and Pouring Rain*; *Sacred Games*
Chandra, Vinita 133, 140
Chandrahas 58
Chariandy, David 71, 75
Chattopadhyay, Bankimchandra 127
Chatterjee, Upamanyu xx, 23, 128
Chaudhuri, Amit xviii, xx, 11, 27, 32, 169
Chemmeen (film adaptation) 43
chick lit 19–21, 151–2, 156–8, 161–2
Chokher Bali (Ghose, Rituparna) 39
Chopra, Vidhu Vinod 26, 39
Christianity 38
Christian Science Monitor (Marquand, Robert) 2
Circle of Reason, The (Ghosh, Amitav) 130, 136
Clifford, James 56, 65, 130
CNN 54–5, 65

Coetzee, J. M. 53
Cohen, Katharine 153
Cohen, Robin 130
'Colonel Bogey March' (Mistry, Rohinton) 120
colonialism 4, 12, 72, 103, 110, 121, 139
Columbia Guide to East African Literature in English Since 1945 (Gikandi, Simon) 68, 75
Commonwealth Writers' Prize xv, 10, 67, 114, 116, 137
Conradian primitive myths 47
Continuum Contemporaries series 48
Costa Book Awards 65
cosmopolitan xi, xviii, 12, 44, 46, 51, 77–8, 84, 128, 134, 141, 148, 167, 169, 180–81
Cosmopolitanism Now (Brennan, Timothy) 64
Cricket World Cup (1987) 55
Critique of Postcolonial Reason, A (Adiga, Aravind) 53
Crossette, Barbara 21
Crown Publishing Group 155
culturalist reductionism xii
Cum Laude (von Ziegesar, Cecily) 156
Curran, James 16, 18
Cusack, John 19
CW Television 156

D

Dabydeen, Cyril 75
Dan David Prize 136
Darkness and Other Stories (Mukherjee, Bharati) 128, 139
Daruwalla, Keki N. 104
'Death in Kashmir' (Mishra, Pankaj) 4–5
Delhi 2–3, 20, 22, 55, 60–62, 105, 129, 132, 145, 167
Dell 59
Delacorte Press 155
Democracy and the Nation State (Hammar, Tomas) 78
Desai, Anita 20, 73, 143, 149
Desai, Jigna 93, 100
Desai, Kiran xv, xix–xx, 10–12, 14, 17, 44, 53, 65, 167–83; see also

Hullabaloo in the Guava Orchard;
Inheritance of Loss
Desai, Morarji 79
deshi 11
desi 92
desi-diaspora 168
Devil Wears Prada, The 19
Dharna 42
diaspora xii–xii, xix–xx, 11–12, 14, 39, 67, 72–3, 77–8, 82, 87–9, 92–5, 97–100, 103, 111–12, 114, 120, 129–31, 139–40, 150, 167–8, 170, 185–6, 190–2
Dickens 36, 43, 113, 116, 120, 123
Dickey, Jerome 19
Didur, Jill 1–3
Dil Chahta Hai 23
Dirlik, Arif 181
'Disjuncture and Difference in the Global Cultural Economy' (Appaduri, Arjun) 56, 64, 66, 183; ethnoscapes 64, 177, 183; financescapes 56, 64, 183; ideoscapes 64, 183; mediascapes 64, 183; technoscapes 64, 183
Divakaruni, Chitra Banerjee xx, 185, 187–93
'Divali' (Seth, Vikram) 146
Diwali 153
Donne, Jon 143
Doon School in Dehra Dun 129
Doordarshan 33
Doubleday 73
Douglas, Michael 19
Doyle, Roddy 53
Dreams, Illusions and Other Realities (O'Flaherty, Wendy Doniger) 189
DreamWorks 154, 156
Dudrah, Rajinder Kumar 94
Dugger, Celia 47
Dvorak, Marta 47

E

East, the 2, 93, 127, 139, 168
East Africa 68, 70, 72, 75
Eastwood, Clint 37
Economist 57, 87, 89
'Edmund Wilson in Benares' (Mishra, Pankaj) 4–5
Eklavya (Chopra, Vidhu Vinod) 39
Eliade, Mircea 189
Emblidge, Dr David 157–8
Emerson College 157
empire 10, 54, 123, 139, 167, 176, 178
Empire Writes Back: Theory and Practice in Postcolonial Literature (Ashcroft, Bill) 10, 139
Enchantress of Florence, The (Rushdie, Salman) xvi
Encore Award 104
'End of Imagination, The' (Roy, Arundhati) 42
End to Suffering: The Buddha in the World, An (Mishra, Pankaj) 2–4; majoritarianism 3–4; memoir 2; religious extremism 3; Vinod 4
English August (Chatterjee, Upmanyu) 23
'English Spoken Here' (Choudhury, Chandrahas) 58
Enright, Anne 53
Equal Music, An (Seth, Vikram) 141, 143–5, 147–8; Julia McNicholl 144; London 143–4, 147–8; Michael Holden 144; Rochdale 144
Essay on Exoticism: An Aesthetics of Diversity (Segalen, Victor) 45, 49
Eugene Onegin (Pushkin, Alexander) 142
Eurocentric xii
Everything is Illuminated (Foer, Johnathan Safran) 157
exoticism 34, 36, 45, 47, 89, 99, 103, 169, 181

F

'Fabricating Community: Local, National and Global in Three Indian Novels' (Sharrad, Paul) 130
Family Matters (Mistry, Rohinton) 114–15, 117; Nariman 115; Roxana 115; Yezad 115
Farsi xii–xiii
Female Eunuch, The (Greer, Germaine) 83
fetishize 191–2
Fielding, Henry 35
Filming: A Love Story (Khair, Tabish) 104–5, 107–8, 111; *Aakhri Raat* 108; Anjangarh 108; Ashok 108; Batin

107; Chotte Thakur 108; Durga
  108–9; Gandhi 109; Harihar 108–9;
  Hinduism 109; Malikini 108;
  Saleem 109
Fine Balance, A (Mistry, Rohinton) 45,
  70, 114–17, 119, 123; Booker
  nomination 114; Dina 115; Indira
  Gandhi's Emergency 115; Ishvar
  115; Maneck Omprakash 115
First Gulf War 55
First World 93, 138, 177
Five Point Someone: What Not to Do at IIT
  (Bhagat, Chetan) xv, 20, 22–3
Flaubert, Gustave 1–2, 5, 123; see also
  Sentimental Education, A
Foer, Jonathan Safran 157
Forster, E. M. 116
France xiii, 136
Freud, Sigmund 120, 189
From Heaven Lake (Seth, Vikram)
  142, 146
Fung, Richard 123

G

Gabel, Claudia 155
Gagnon, Monika Kin 123
Gairola, Rahul 1–2
Gandhi, Indira 54, 59, 79, 109, 115–16,
  119, 129
Gandhi, Leela 139
Gangopadhyay, Sunil 137
General Electric 59
Ghose, Rituparna 39
Ghose, Zulfikar 75
Ghosh, Amitav xv, xix, xxi, 10, 12–13,
  18, 21, 32, 65, 104, 112, 127–40,
  185–6, 192
'Ghost of Firozsha Baag' (Mistry,
  Rohinton) 115; Kersi Boyce 115
Gikandi, Simon 68, 71, 75
Giller Award 67
Giller Prize 70, 114
Gillespie, Mary 98
Gilroy, Paul 135
Ginsberg, Allen 59; 'America' 59; Cold
  War 59; Eisenhower-era US 59
Girl Alone (Gulab, Rupa) 20
Gladwell, Malcolm 161

Glass Palace, The (Ghosh, Amitav)
  132–3, 136–7; Herculean 132;
  Rajkumar 132
Global Diasporas: An Introduction (Cohen,
  Robin) 130
globalization xv, xvii–xx, 1, 4–5, 14–15,
  23, 51–2, 54, 56, 58–62, 67, 72, 74,
  77–8, 81, 84, 88, 95, 109–10, 122,
  130, 175, 177, 181, 186
Globe and Mail 71
'glocalization' 175
Gluck, Suzanne 153
Glum Peacock, (Kapur, Akash) 104
Gödel, Kurt 189
God of Small Things, The (Roy, Arundhati)
  xv, xviii, 3, 10, 41–8; Abhilash
  Talkies 48; America 43, 46; Ammu
  42, 48; Ayemenem 42–3, 47; Baby
  Kochamma/ Navomi Ipe 43; E. M.
  S. Namboodiripad factor in Kerala
  politics 42; Estha 42–3, 47; Farmer
  revolt in West Bengal 42; Father
  Mulligan 43; Kerala 41–3, 45–6, 48;
  Meenachal River 42; moon landing
  42; Naxalite movement 42; Rahel
  42–3, 48; Velutha 45; Vietnam
  War 42–3
'God's Own Country' 45, 48
Godwin, David 41, 46
Gokhale, Namita xx, 144, 148
Golden Gate, The (Seth, Vikram) 141–2,
  146–7
Golding, William 53
Gombrich, Ernst 189
Goodwin, Doris Kearns 162
Gopalkrishnan, Lakshmi 46
Gopal, Sangita 95
Gordimer, Nadine 53
Gossip Girl 156; Serena van der
  Woodsen 156
*Gothic, Postcolonialism and Otherness,
  The* (Khair, Tabish) 104
Grand Prize for fiction (Frankfurt
  International e-Book Awards) 136
Grant, Hugh 19
Granta 2
'Greater Common Good, The' (Roy,
  Arundhati) 42

'Great Indian Dream, The' 87
Great Indian Novel, The (Tharoor, Shashi) 12
Greer, Germaine 83, 116
Guardian 2, 14, 111, 157
Gujarat 27, 42, 114, 152–3
Gulab, Rupa 20
Gunnarsson, Sturla 114
Gunny Sack, The (Vassanji, M. G.) 68, 71–2, 74
Gurnah, Abdulrazak 81

H

halal 153
Hamid, Mohsin 23–4
Hammar, Tomas 78
Hardt, Michael 78
Hardy, Thomas 116
HarperCollins 3, 14, 21, 41, 46, 73, 104
Harrison, George 162
Harshe, Rajan 54
Harvard Crimson 151, 159
Harvard University 129, 151–4, 157–9
Hawley, John C. 129
Heart of Darkness 47, 62
Heathrow Travel Product Award 31
Heble, Ajay 120
Heinemann 11, 73–4
Hello 25
Herbert, Caroline 120
Hermes scarves 154
He's Just Not That Into You 19
Hewlett-Packards 55–6
Hidier, Tanuja Desai 161
High Fidelity (Hornby, Nick) 19
Hindi xi–xii, 22, 27, 34, 38, 88–9, 94, 98–9, 137, 141, 143, 145
Hindu 23, 110
History Man, The (Kirk, Howard) 27
Holbrook, Morris 157
Hollywood 19, 37, 42, 92, 154
Hornby, Nick 19, 28
Hosain, Attia xiii
How Opal Mehta got Kissed, Got Wild and Got a Life (Viswanathan, Kaavya) 151–62; Diwali party 153; Gujarati community 152–3; Haute Bitchez 153, 156; How Opal Mehta will get a Life 153; How Opal will get into Harvard 152; Kaavyagate 159–60; Kali 152; Opal Mehta xix, 152–5; Patel Cash-and-Carry 152; Priscilla 161
How to Lose Friends and Alienate People 19
Huggan, Graham 44, 47, 51–2, 63, 169, 174–5, 177, 181
Hugo, Victor 116
Hullabaloo in the Guava Orchard (HGO) (Desai, Kiran) 168, 170–73, 175; Kulfi 172–3; Sampath Chawla 170–73; Shahkot 170–71, 173, 175
'Human Pseudo-Event, the' (Boorstin, Daniel) 159
Humble Administrator's Garden, The (Seth, Vikram) 145
Hungry Tide, The (Ghosh, Amitav) 134, 136–7; Fokir 134; Kanai 134; Nilima 134–5; Nirmal 134–5; Piya 134; Shrimati Bina Kanjilal 135; Sri Tushar Kanjilal 135
Hussein, Saddam
Hutch Crossword Book Prize 136
Hutcheon, Linda 119

I

IBM 55–6, 59
identity xviii–xix, 12, 16, 37, 67, 77–8, 81, 83–5, 88, 90–91, 94, 98, 105, 108–9, 113–14, 116, 120–23, 127–31, 133–4, 139, 146–7, 172, 174, 176, 179–81, 185–6, 190–92
Idikkula, G. M. 46
Illustrated History of Indian Literature in English, An (Mehrotra, Arvind Krishna) 11, 17, 28
immigrant xx, 53, 70, 72, 77–84, 99, 121–2, 138, 146, 148, 160, 177–8, 185–8, 190–92
Immigrant (Raman, Menaka) 82
Immigrant, The (Kapur, Manju) xviii, 77–9, 82–5; Ananda 77–81, 84–5; Anton 84; Canada 77–8, 80–81, 84; India 77–84; Indian Oberoy 83; Nina 77–84
immigration xviii, 14, 70, 77, 79, 81–2, 84, 177, 180, 186, 191
In-Between World of Vikram Lall, The (Vassanji, M. G.) 68, 71–2

INDEX

Independent 110–11
India Today 14, 72, 104
Indian English Literature 1980–2000: A Critical Survey (Narayan, Shyamala A.) 11
Indian Institute of Technology (IIT) 20, 22–3, 115
Indianness xviii, xx, 12, 16, 23, 45, 77, 84, 92, 127–8, 133, 139, 141, 176, 181, 187
Indian Express 129
Indian Supreme Court 42
In Diaspora: Theories, Histories Texts (Paranjape, Makarand) 139
'Indo Chic' 50
Inheritance of Loss, The (Desai, Kiran) xv, 10–11, 13–14, 53, 168, 172–5, 177, 180; Biju 177, 179; Gyan 176; Sai 178–80; Sherpa-servant 179
Inscrutable Americans, The (Mathur, Anurag) 19–20
International Darmaka 94
Internet 36, 94–5, 157, 159
Interpreter of Maladies (Lahiri, Jhumpa) xv, 10
Islam 38, 109
Ishiguro, Kazuo 53
Itwaru, Arnold 75
Ivy League 151, 153
IvyWise 151, 153
Iyengar, K. R. Srinivasa 16
Iyer, Pico 116

J

Jameson, Frederic 51
Jana, Reena 47
Janata Party 79
Japanese Wife, The (Basu, Kunal) 13–15
Jawaharlal Nehru University 2
Jew 144, 147
Jha, Ashok 143
Jhabvala, Ruth Prawer 53
Johar, Karan xvii, 91–3; see also *Kal Ho Naa Ho*; *Kuch Kuch Hota Hai*
John Simon Guggenheim Memorial Fellowship 142
Jonathan Cape 46
Jung, Carl 189
Jussawalla, Adil 104

K

Kafkaesque 199–20
Kai Po Che (Bhagat, Chetan) 27
Kakutani, Michiko 43
Kala, Advaita 20
Kal Ho Naa Ho (Advani, Nikhil; Johar, Karan) 91–4
Kanjilal, Shrimati Bina 135
Kanjilal, Sri Tushar 135
Kanthapura (Rao, Raja) xiii, 13, 17, 32, 132
Kapur, Akash 5–6
Kapur, Manju xviii, 77–82, 84–5; see also *Immigrant, The*
Kapur, Shekhar 39
Kariat, Ramu 43
Karo, Aaron 19
Karthika, V. 21
Kashmir 2–5, 36–7
Katrak, Keru 146, 148
Kaushal, Swati 20
Kelman, James 53, 64
Kerala (God's Own Country) 41–3, 45–6, 48
Kermode, Frank 116
Khair, Tabish xix, 6, 103–5, 107–11; see also *Aakhri Raat*; *Angel in Pyjamas, An*; *Babu Fictions: Alienation in Contemporary Indian English Novels*; *Babu Fictions: Alienation in Indian English Novels*; *Bus Stopped, The*; *Filming: A Love Story*; *Glum Peacock, The*; *Gothic, Postcolonialism And Otherness, The*; *Man of Glass*; *Thing About Thugs, The*; *My World*
Khan, Aamir 26
Khan, Salman xvii, 25, 27
Khan, Shah Rukh 94, 98
King, Stephen 158
Kingstone Bookstore 31
Kinsella, Sophie 161
Kirk, Howard 27
Kirkus Review 14
Kitschiness 96
Knopf 73
Kuch Kuch Hota Hai (Johar, Karan) 91, 93–4
Kuhn, Thomas 189
Kumar, Amitava 57–8, 62

Kumar, Shiv K. 104
Kunzru, Hari 104
Kureishi, Hanif xiii

L

LA Times Art Seidenbaum Award for First Fiction 6
lad lit xvi–xvii, 19–21, 23, 25
Ladoo, Harold Sonny 75
Lahiri, Jhumpa xv, xx, 10, 12, 159, 187, 191
language nationalist xi
Laurence, Margaret 123
Lee, Hermione (Head Judge of the Booker Foundation) 180
'Lend Me Your Light' (Mistry, Rohinton) 115, 118
Lenin 53
Lévi-Strauss, Claude 185
liberalization xv, xix, 1, 4–5, 12, 15, 23, 53, 74, 79, 93, 95, 109–10, 128, 138, 142, 148, 170
Little, Brown 152, 154, 157–8, 160, 162
London xiii, 41, 44, 94, 103, 116, 143–4, 147–8
London Review of Books 116

M

Macaulay, Thomas Babington 176, 183
Macbeth, Lady 61
Maguire, Toby 19
Mahabharata 12; Ganga 60, 62–3
Mahanta, Aparna 138
Mahomed, Deen xiii
Majithia, Sheetal 191
'Making and Marketing of Arundhati Roy, The' (Mongia, Padmini) 46
Maoists 36
Malieckal, Bindu 117
Mallon, Thomas 162
Man Booker Prize xv, 10, 44, 114, 168
Mangal Pandey: The Uprising (Mehta, Ketan) 39
Man Group PLC 44
Manguel, Alberto 122
Man of Glass (Khair, Tabish) 104
Manolo Blahniks 154

Mappings (Seth, Vikram) 145–6; 'To a Fellow Traveller' 146
Marchandani, Ravi 57
Marquand, Robert 2
Mathur, Anurag 19; see also *Inscrutable Americans, The*
Mathur, Ashok xx, 75, 123, 125
Maximum City (Mehta, Suketu) xviii, 87–90, 93–5, 97–8; Monalisa 97
Mazumdar, Suchetta 186
McCafferty, Megan 152, 155, 160–62
McEwan, Ian 162
McClelland & Stewart 73
Means Without End: Notes on Politics (Agamben, Giorgio) 78, 85
Mee, John 11–13
Meeting of Streams: South Asian-Canadian Literature, A 68–9
Mehrotra, Arvind Krishna 11, 17–18
Mehta, Deepa 39
Mehta, Dina 114
Mehta, Ketan 39
Mehta, Suketu 87–9, 91, 93, 97, 99: see also *Maximum City*
Menon, Ritu 45, 47
Mercedes Benz 120
Midnight's Children (Rushdie, Salman) 10–12, 38, 43, 53, 72, 128, 138; Saleem Sinai 46
migration xviii, xx, 67, 71, 73–4, 77–8, 81–4, 130, 146, 170, 177, 180, 185–6
Miniaturist, The (Basu, Kunal) 13, 15; Akbar 15; Bihjad 15
'Minute on Education' (Macauley, Thomas Babington) 176
Mirrorwork (Rushdie, Salman) 174
Mishra, Pankaj xvi–xvii, 1–7, 32, 41, 46, 93, 105; Afghanistan 2, 4; Allahabad 1–2; Ayodhya 5; Benares 1–2, 4–5; Kashmir 2, 4–5; Nepal 2, 4; Pakistan 2, 4; School of Languages 2; Tibet 2, 4; *see also* 'Afghanistan: Communists, Mullahs, and Warlords'; 'Ayodhya: The Modernity of Hinduism'; 'Behold the Good European'; 'Benares: Learning to Read';

'Bollywood: India Shining'; *Butter Chicken in Ludhiana: Travels in Small Town India*; 'Death in Kashmir'; 'Edmund Wilson in Benares'; *End to Suffering: The Buddha in the World, An*; 'Nepal: The "People's War"'; 'New, Nuclear India, A'; 'Pakistan: Jihad Globalized'; *Romantics, The*; 'Sepulchral Chill in the Soul, A'; *Temptations of the West: How to be Modern in India, Pakistan and Beyond*; 'Tibet: A Backward Country'
Mishra, Vijay 89–90, 95–6
Mistress of Spices, The (Divakaruni, Chitra Banerjee) 187–90
Mistry, Rohinton xix, 10, 45, 48, 70–71, 75, 113–22, 124–5, 146; diasporic Canadian 115; Indo-Canadian 113; see also *Bridge on the River Kwai*; 'Colonel Bogey March'; *Family Matters*; *Fine Balance, A*; 'Ghost of Firozsha Baag'; 'Lend Me Your Light'; 'Of White Hairs and Cricket'; *Other Stories From Firozsha Baag*; *Scream, The*; 'Squatter'; *Such a Long Journey*; 'Swimming Lessons'; *Swimming Lessons and Other Stories from Firozsha Baag*; *Tales from Firozsha Baag*
MIT (Massachusetts Institute of Technology) 68
Mongia, Padmini 46
Moor's Last Sigh, The (Rushdie, Salman) 38, 45
Mootoo, Shani 75
Mordecai Richler (Vassanji, M. G.) 68
Morey, Peter 119
Morgenstein, Leslie 155
Morrison, Toni 158
Moseley, Merritt 43–5
Moss, Laura xviii, 121
Moth Smoke (Hamid, Mohsin) 23–4
Muchnick, Asya 154, 161
Mughal 15
Mukherjee, Arun 68–9, 75
Mukherjee, Bharathi 128, 146, 187, 191; see also *Darkness and Other Stories*
Mukherjee, Meenakshi 127, 132–3, 139

Mullaney, Julie 48
multiculturalism 10, 70, 78–80, 84, 116, 118, 121, 132, 147, 186
multinational xviii, 37, 52, 62–3, 67, 73, 75, 94, 109, 142
Mumbai University 48
Munro, Alice 123
Muslim 4, 36, 104, 109, 117
'My Sweet Lord' (Harrison, George) 162
My World (Khair, Tabish) 104

N

Naik, M. K. 11, 16–17
Naipaul, V. S. xv, 3, 53
Nair, Mira 39
Narasimhaiah, C. D. 17, 143
Narayan, R. K. 20, 73, 105
Narayan, Shyamala A. 11
Narmada Bachao Andolan (Save the Narmada movement) 42
Narmada valley 42
nation 3, 10, 12–13, 16, 38, 42, 58–9, 71, 78, 84, 87, 93–4, 108, 122, 128–33, 136, 138–9, 143, 175, 178, 186
nationality xviii, 16, 67, 73, 78, 132, 176
nation-state 12, 78, 87, 93–4, 122, 128, 143, 175, 178
Naxalite 15, 42, 65
Nayar, Pramod 17; see also *Postcolonial Literature: An Introduction*
Negri, Antonio 178, 183
'neocolonial commodification' (Dvorak, Marta) 47
Nepal 2, 4, 146, 178, 180
'New Canadian and World Writing' 69
'New, Nuclear India, A' (Mishra, Pankaj) 4–5
New Statesman 2, 4, 99
New Yorker 116, 156
New York Review of Books 2, 4, 116
New York Times 21, 41, 43, 46–7, 159
Nezhukumatathil, Aimee 159
Nobel Prize in literature 51
No New Land (Vassanji, M. G.) 68–9; Lalani family 69
nonresident Indian (NRI) 14, 24, 91

O

'Of White Hairs and Cricket' (Mistry, Rohinton) 115
O'Hara, P. A. 54, 58
O'Flaherty, Wendy Doniger 189
Okri, Ben 53
Ondaatje, Michael 53, 71
One Night @ the Call Centre (*ON@TCC*, Bhagat, Chetan) 23–7
Onge 34, 36–7
Opium Clerk, The (Basu, Kunal) 13, 15, 18; Hiran 15
Oprah 114, 123
Oprah's Book Club 114
Order of Canada 67
Oriental xii, 36, 47, 82, 110, 140, 174, 182, 191
Orion 143–4
Orwellian 54
Oscars 31
Other Routes xiii, 104
Other Stories from Firozsha Baag (Mistry, Rohinton) 113–14
Outlook 2, 111, 149
Oxford University 13, 129
Oxford University Press 103

P

Paheli (Palekar, Amol) 39
Pakistan xiii, 2, 4, 6, 23, 55, 72, 128, 131, 138
Palekar, Amol 39
Palgrave Macmillan 104
Pantheon 73
Parameswaran, Uma 75
Paranjape, Makarand 139
Parekh, Bikhu 147–8
Paris Book Fair 31
Parsi xix, 113–18, 120–21, 135
Pathak, R. S. 149
Patkar, Medha 42
p'Bitek, Okot 73
Penguin xx, 14, 17, 68, 71, 73–4, 104
People Magazine 47
Perishable Empire, The (Mukherjee, Meenakshi) 139
Permanent Black 104
Picador 73, 104

Piece of Cake (Kaushal, Swati) 20
Pillai, T. S. 43
Pinto, Jerry xvi
Pioneer, The 2
'Pity the nation that has to silence its writers' (Roy, Arundhati) 42
Place Within: Rediscovering India, A (Vassanji, M. G.) 68, 71, 74
Plato 189
Pokhran 42
Ponzanesi, Sandra 186–7
Portillo, Michael 57–8
postcolonial xi–xiii, xv, xvii–xviii, 3–4, 10, 12, 16, 43–4, 47, 51–3, 57, 62–3, 72–3, 99, 103–5, 109–10, 113, 116–17, 119–21, 123, 128, 130–33, 137–41, 148, 167–9, 175, 177
Post-Colonial Exotic: Marketing the Margins, The (Huggan, Graham) 44, 51
Postcolonial Theory: A Critical Introduction (Gandhi, Leela) 139
postliberalization xv–xviii, 1, 10–13, 44, 48, 51, 53–6, 58, 60–61, 74, 77–8, 84, 109, 131, 141, 169
postmodern 12, 16, 43, 113, 117, 123, 138, 164
postnational utopia xix, 127, 132, 139
Prasad, Murari 132
Premji, Azim 31
Prix Medicis Etranger 136
Pulitzer Prize xv, 10
Pushkin, Alexander 142

Q

Qadeer, Haris 174
Q & A (Swarup, Vikas) xviii, 31, 34–5
Queen of Dreams (Divakaruni, Chitra Banerjee) 187, 189
Queen of England 121
Quill & Quire 71

R

Racists (Basu, Kunal) 13, 15
Radio 4 (BBC) 31
Rajan, Gita 99
Rajmohan's Wife (Chattopadhyay, Bankimchandra) 127

Raman, Menaka 82
Ramraj, Victor 146
Randhawa, Ravinder 147
Random House 2, 46, 73, 155
Rao, Raja xiii, xviii, 11, 13, 17, 32, 73, 132
Rasa 107
Ratnam, Mani 39; see also *Guru*
Ray, Manas 92–3
Red Earth and Pouring Rain (Chandra, Vikram) xv
'Remaking India' (Rajan, Gita) 87
Revolution 2020: Love, Corruption, Ambition (Bhagat, Chetan) 27
Richardson, Samuel 35
'Rising Elephant' (Rajan, Gita) 87
River of Smoke (Ghosh, Amitav) 130, 136
Roberston, Roland 175
Rock Hard Apps: How to Write the Killer College Application (Cohen, Katherine) 153
Rollason, Christopher 144, 147
Romantics, The (Mishra, Pankaj) 2, 5–7; Anand 3; Arjun 2; Benares 5; Catherine 3; Debbie 3; Mark 3; Miss West 3; Panditji 2; Rajesh 2; Samar 2–3, 5; Sarah 3; Shyam 3; Sitadevi 3; Vijay 2
Ross, Robert L. 116
Routledge 48
Roy, Suzanna Arundhati xv, xx–xxi, 3, 10, 12, 31–2, 41–9, 53, 66; Corpus Christi (*Pallikoodam*) 3; *see also* 'End of Imagination, The'; *God of Small Things, The*; 'Greater Common Good, The'; 'Pity the nation that has to silence its writers'; *Shape of the Beast, The*
Roy, Mary 3, 41
Rupa 11, 20, 104
Rushdie, Salman xiii, xv–xvii, xix, 9–12, 14, 17, 20–21, 31–2, 38–9, 41, 43–6, 53, 63, 72, 105, 113, 128, 138, 140, 146, 161, 163, 168, 170, 174, 182; see also *Enchantress of Florence, The*; *Midnight's Children*; *Mirrorwork*; *Moor's Last Sigh, The*; *Satanic Verses, The*; *Vintage Book of Indian Writing, 1947–1997, The*

S

Salman Rushdie and the Third World (Brennan, Timothy) 128
Sacred Games (Chandra, Vikram) xviii, 87–90, 93–4, 97–9; Ganesh Gaitonde 90–91, 94, 97–8; Sartaj Singh 91, 94, 97
Sahitya Akademi 137
Sahitya Akademi Award 136
Sam, David 81, 84
Sanskrit xii, 107
Sarang, Vilas 104
Sardar Sarovar dam 42
Sassen, Saskia 183
Satanic Verses, The (Rushdie, Salman) 38
Sawka, Karma 117
Sayal, Meera 147
Schadenfreude 160
Schopenhauer 1
Scream, The (Mistry, Rohinton) 114
Sea of Poppies (Ghosh, Amitav) xv, 135, 137
Second Helpings (McCafferty, Megan) 152
Second Sex, The (Beauvoir, Simone de) 83
Segalen, Victor 45, 49
Sehgal, Nayantara 20
Selvon, Sam 75
Sen, Aparna 13
Sengupta, Somini 47
Sentimental Education, A (Flaubert, Gustave) 2; Frederic Moreau 2, 5
'Sepulchral Chill in the Soul, A' (Mishra, Pankaj) 4–5
Seth, Vikram xv, xix, xxi, 10–12, 31–2, 141–50; Nanjing University 142; Stanford University 142; see also *All You Who Sleep Tonight*; *Arion and the Dolphin*; *Beastly Tales From Here and There*; *Equal Music, An*; *From Heaven Lake*; *Golden Gate, The*; *Humble Administrator's Garden, The*; *Mappings*; *Suitable Boy, A*; *Three Chinese Poets*; *Two Lives*
Sethi, Ali 138
sex 12, 19–20, 24, 34, 36, 46, 55–6, 66, 69, 81, 83–4, 89, 92, 106, 157, 189, 191
Sex and the City 19
Shadow Lines, The (Ghosh, Amitav) xxi, 12–13, 18, 128, 131–3, 136, 140

Shakespeare, Nicholas 145
Shallow Grave (Boyle, Danny) 31
Shamela 35
'Shaping India of our Dreams' 87
Shape of the Beast, The (Roy, Arundhati) 49
Sharrad, Paul 130–31
Shields, Carol 123
Shiffrin, Richard 162
Sidhwa, Bapsi 114, 116
Siemens 59, 61
Signal Books 104
Sikh 105
Simon Pulse 161
Singh, Khushwant xvi, xxi, 20, 104
Sisterhood of the Traveling Pants, The (Brashares, Ann) 155–6
Six Suspects (Swarup, Vikas) xviii, 31–2, 34–7; Shabnam Saxena 34, 36
Sloppy Firsts (McCafferty, Megan) 152, 161; Bridget 161; Burke 161; Hope 161
Slumdog Millionaire (Boyle, Danny) 31–3, 87, 99; Arun Advani 37; Babu Pillai 34; Dominic Thomas 33; Kunwar Shankar Singh 38; Mustafa 34; Neelima Kumari 37; Nita 37; Punnoose 34; Ram Mohammad Thomas (RMT) 33–8; Salim 33; Shantaram 37; Swapna Devi 38
Smith, Stan 56, 65
Smith, Zadie 157; see also *White Teeth*
Social Sciences and Humanities Research Council 121
Society Young Achievers' Award 26
Soucouyant (Badami, Anita Rau) 71
Sound of Music, The (1965 film) 43
Soyinka, Wole 73
Spivak, Gayatri 53, 57, 65, 76, 171
'Squatter' (Mistry, Rohinton) 113, 118, 120, 122; Clark Gable 120; Nariman 120
standardization 64, 157
Stendhal 116
Sterne, Laurence 162
Strange and Sublime Address, A (Chaudhuri, Amit) 11
Such a Long Journey (Mistry, Rohinton) 10, 48, 114–15; Dilnavaz 115; Gustad Noble 115; Jimmy Bilimoria 115; Sohrab 115
Sugunasiri, Suwanda H. J. 75
Suitable Boy, A (Seth) xxi, 10–12, 141–5, 147–9; researched epic 142–3; Chatterjis, the 143; Kapoors, the 143; Khans, the 143; Lata 143; Mehras, the 143; Rupa Mehra 143; Savita 143
Sunday Times bestsellers list 41
'Suppressed Memory and Forgetting: History and Nationalism in *The Shadow Lines*' (Chandra, Vinita) 133, 140
Swarup, Vikas xvii–xviii, 31–9; see also *Q & A*; *Six Suspects*
'Swimming Lessons' (Mistry, Rohinton) 115, 117, 120, 122
Swimming Lessons and other stories from Firozsha Baag (Mistry, Rohinton) 113–14, 124
Sydney Morning Herald 14

T

Tagore, Rabindranath 73
Tait, Theo 64
Taleb, Abu xiii
Tales from Firozsha Baag (Mistry, Rohinton) 114, 117, 120, 124
Tamil xi–xii, 26
Tapping, Craig 146, 150
Taraporevala, Sooni 114
Telegraph 150
Temptations of the West: How to be Modern in India, Pakistan and Beyond (Mishra, Pankaj) 2, 4–7, 100
Tharavaad 43
Tharoor, Shashi 12, 149
Theroux, Paul 3
Thien, Madeleine 71
Thing About Thugs, The (Khair, Tabish) 104
Thiong'o, Ngugi wa 73
Third World xviii, 11, 44, 128, 138–9, 177, 180
'Third World Cosmopolitans' (Brennan, Timothy) 128
Third World literature in English 44
Thomas, Sabu 46

Three Chinese Poets (Seth, Vikram) 141, 145; Du Fu 145; Emperor Ming Huang of the Tang Dynasty 145; Li Bai 145; Wang Wei 145
Tickell, Alex 48
Time Out 104
Times Literary Supplement 2, 14, 18, 111–12, 140, 150
Times of India 7, 124, 149
Tivnan, Tom 64; *see also* 'Rising Tide'
Tiwari, Shubha 174, 182
'To a Fellow Traveller' (Seth, Vikram) 146
Tolstoy 113, 149
Tolstoyan 116
Toronto Review of Contemporary Writing Abroad 68
Toronto South Asian Review (*TSAR*) 68–71, 73, 75
Trainspotting 31
transnationalism 16, 128, 136, 138, 148
travel book 2
travelogue xvii, 2, 4, 142, 146
Turgenev 1
Tutuola, Amos 73
tween lit 19, 155
tweens 19, 155
Two Lives (Seth, Vikram) xv, 141, 144–5, 147–50; Helga Gerdo Caro/ Henny 144–5, 147; Lola 145; Shanti Behari Seth 144–5, 147; Vicky 144

U

Uhuru Street (Vassanji, M. G.) 68
Untouchable, The (Anand, Mulk Raj) 11
Updike, John 116
Urdu xi–xii, 105, 143
Urquart, Tony 114
USA xiii, 68, 136, 142, 177, 197
utopia xix, 15, 127, 132, 139
UTV Spotboy 27

V

Vajpayee 42
Vassanji, M. G. xviii, xxi, 67–76; Lalani family 69; Mau Mau uprising 72; Order of Canada 67
verse libretto 146

Vintage Book of Indian Writing, 1947–1997, The (Rushdie, Salman) 46, 49
Viswanathan, Kaavya xix, 28, 151–65; Harvard sophomore 151; *see also* 'How Opal Mehta got Kissed, Got Wild and Got a Life'
Visweswaran, Kamala 186, 192
Vodafone Crossword Award in India 58, 104

W

Walsh, Jennifer Rudolph 153–4, 158
Washington Post 101, 149, 192
Weinreb, Michael 19
West, Elizabeth 49, 182
West, the xiii, xviii, 2, 6–7, 39, 42, 44, 48, 57, 65, 81–2, 87–8, 92–3, 95, 99–100, 111, 117, 127, 138–9, 143, 146, 168, 174
Western xv, xvii, 2, 4, 11, 17, 39, 47, 51, 53, 63, 77, 80, 83–4, 87–9, 92–3, 97–9, 111, 123, 138, 143, 147, 169, 174, 188–9
Watergate scandal 160; President Nixon 160; lynch mob 160
What We All Long For (Brand, Dionne) 71
When She Was Queen (Vassanji, M. G.) 68, 70
White Teeth (Smith, Zadie) 157, 164
White Tiger, The (Adiga, Aravind) xv, xvii, 51–2, 54–65; Balram Halwai 55–6, 59–63, 66; Bangalore 55, 59–62, 65; Benaras 62–3; Bodh Gaya 62; Himalayas 62; Mr Ashok 56, 59; Mr Jiabao 60, 63; Mr Premier 62; Vodafone Crossword Book Award 58
Wikipedia 168, 182, 192
William Morris Agency 153, 157–8
Wilson, Frances 145, 150
Winfrey, Oprah 116–17
Wise, Robert 43
Wonder Boys 19
'Work of Art in the Age of Mechanical Reproduction, The' (Benjamin, Walter) 96
World Literature Today 124
world literature written in English (WLWE) 73
Woolf, Virginia 162

World Literacy of Canada 114
WWI xiii
WWII xiii, 131, 141, 144, 147

Y

Yellow Emperor's Cure, The (Basu, Kunal) 13
Yogavasistha 189

Z

Zhou, David 164
Ziegesar, Cecily von 156; see also *Cum Laude*
Zoroastrian Parsis 114
Zubaan Books 104

www.ingramcontent.com/pod-product-compliance
Lightning Source LLC
Chambersburg PA
CBHW021824300426
44114CB00009BA/312